I0793019

IMAGES
of America

DAVENPORT'S WOC AM-FM-TV

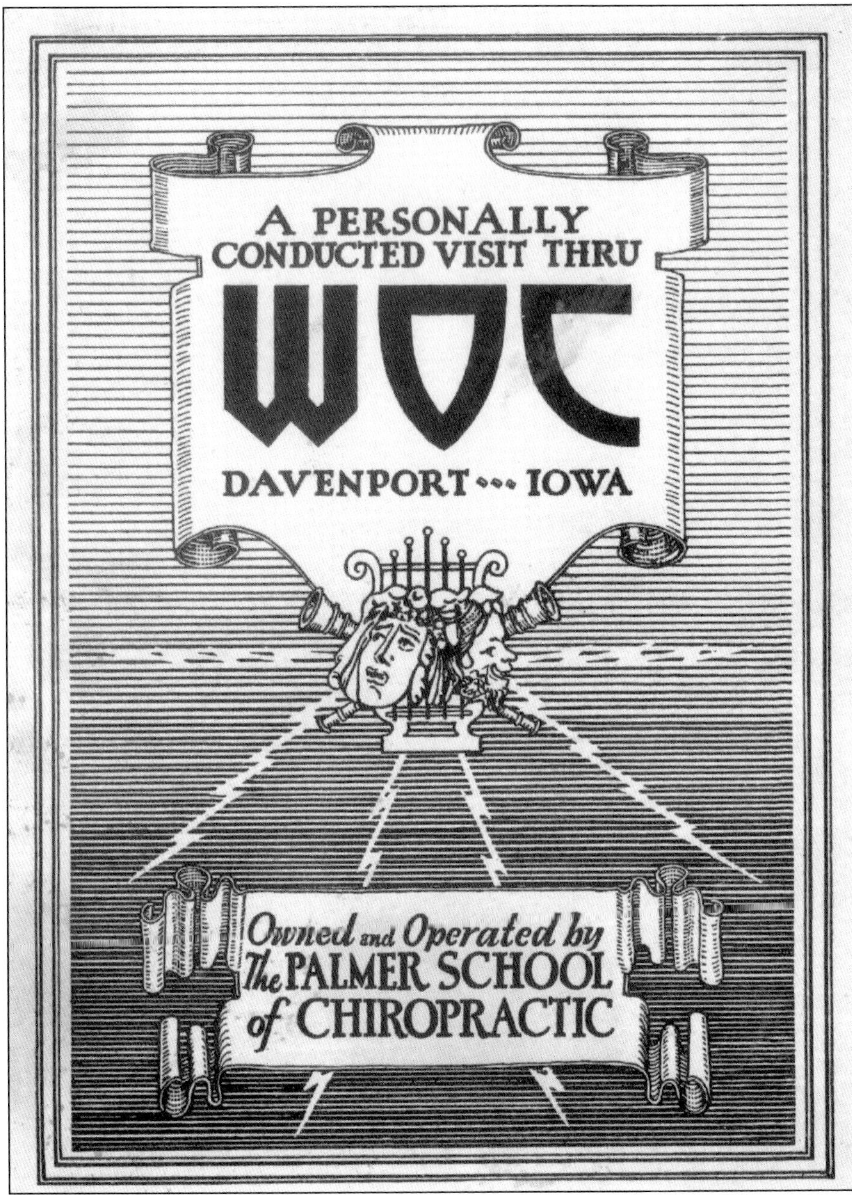

The concept of voice and music coming out of the air and into something called a radio was still new to many people in the early 1920s. To promote this new medium, WOC published several booklets that described what radio was, how it worked, and what a radio station looked like. Photographs of the facility, equipment, and personnel were included to illustrate the narrative copy, similar to this volume.

On the Cover: This behind-the-cameras photograph offers a view of WOC-TV's popular hostess Pat Sundine as she welcomes viewers to *Especially for You*. The show was in production for nearly 17 years and was the premier program of its kind on local television. The show entertained and informed with musical segments, interviews with both local and national celebrities, and various topics of interest for its female audience. (Courtesy of Rock Island County Historical Society Library.)

IMAGES
of America

DAVENPORT'S WOC AM-FM-TV

David T. Coopman

ARCADIA
PUBLISHING

ISBN 978-0-7385-7780-7

Published by Arcadia Publishing
Charleston SC, Chicago IL, Portsmouth NH, San Francisco CA

Printed in the United States of America

Library of Congress Control Number: 2009940513

For all general information contact Arcadia Publishing at:
Telephone 843-853-2070
Fax 843-853-0044
E-mail sales@arcadiapublishing.com
For customer service and orders:
Toll-Free 1-888-313-2665

Visit us on the Internet at www.arcadiapublishing.com

This book is dedicated to all the former employees of the WOC stations who helped pioneer and create the quality programming heard and seen on their airwaves. It is also dedicated to the employees of WOC's predecessor stations, may they continue the tradition.

Contents

ACKNOWLEDGMENTS

The research represented here could not have been accomplished without the help of a great many people who shared their photographs, documents, and information. My thanks go to the following: former WOC employees Wally Boller, Bob Danico, Ed Jones, Gwen Korn, Don McGonegle, Ivan Owens, Don Rhyne, Phil Roberts, Stan Straight, Anita Sundin, Russ Wingo, and Ed Zack; Tracey Allard, Doug Bierman, Judith Carls, Scott Childers, Bill Coopman, Kelly Crawford, Ron and Linda Crouch, John Flambo, David Gleason, Ray Johansen, Rick McGuire, Stephanie Nelson, Jim O'Hara, and Curtis Roseman.

Thanks to Alana Callendar, Glenda Wiese, and Justin Snider of the David D. Palmer Health Science Library Special Collections Archive at Palmer College of Chiropractic; Laura Yeater and the *Dispatch/Argus*; and the staff of the Rock Island County Historical Society Library.

Special thanks go to current WOC engineer Jon Book, Rich Birley (creator of the web site www.captainerniesshowboat.com), and KWQC promotions manager Michelle Makelbust for valuable background information and photographs.

Photographs not credited and source materials, including magazine and newspaper articles, pamphlets, and one-sheets, are from the author's collection.

My sincere gratitude goes to Arcadia Publishing publisher John Pearson and editor Ted Gerstle for their guidance and encouragement in putting this project together.

INTRODUCTION

Radio station WOC can trace its history as far back as 1907 when the system for generating and receiving long-range radio signals captured the fancy of thousands who wanted to learn and experiment with this new technology. Included with this group of radio amateurs, or "hams," was Robert Karlowa of Rock Island, Illinois. Karlowa operated the radio department of the Young and McCombs Department Store and had been experimenting with Morse code radio transmissions.

With the development of the vacuum tube, Karlowa was able to graduate from code to voice broadcasting, and he received the call sign 9-BY for his radiophone station in June 1919. He began to air news, sports scores, and phonograph music on a regular nightly schedule. A new commercial license was issued to Karlowa on February 18, 1922, with the call letters WOC.

Throughout this same period, Dr. B. J. Palmer, owner and president of Palmer School of Chiropractic, and his son David were developing their own interest in this new technology. David and several of his friends established a wireless station in the attic of the Palmer home on Brady Street in Davenport, Iowa. Formation of the PSC Radio Club followed in January 1921.

Dr. Palmer's interest began with the installation of a Western Electric public address system at the Palmer School. According to Western Electric, it was the first installation of its type in an institution of learning. The system allowed lectures to be heard throughout the school. During the school's August 1921 Lyceum program, with an overflow crowd of alumni seated on the rooftop garden of the administration building listening via that system, it occurred to Dr. Palmer that he could reach not only the school's alumni, but many others through the use of radio. It would be a means of presenting chiropractic in a positive, favorable manner.

Since the sale of advertising time was yet unheard of in this new industry, operating costs were born totally by the station owner. In March 1922, Karlowa realized that he could no longer afford to operate his station. B. J. Palmer purchased the station that month, and the Palmer School of Chiropractic became the licensee of WOC. The station's license was transferred, and the equipment was moved to the Palmer School campus in Davenport. This was the first instance of a radio station being sold and moved from one state to another.

Prior to WOC's dedication week beginning October 8, 1922, the station increased its range with the installation of a 500-watt transmitter. With the increase came notices by mail that the station was being heard in Europe, Russia, China, and South America. Programming included weather and market reports, news, sports, educational lectures, and musical concerts by local soloists, ensembles, and choirs.

As programming evolved, some rather unique shows were heard. Gilson "Radio Rex" Willets created a homemaking program that aired recipes and was wildly popular with housewives. Pat Flanagan, who later became a famous sports announcer, inaugurated physical exercising over the air. Val McLaughlin, as the "Sandman Story Teller," broadcast bedtime stories for children.

WOC is credited with achieving an impressive list of many firsts in the field of broadcasting. In 1922, it was the first commercially licensed station west of the Mississippi River. It was the first station to build log records for electrical consumption, tube values, voltage, and current every half hour and program schedules to the second. Stations adopted and were later required to perform many of these same logging procedures. It was the first station to broadcast from both houses of the Iowa Legislature. It was the first station to build and use a fader panel that allowed the use of multiple microphones in one studio. WOC was also the first station to establish an absolute minute and second time for the beginning and ending of all programs. Another practice initiated by WOC, and quickly followed by other stations, was the use of time signals at the beginning of programs.

In 1928, a government realignment of frequencies put WOC in Davenport and WHO in Des Moines on the same clear-channel frequency with the same 5,000 watts of power. This created a problem for each station's interests and audience. One of the issues was solved by the Palmer School of Chiropractic creating Central Broadcasting Company and purchasing WHO from Banker's Life Insurance Company. The stations split time on the frequency until the use of synchronized signals was perfected, so programming could be heard from either station. During that period, the stations were known as WOC-WHO or WHO-WOC, depending on which facility was actually on the air.

WOC's most famous employee was hired in 1932. Fresh out of college, the Dixon, Illinois, native Ronald "Dutch" Reagan was hired as a sports and general staff announcer. Reagan made Davenport his home until April 1933. At that time, a new single transmitter for both stations took to the air from the Des Moines area, with 50,000 watts of power, and both of the old 5,000-watt transmitters were shut down. Reagan was transferred to WHO, where he announced a variety of sporting events until he left for Hollywood in 1937.

The rather unique situation of WOC-WHO operating as one station covering all of Iowa had some drawbacks; one of which was that local advertising was not aired. Dr. Palmer felt that Davenport was not being well served. In November 1934, he split the operations of WOC-WHO and put WOC back on the air, as an individual station, from Davenport. To accomplish this, Palmer formed Tri-City Broadcasting Company to purchase the license and transmitting equipment of KICK in Carter Lake, Iowa.

WOC-FM was added in October 1948, duplicating the signal of WOC-AM. WOC-TV began its telecasts on October 31, 1949. It was the first television station in Iowa, as well as the first station in the Quad Cities. Originally on channel 5, its signal was moved to channel 6 in November 1953. Like the radio station, WOC-TV was an affiliate of the NBC network. Also similar to WOC radio, the news and public-service programming was an important part of the television broadcast schedule over the years. Channel 6's newscasts have consistently topped the ratings for well over 30 years.

In 1972, WOC-FM changed its call letters to KIIK-FM and began airing current rock-and-roll hits, 24 hours a day. In 1979, WOC switched formats from playing hit standards to the news and talk programming it still uses today. KIIK became KUUL-FM in 1989, playing rock-and-roll hits of the 1950s though the 1980s.

In 1986, Palmer Communications sold WOC-TV (now KWQC-TV) to Broad Street Communications and sold WOC-AM and KIIK-FM to Signal Hill Communications, which was owned by Dr. David Palmer's daughter Vickie. In 1996, KWQC-TV was sold to present owner Young Broadcasting. Signal Hill Communications was sold to Sconnix Broadcasting in 1996 and is now owned by Clear Channel Communications.

For over 70 years, the Palmer family and their stations set benchmarks in quality radio and television and created an enduring legacy that has been hard to follow. The Palmers and their stations put Davenport and Iowa on the map—"WOC, Davenport, Iowa, Where the West Begins, in the State Where the Tall Corn Grows."

One

On the Air from Signal Hill

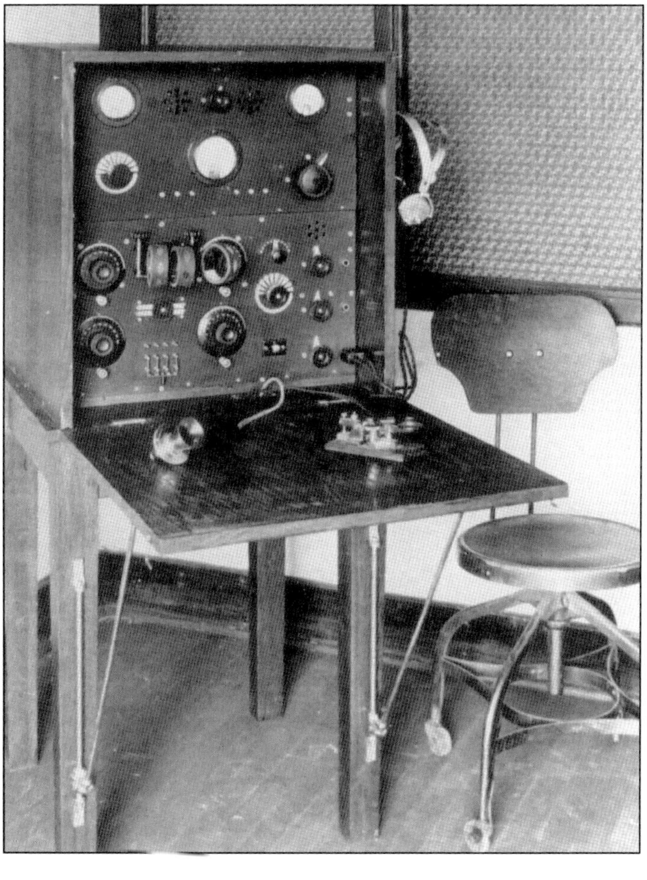

Pictured around 1921, this is the original experimental station 9-BY owned by Robert Karlowa. On the right side of the tabletop is the "key" for sending Morse code. On the left is the microphone for broadcasting voice. Music was broadcast by placing the microphone next to a Victrola speaker. In 1922, this amateur equipment became radiophone station WOC and was purchased by the Palmer School of Chiropractic. (Courtesy of Vern Peterson.)

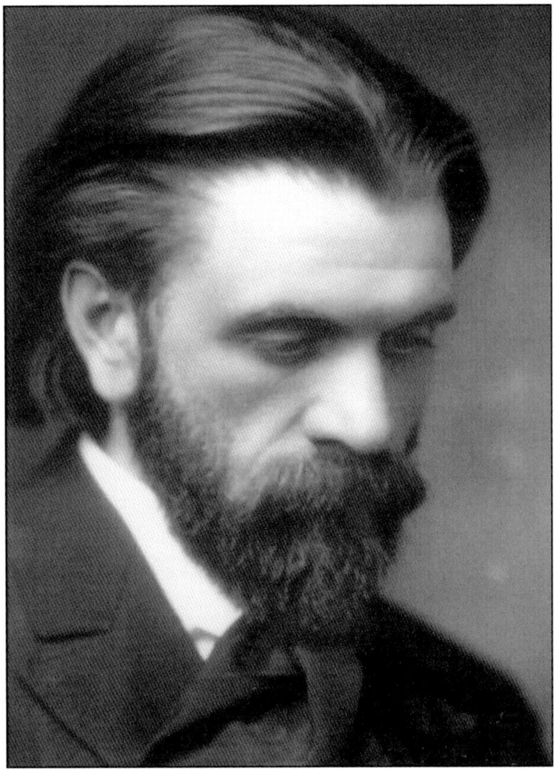

Pres. B. J. Palmer, the driving force behind the Palmer School of Chiropractic, saw radio as a way to reach the school's many alumni and present chiropractic to the general public in a positive, favorable manner. He was not only a shrewd businessman but also a strong promoter of both Davenport and the state of Iowa. (With permission of Palmer College of Chiropractic, Special Collections and Archives.)

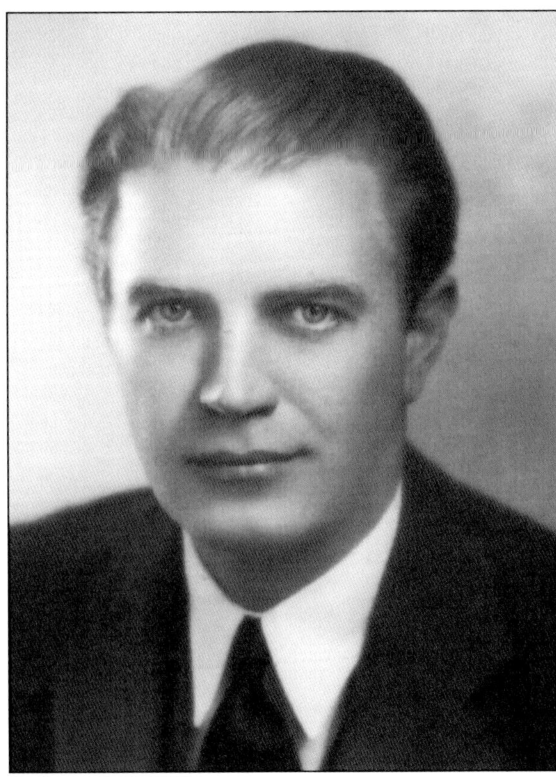

With an interest in amateur radio, David Palmer and a group of like-minded friends started the Palmer School PSC Radio Club. This may have helped inspire B. J. Palmer to purchase radiophone station WOC from Robert Karlowa. David Palmer would later become the president of the WOC stations and the Palmer College of Chiropractic. This portrait is from around 1930. (With permission of Palmer College of Chiropractic, Special Collections and Archives.)

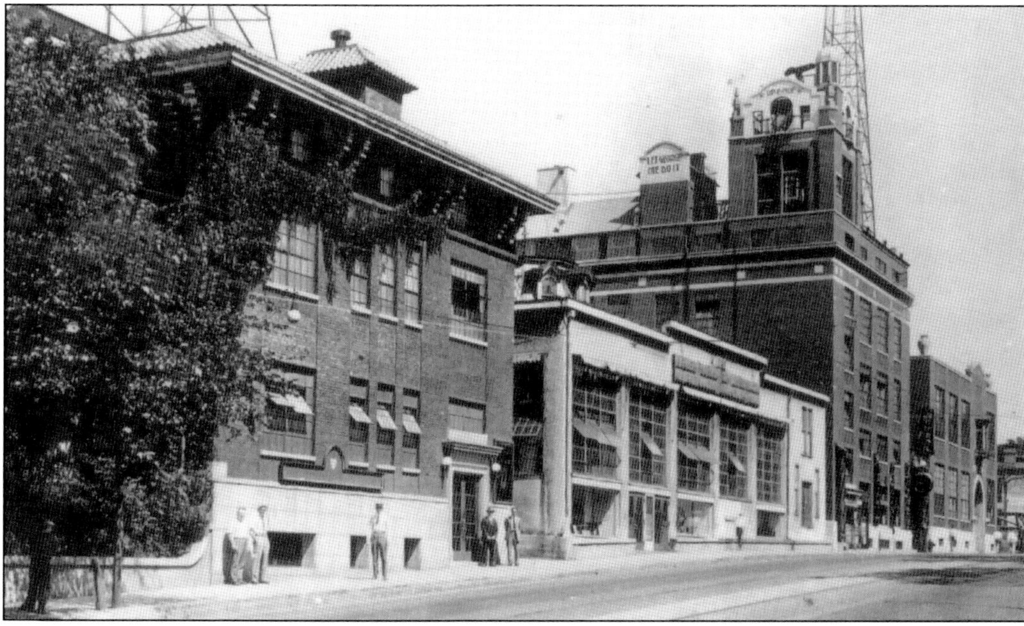

This postcard from the late 1920s provides a great view of the Palmer School of Chiropractic, home of WOC Radio, on Brady Street hill. The radio studios were located in the second building from the right. It was atop this building that colored flags were flown to denote weather conditions. From this practice, the name Signal Hill was coined. (With permission of Palmer College of Chiropractic, Special Collections and Archives.)

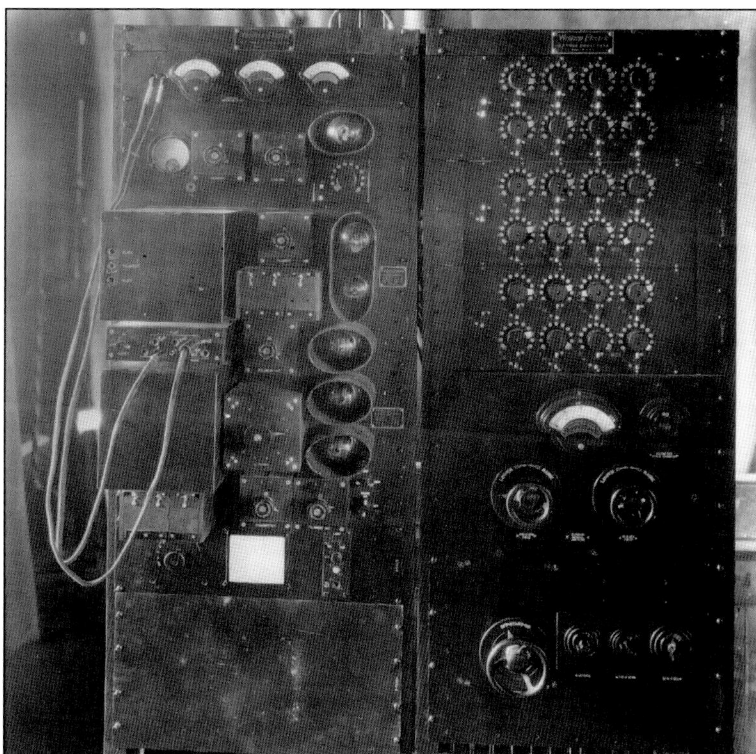

This is the piece of equipment that started it all; the Western Electric public address system. It was the first such system installed in an educational institution. Upon witnessing how an overflow crowd at a Palmer School lyceum could hear the program of lectures, B. J. Palmer realized that radio might be able to promote the practice of chiropractic to a wide audience. (With permission of Palmer College of Chiropractic, Special Collections and Archives.)

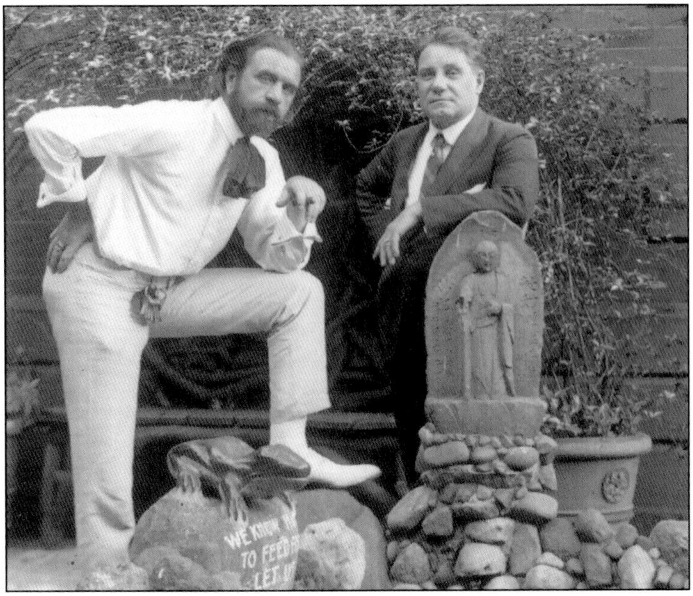

B. J. Palmer (left) and Wisconsin governor John J. Blaine meet at the Palmer residence. While the meeting initially pertained to chiropractic issues in Wisconsin, no doubt the two gentlemen had long discussions on the subject of radio. The University of Wisconsin's educational radio station, WHA, began broadcasting in January 1922, just prior to WOC. (With permission of Palmer College of Chiropractic, Special Collections and Archives.)

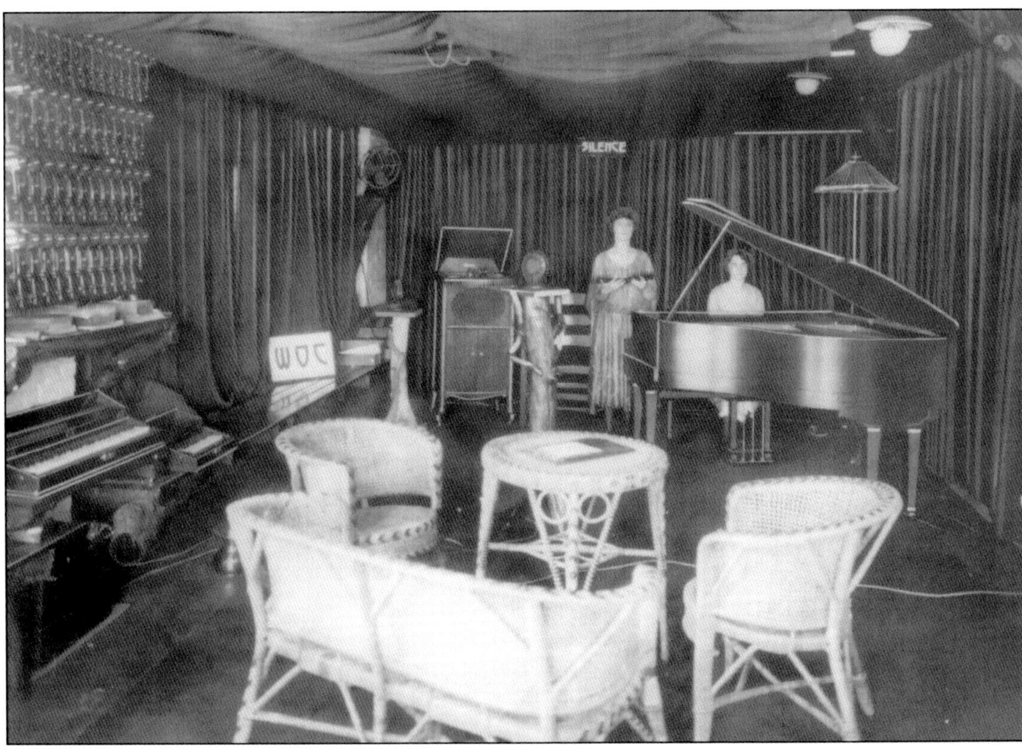

This was WOC's first broadcasting studio. Deep pile carpeting and heavy curtains hung on the walls and ceiling helped eliminate street noise and echoes. The studio was large enough for small orchestras, and an adjoining reception room was used for even larger groups. In addition to an organ and the piano, a keyboard for the bell tower chimes was located here. (With permission of Palmer College of Chiropractic, Special Collections and Archives.)

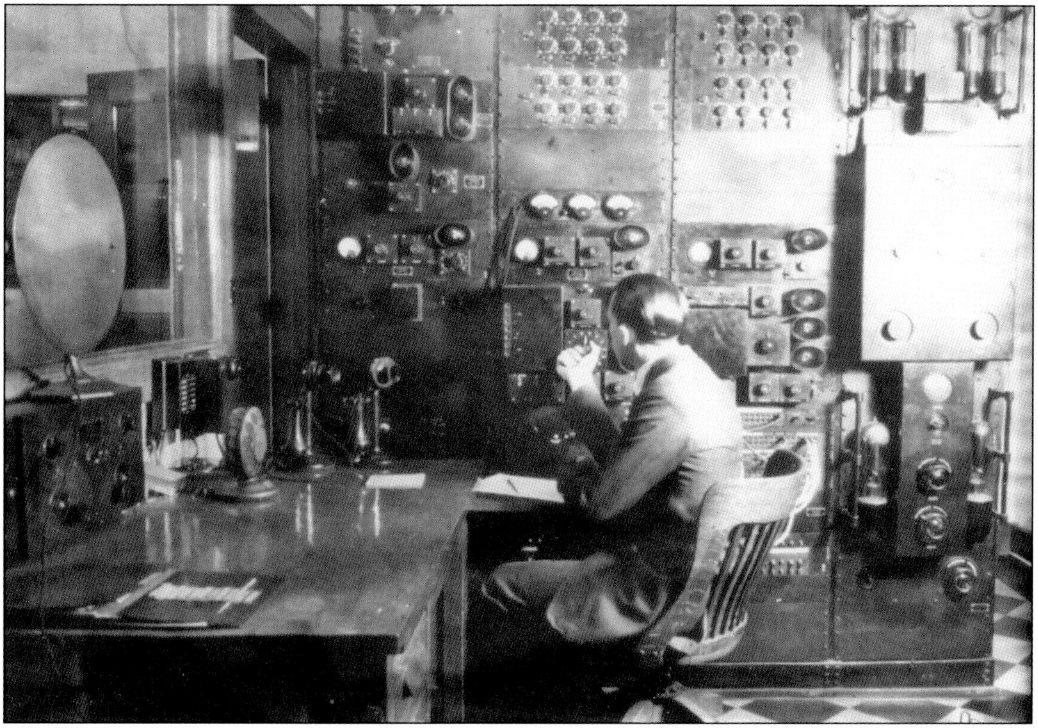

Chief engineer Frank Pierce watches over equipment in the master control room in this photograph from 1924. All studio audio programming passed through this point on its way to the transmitter. The large unit on the right was part of the public address system that allowed radio programs or announcements to be carried throughout the entire facilities of the Palmer School of Chiropractic. (Courtesy of Vern Peterson.)

Pictured is a rather interesting view of one of the antenna towers and the building atop Palmer School of Chiropractic that housed WOC's technical and transmission equipment. Through the windows on the left are the 5,000-watt transmitter, electrical generator, and batteries. Master control and the school's public address system are in the center. On the far right is a small announcing studio. (Courtesy of Vern Peterson.)

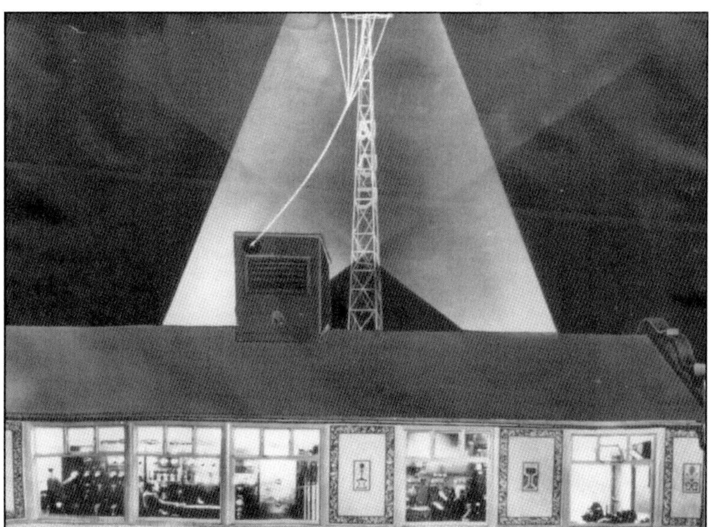

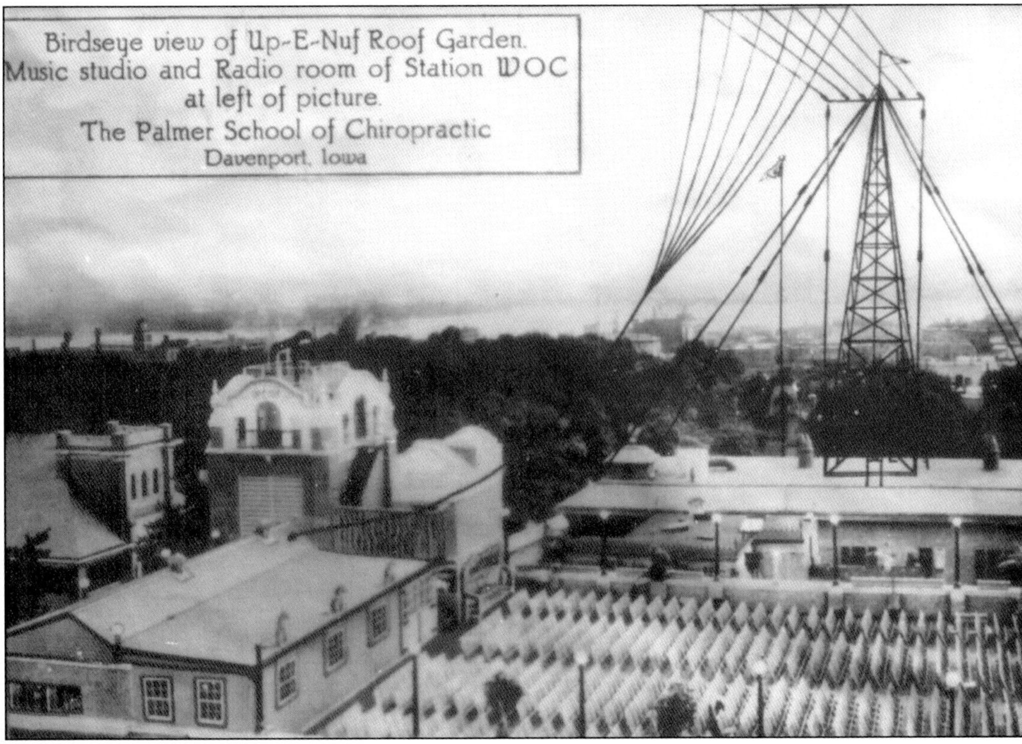

This early postcard photograph displays the 1922-era facilities of radio station WOC on the Up-E-Nuf Roof Garden of Palmer School of Chiropractic. The building beneath the tower houses the transmission and power-generating equipment. The building to the left contains the reception area, announcers' studio, and a larger studio used for musical programs. (Courtesy of Vern Petersen.)

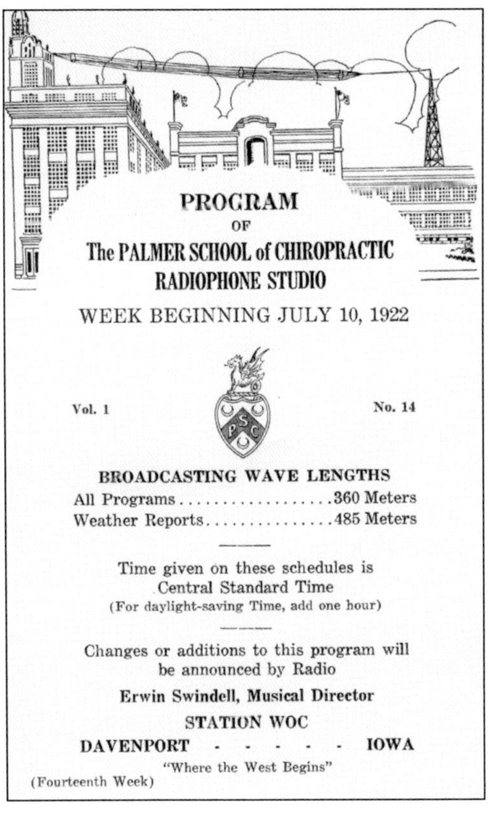

PROGRAM
OF
The PALMER SCHOOL of CHIROPRACTIC
RADIOPHONE STUDIO

WEEK BEGINNING JULY 10, 1922

Vol. 1 No. 14

BROADCASTING WAVE LENGTHS

All Programs..................360 Meters
Weather Reports...............485 Meters

Time given on these schedules is Central Standard Time
(For daylight-saving Time, add one hour)

Changes or additions to this program will be announced by Radio

Erwin Swindell, Musical Director
STATION WOC
DAVENPORT - - - - - IOWA
"Where the West Begins"
(Fourteenth Week)

With radio being a totally strange, new medium, WOC published program guides so listeners would know what would be broadcast and at what time it could be heard. When the government first allowed voice broadcasting, all radio stations used the same two frequencies as noted on the guide. As more stations took to the air, or began to increase their signal power, the government saw the need to create individual frequency assignments.

The broadcast day in 1922 was nothing like it is now. While today's radio audience can find programming around the clock, early radio might broadcast for only a brief period. It would then inform the audience to tune in again at a particular time to hear another program, as this schedule indicates. Needless to say, the educational talk scheduled at 3:30 p.m. did not last for over two hours.

MONDAY, JULY 10, 1922

12 Noon........................Chimes Concert
12:15 P. M......................Weather Report
1:30 P. M....Closing Stock & Market Quotations

3:30 P. M.—EDUCATIONAL TALK

"Turn On the Button" ....
Delivered by J. K. Hawkins

5:45 to 6:00 P. M................Chimes Concert
6:30 P. M.......................Baseball Scores

7:00 to 8:00 P. M.—MUSICAL (Indian Program)

ARTISTS

Erwin Swindell, Musical Director
Margaret Louise Frank........................Soprano
Erwin Swindell ....Pianist

PROGRAM

"From the Land of the Sky Blue Water"........................Cadman
"The White Dawn Is Falling".................................Cadman
Margaret Louise Frank
Selection—Duo Art
"The Moon Drops Low"..................................Cadman
"Pow-wow" ....Lane
Erwin Swindell.
"Pale Moon" ....Logan
Margaret Louise Frank
Selection—Duo Art

Livestock and grain quotations are official Chicago Board of Trade quotations, furnished by courtesy of W. H. Hutton Co., Blackhawk Bldg., Davenport, Iowa

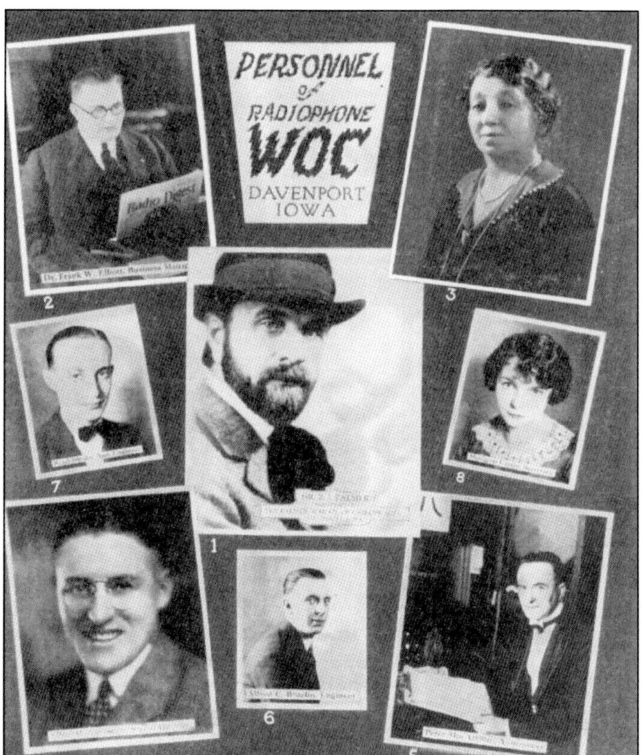

A *c.* 1925 promotional piece displays the faces of the people heard by the WOC audience. In the center is president Dr. B. J. Palmer; clockwise from the upper left are vice president Dr. Frank Elliott, musical director Amalia Schmidt-Gobble, hostess Marigold Cassin, announcer Peter MacArthur, chief engineer Alfred Bruzlin, studio director and announcer Edgar Twamley, and operator and announcer Reed Snyder. The announcers did not use names, only their initials.

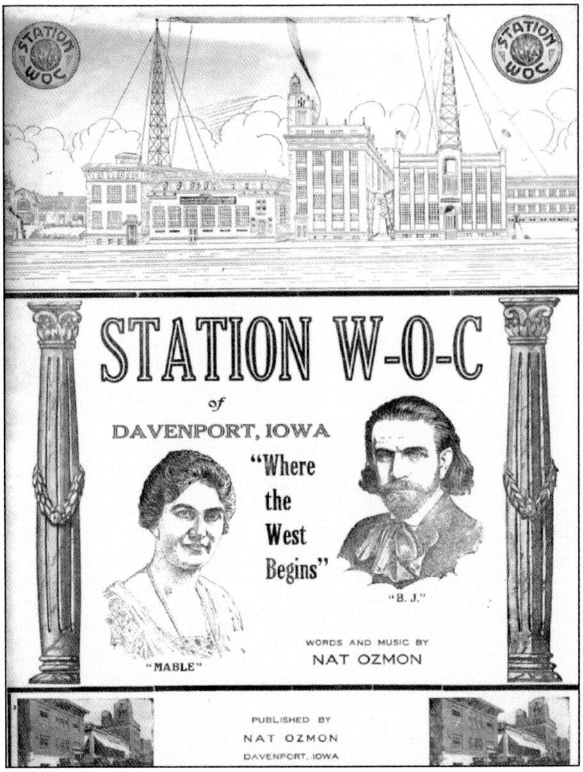

It is not often that a radio station has an actual song written about it, but WOC did. Nat Ozmon was a singer and dancer who had appeared on the vaudeville stage. He also sang on WOC. In 1923, Ozmon composed both the lyrics and music to "Where the West Begins" as a tribute to Dr. B. J. Palmer and his wife, Mabel. The cover rendering provides a great image of WOC's antenna system.

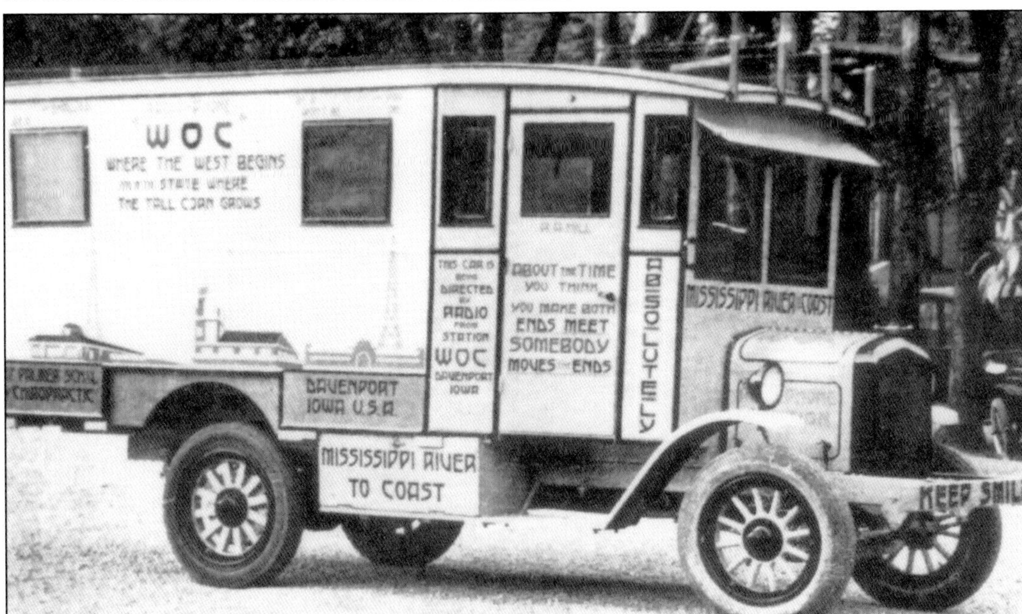

WOC employed this vehicle as a radio mobile unit, broadcasting live from important events around the area during the 1920s. The unit also made a cross-country trip, stopping at interesting places along the way to send reports back to Davenport. B. J. Palmer was a fan of epigrams, which are concise clever statements. A few are seen on the side of the truck, and many can still be seen today around the Palmer College campus.

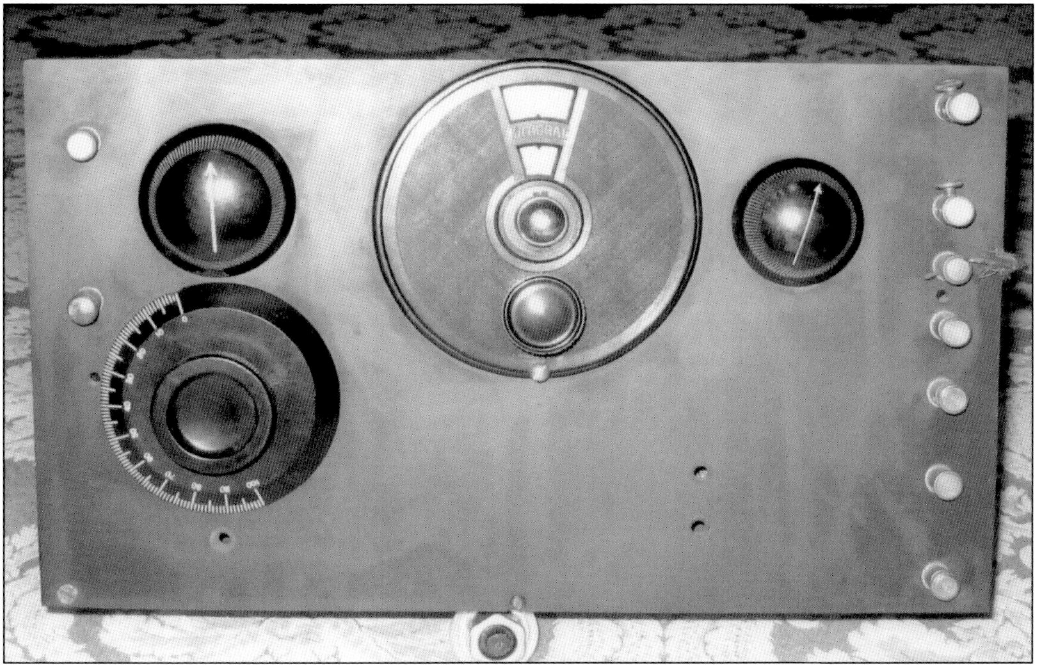

Radios of the 1920s era might qualify as the first component sets. This is the tuner portion of the grouping. A power supply, in the form of three dry-cell batteries, a power transformer, and a speaker, are still needed to complete a working radio set. The batteries and transformer were wired to the connectors on the right side of this tuner panel, and the speaker was wired on the left.

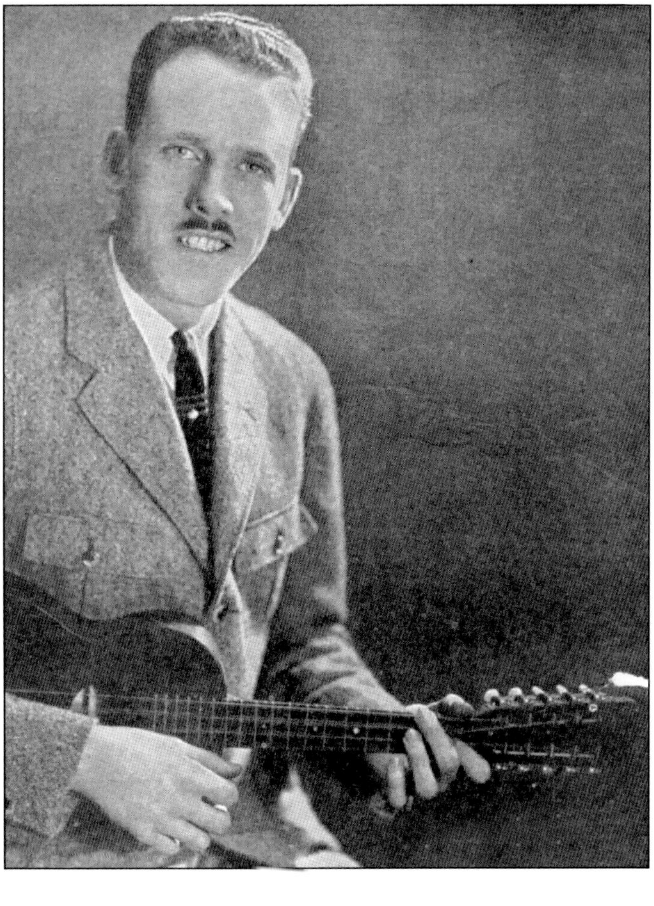

Wendell Hall, the "Red-Headed Music Maker," was one of WOC's most popular musicians. He spent several weeks at the station playing his ukulele and singing his million dollar–selling song "It Ain't Gonna Rain No Mo.' " Newspaper reports noted WOC received over 40,000 fan letters while Hall was in Davenport. He went on to host the *Eveready Hour* on WEAF in New York, the first station to provide a "chain," or network, radio hookup.

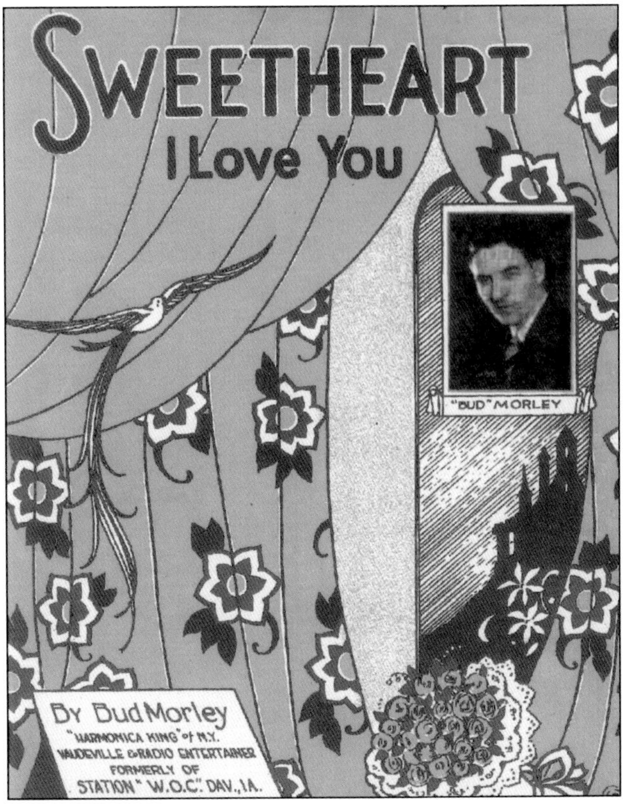

Needing plenty of entertainment to fill a broadcast schedule, WOC hired many musicians to provide programming. At one point, over 400 musical acts had been heard on the station. In the mid-1920s, the publishers of this song and sheet music felt it would help sales and give credence to former vaudevillian and harmonica player Bud Morely if it was noted that he had been heard on station WOC.

Freeman Gosden (left) and former Rock Island resident Charles Correll were the creators of *Amos 'n' Andy*, a radio situation comedy set in the African American community. The show premiered on NBC in 1929 and ran nightly on WOC until 1934. Over the course of the nightly shows, the duo portrayed all the male roles and had created over 170 voice characterizations. (Courtesy of Rock Island County Historical Society.)

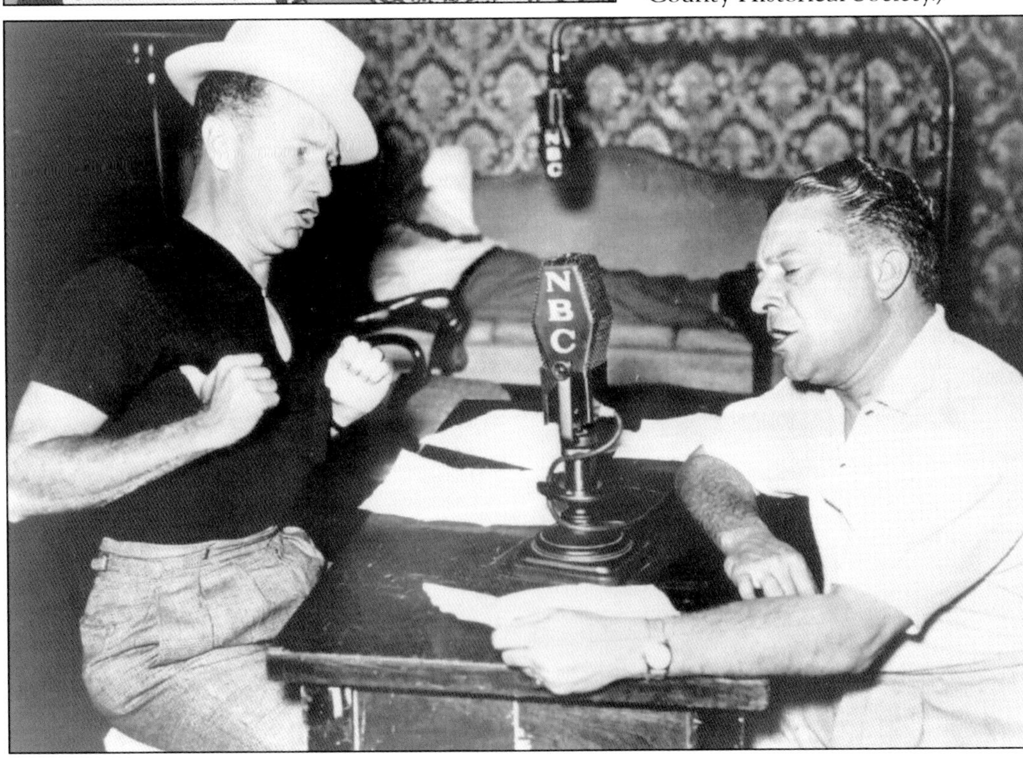

Cowboy music was extremely popular during the Depression years. Ken Houchins, who some say sounded like Gene Autry, performed on his own show heard on WOC in 1930. By 1933, he had joined the Prairie Ramblers and was part of the National Barn Dance program from Chicago, also carried by WOC. Houchins would return to Davenport in 1950 and appear as "Cowboy Ken" on a WOC-TV children's program.

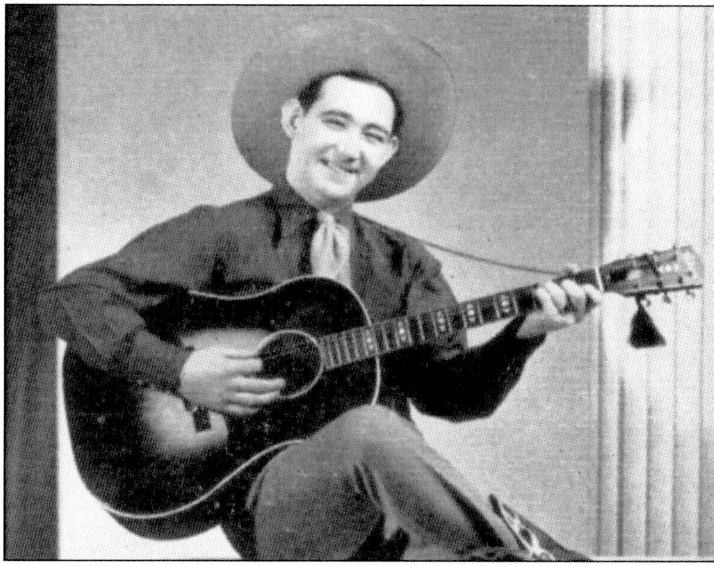

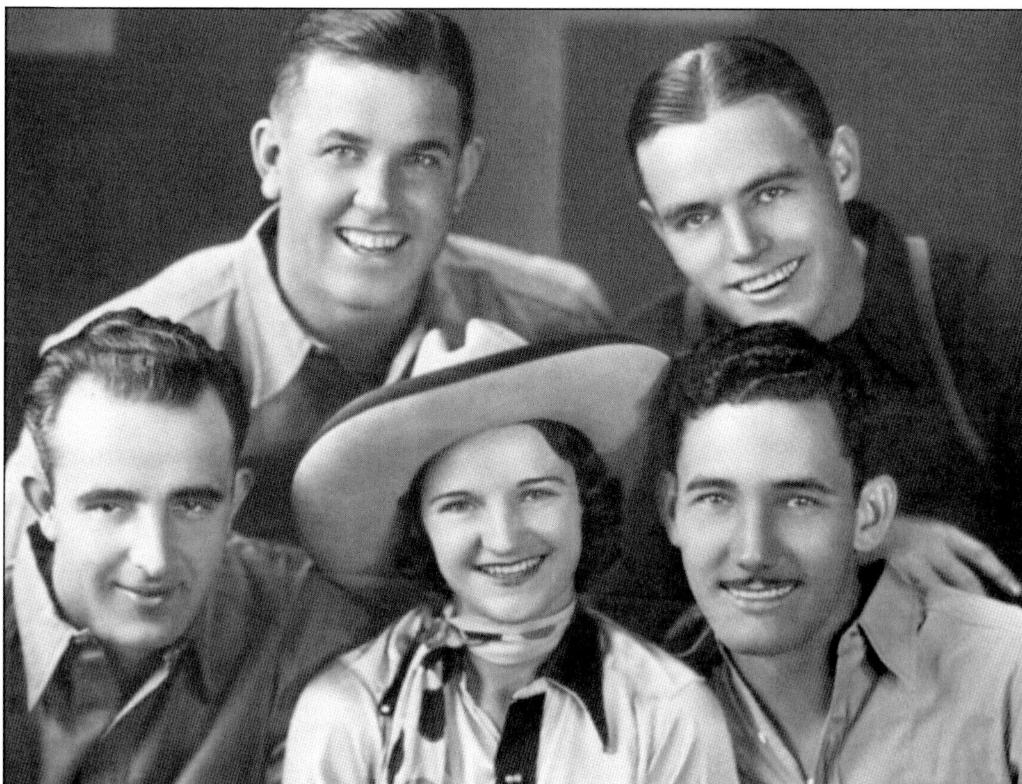

Known as the Kentucky Ramblers, this group received its first radio job at WOC in 1932. After six months, the group moved on to the *National Barn Dance* program and was chosen as one of the most popular acts on that program. Members of the group, seen here from left to right, were (first row) Jack Taylor, Patsy Montana, and "Salty" Holmes; (second row) Chick Hurt and Tex Atchison. Later Montana led the group. (Courtesy of Scott Childers-WLSHistory.com)

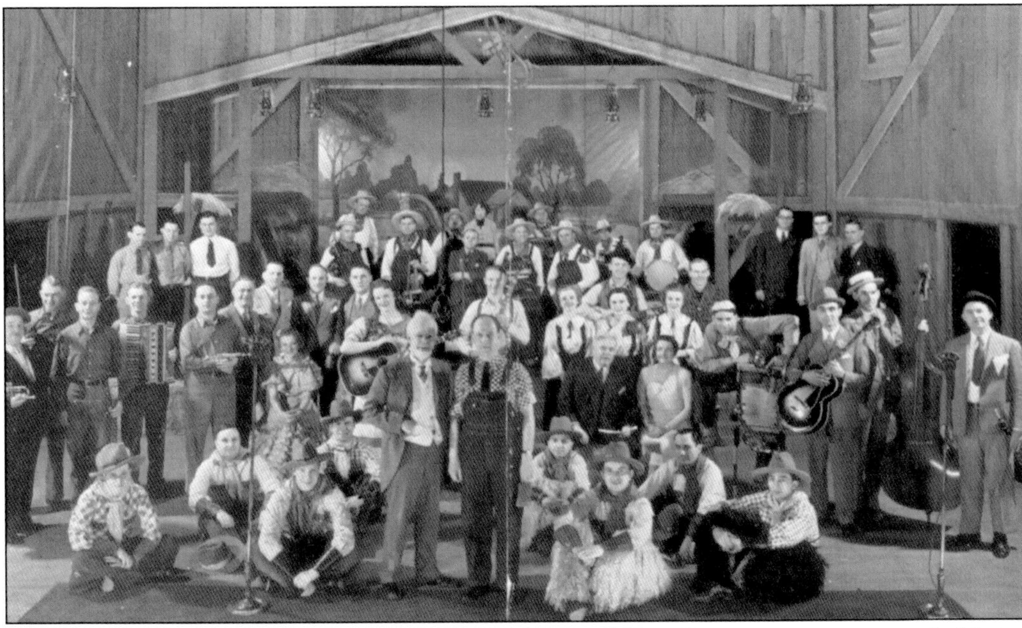

Originating on Chicago radio station WLS, the *National Barn Dance* was a program of old-time music that became hugely popular with both rural and urban audiences. NBC picked up an hour of the program every Saturday night and fed it coast to coast. WOC aired the show locally. Many popular musicians and comedians appeared on the show, including Red Foley, Gene Autry, George Gobel, and radio's "Fibber McGee and Molly."

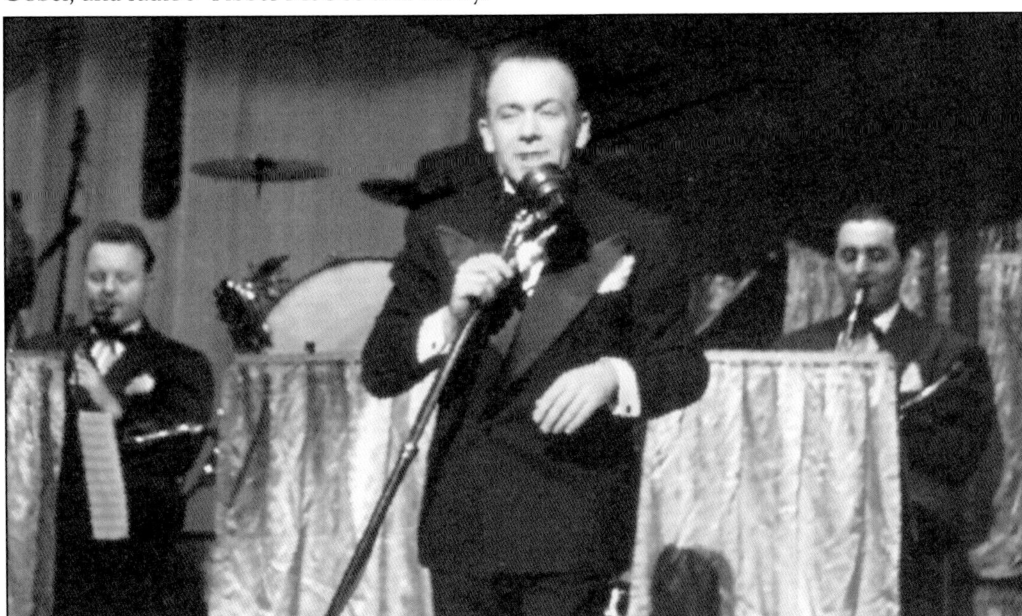

Originally from England, "Little" Jack Little studied at the University of Iowa and played in the university band. In the late 1920s, Little organized his own orchestra and began touring. Little and the orchestra were featured for a period of time on the *Fitch Bandwagon* program that originated on WOC-WHO Radio. He was considered a master of a singing-talking technique that was popular with listeners during the 1930s.

Two

RADIO MATURES

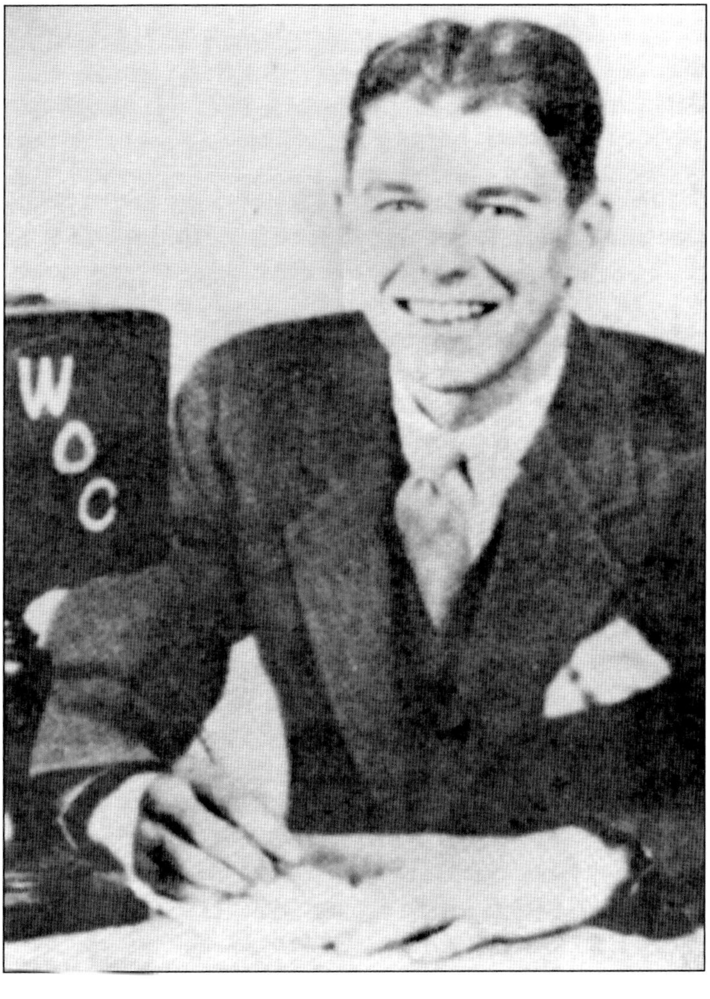

WOC gave 21-year-old Ronald Reagan his first job in radio. Hired in the fall of 1932, Reagan worked as the station's sports announcer through the end of the football season late that fall. In March 1933, he was rehired as both a sports and general staff announcer. Reagan always credited his start in show business to WOC. (With permission of Palmer College of Chiropractic, Special Collections and Archives.)

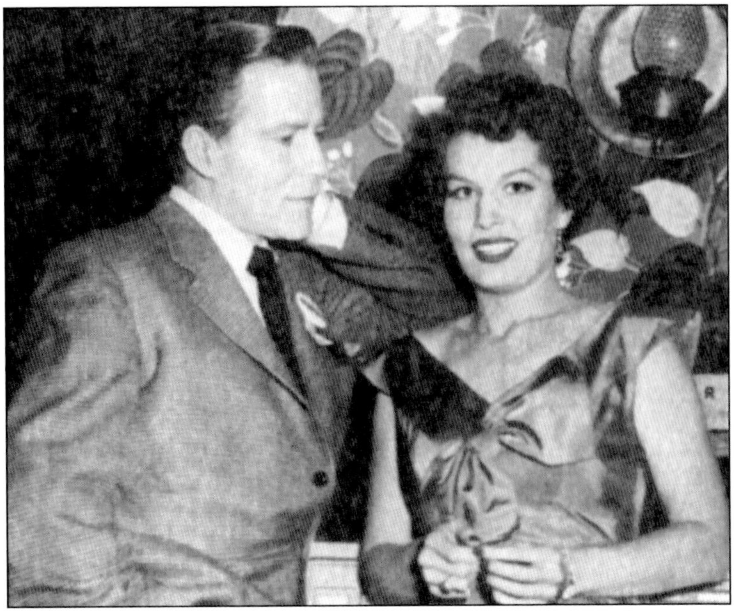

While both were working at WOC, Ronald Reagan asked fellow announcer Hugh Hipple for some advice regarding his commercial delivery. Hipple told him to look for another line of work. Reagan ignored that advice. Hipple went to Hollywood and became actor Hugh Marlowe, shown here with actress Jean Willes in a scene from his television series *Ellery Queen*. Marlowe played many roles in movies and television soap operas.

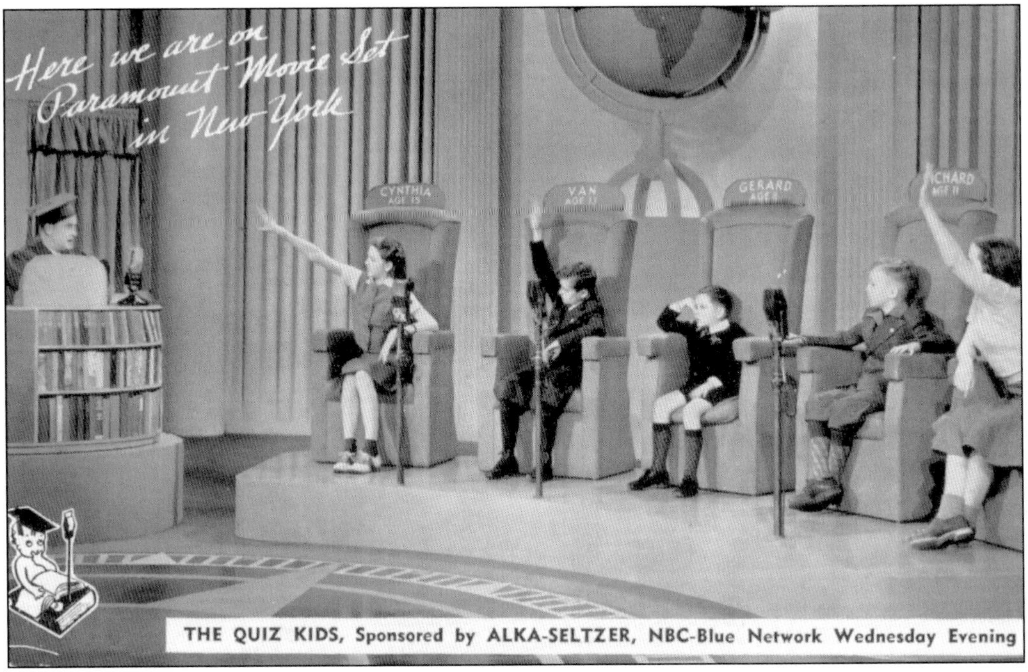

An extremely popular program heard on WOC was *Quiz Kids*. Host Joe Kelly asked questions sent in by the listening audience. The panel consisted of five children who had been chosen because of their high IQs. Kelly often noted that he only knew answers to the questions because he had cue cards; the real intellectuals were the children. The popular program later moved to television and was carried on WOC-TV.

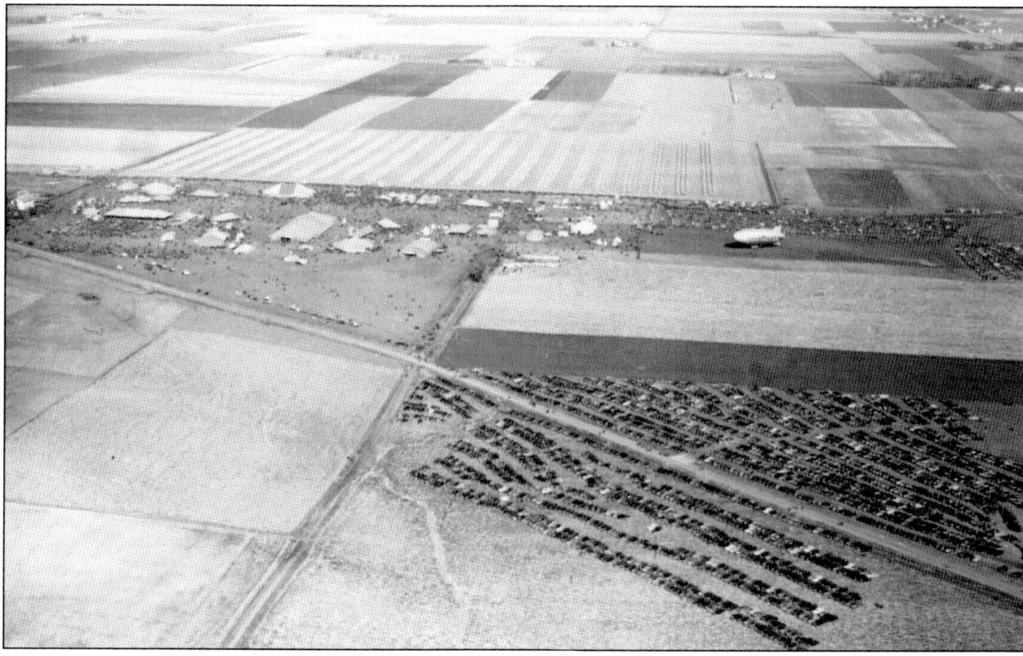

A 1936 issue of *Time* magazine called corn husking "the fastest growing sporting spectacle in the world." That spectacle came to Davenport in the form of the 1940 National Corn Husking Championship. The contest was held on the Henry Keppy farm just northwest of town. According to newspaper accounts, an estimated crowd of 160,000 came to watch the competitors. The national radio networks and WOC were on hand to capture the excitement of competitors husking nearly 50 bushels in 80 minutes. A typical farmer would husk 100 bushels in a full day. The aerial photograph shows the Keppy farm set up for the contest, and yes, that is the Goodyear blimp. The photograph below shows part of the crowd on contest day. How did those toward the back see anything? (Courtesy of Kewanee Historical Society.)

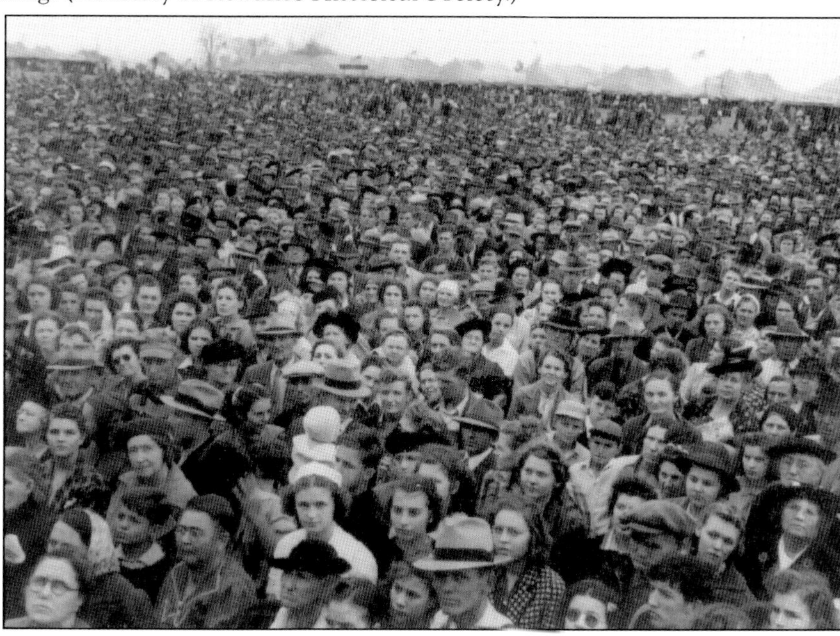

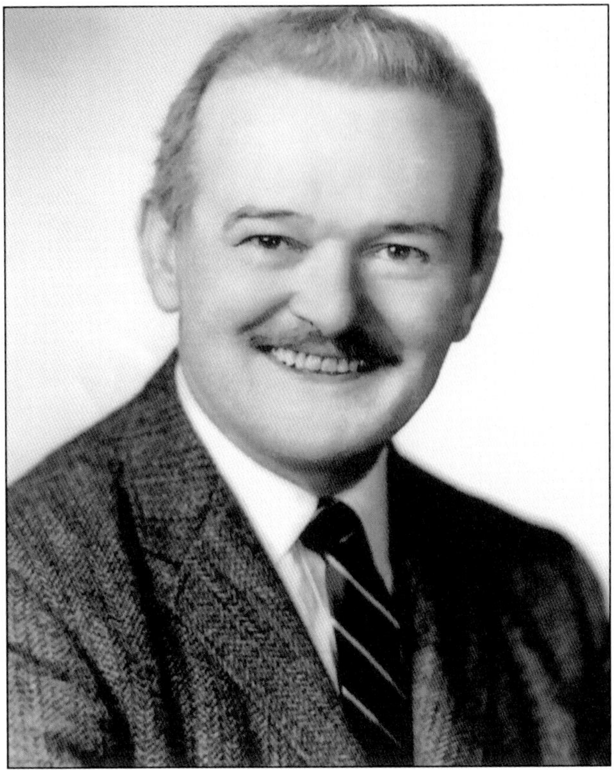

In the earlier days of radio, stations employed staff musicians to provide programming during non-network hours. WOC employed two of the best. Whether behind the scenes or in the studio, solo or together, George Sontag and Marjorie Meinert filled many hours of radio airtime. Sontag had been the pianist with the Orrin Tucker Orchestra from 1932 until the orchestra broke up just prior to World War II. He then joined WOC as musical director. Organist Marjorie Meinert became Sontag's partner in a number of musical programs. A rare talent on the organ, Meinert recorded singles and albums for both the Fraternity and RCA Victor record labels. Along with host Warren Vasen, the two were the stars of WOC-TV's *Trip the Trio* that had viewers send in song titles they thought would stump the group. (Courtesy of Rich Birley.)

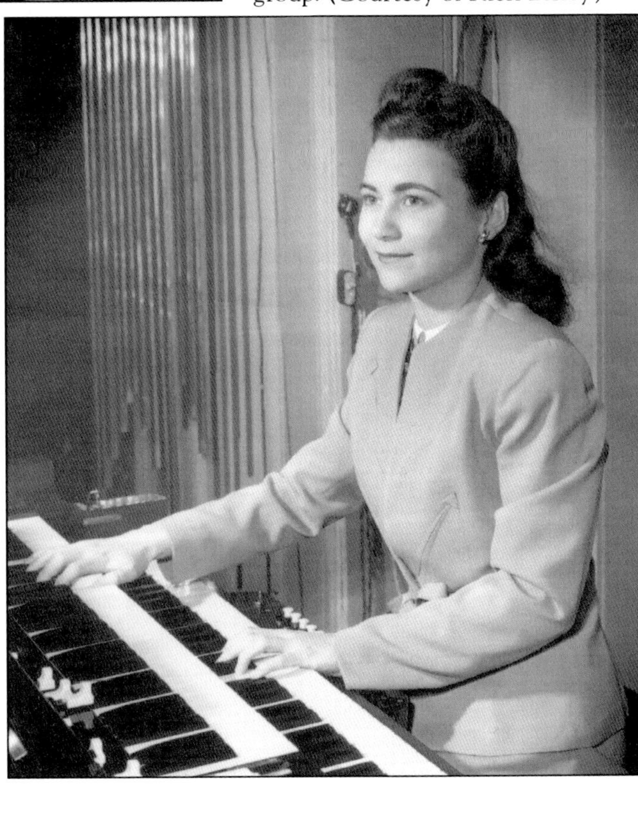

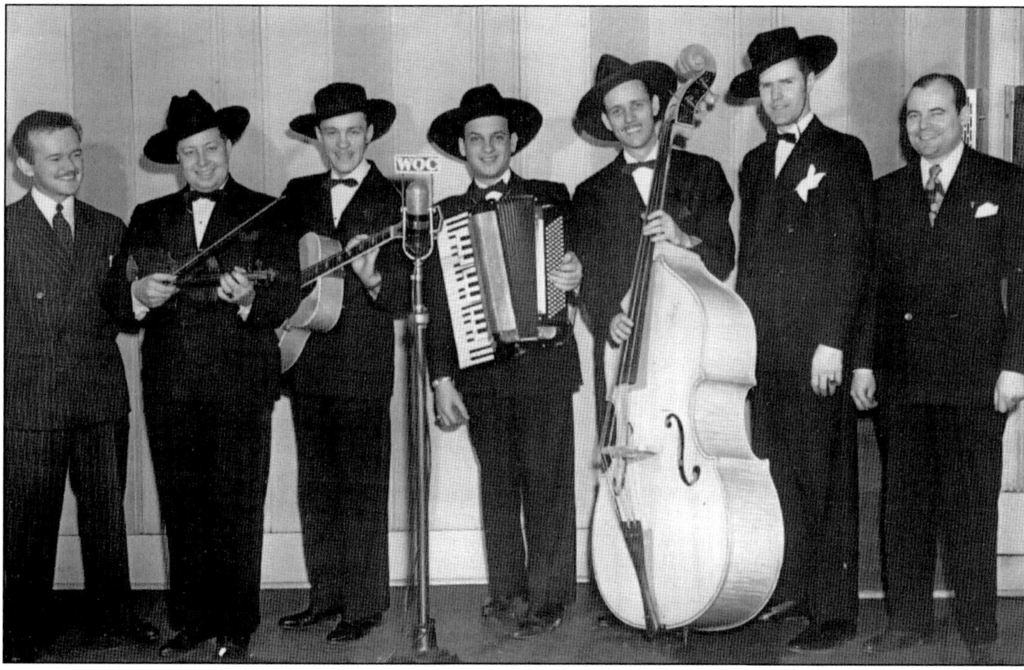

One of the musical groups hired to provide programming and fill non-network airtime was Hi-Pockets Hayden and the Plainsmen. A rather interesting quintet, the group wore tuxedos and cowboy hats and sang Western songs. WOC's musical director George Sontag (far left) and program director Phil Patton (far right), both veterans of the Orrin Tucker Orchestra, are shown with the group in this *c.* 1943 photograph. (Courtesy of Rich Birley.)

During World War II, firms would occasionally use some of their advertising time to help the war effort. This live ad copy, paid for by the Simon and Landauer clothing store, delivered a patriotic message and urged listeners to purchase war stamps and bonds. Note the underlining, no doubt placed there by an announcer. It marks which words should be emphasized while reading the commercial on the air. (Courtesy of Jon Book.)

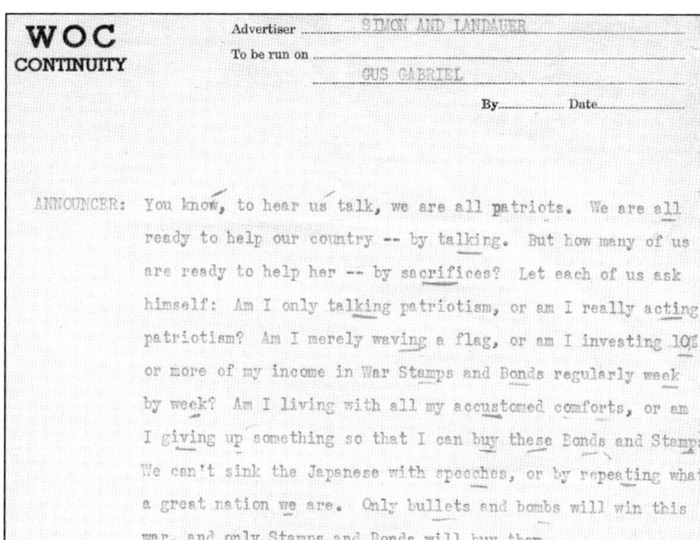

WOC
CONTINUITY

Advertiser SIMON AND LANDAUER
To be run on
GUS GABRIEL
By.......... Date..........

ANNOUNCER: You know, to hear us talk, we are all patriots. We are all ready to help our country -- by talking. But how many of us are ready to help her -- by sacrifices? Let each of us ask himself: Am I only talking patriotism, or am I really acting patriotism? Am I merely waving a flag, or am I investing 10% or more of my income in War Stamps and Bonds regularly week by week? Am I living with all my accustomed comforts, or am I giving up something so that I can buy these Bonds and Stamps We can't sink the Japanese with speeches, or by repeating what a great nation we are. Only bullets and bombs will win this war, and only Stamps and Bonds will buy them.

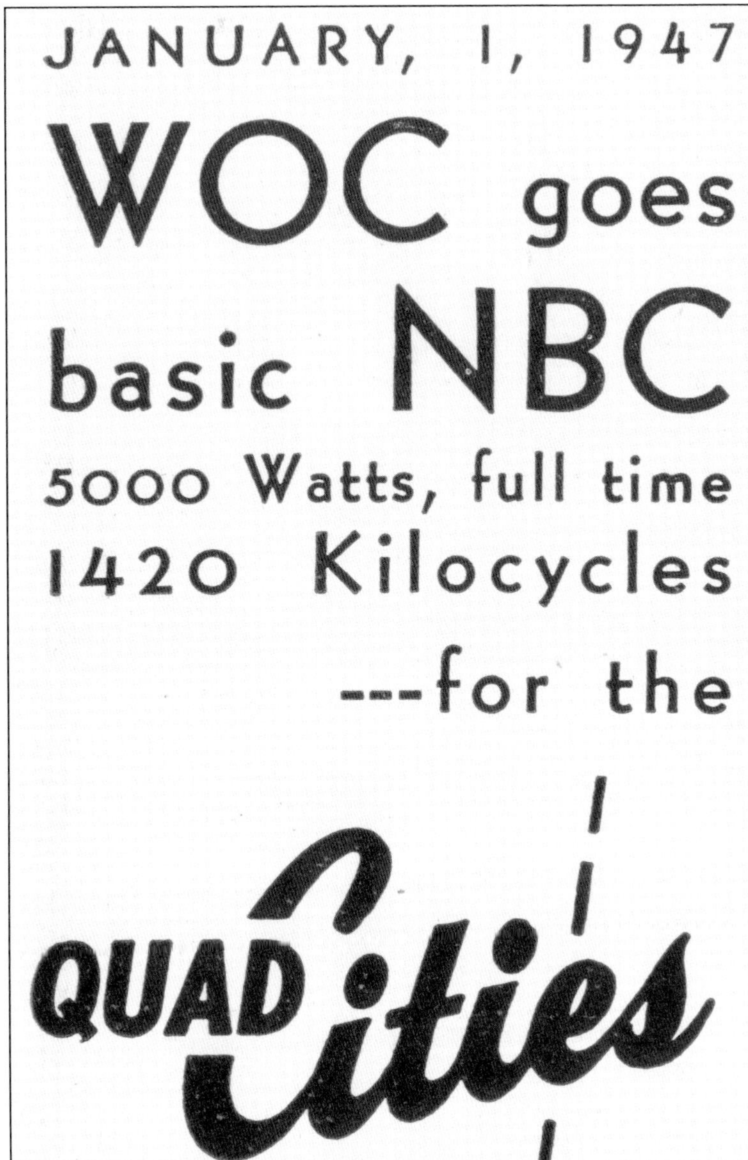

Radio Corporation of America (RCA) created the National Broadcasting Company (NBC) in 1926 by purchasing two radio stations that had each created a loosely structured network of other radio stations. Based on the marketing strategies of those two stations, NBC set up two networks. The Red Network offered sponsored entertainment and musical programs, while the Blue Network carried non-sponsored programs of mostly news and cultural programs. WOC chose to use NBC-Blue. WOC split operations from sister station WHO in 1934 and affiliated with the CBS network for a brief period, then returned to NBC-Blue. By 1939, NBC networks dominated radio audiences and advertising. The Federal Communications Commission (FCC) ordered NBC to divest itself of one of them. The Blue Network was sold in 1945 and became known as the American Broadcasting Company (ABC). When NBC-Blue became ABC, WOC remained with ABC until 1947, then affiliated again with NBC as this advertisement notes. WOC remained an NBC affiliate until 1987, when network parent General Electric sold the radio network.

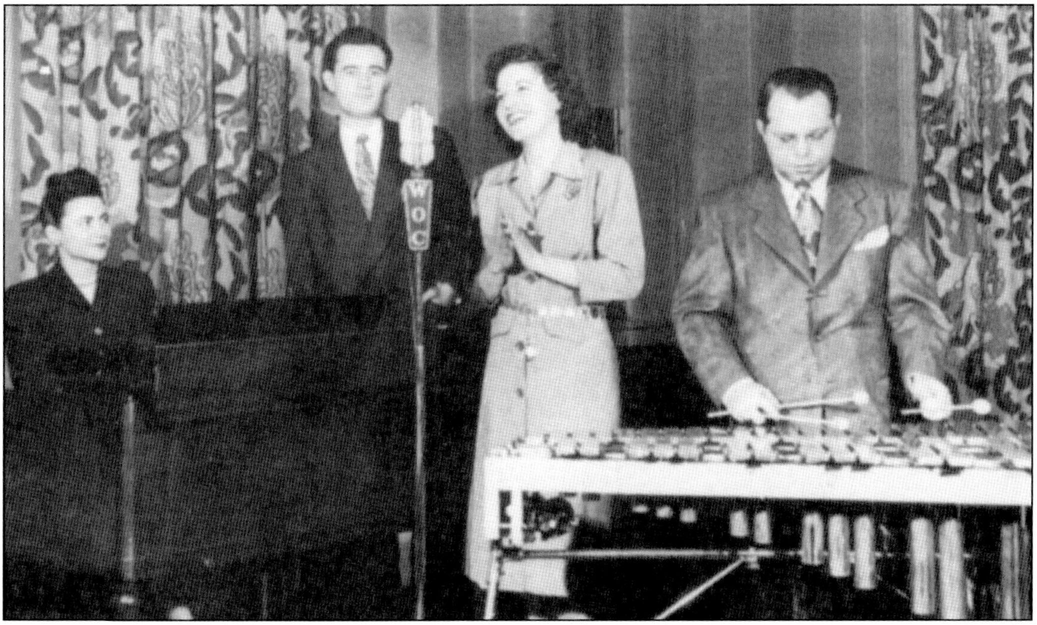

At 12:15 p.m., it's *Time to Sing*. Each afternoon this very popular musical program originated from the WOC studios to entertain its lunchtime audience. Pictured here are, from left to right, Marjorie Meinert, staff musician; Harold Heath, program announcer; Rosemary Schlack, vocalist; and Ralph Coats at the vibes. Heath was also the station's sports announcer, and Coats and Schlack were its transcription librarians.

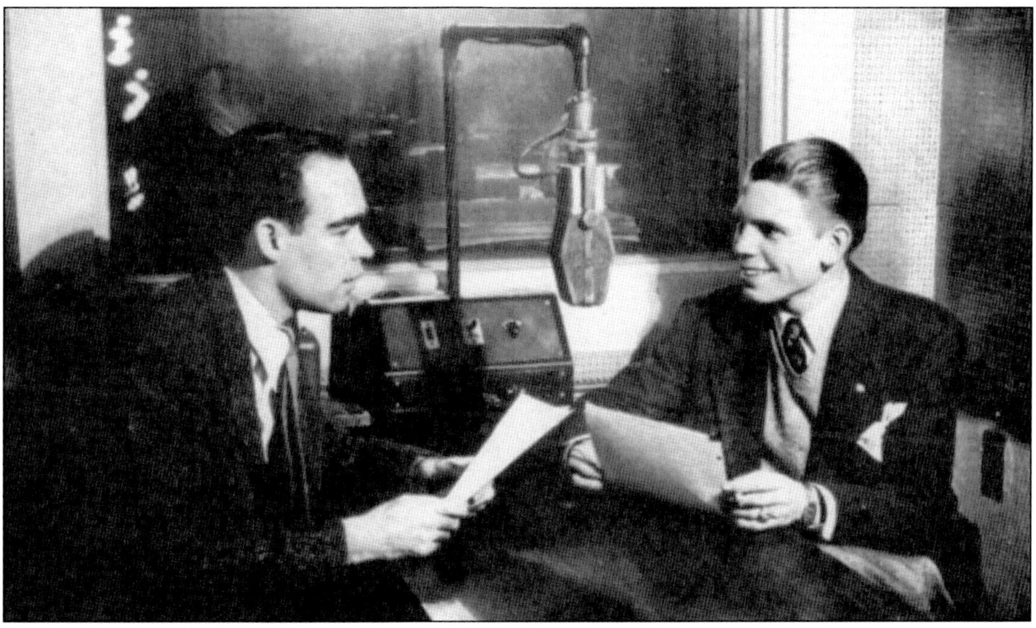

Staff announcer William Ede (left) was the host of many of WOC's recorded musical programs and was also a newsreader. Fenn Horton (right) hosted *Linger Awhile* with Marjorie Meinert and George Sontag. Horton worked only at night, as he attended St. Ambrose College during the day. After college graduation, Horton became a professor of economics at the Naval Postgraduate School in Monterey, California.

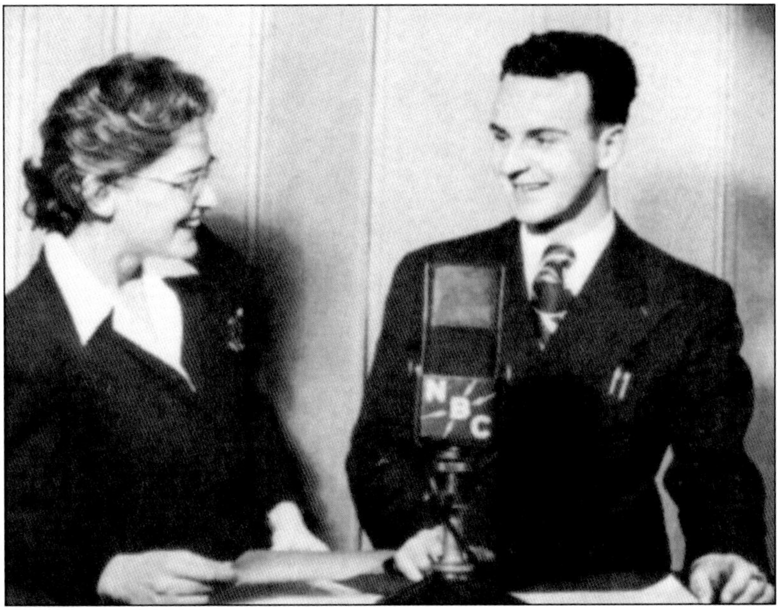

Dorothy Day and Dan Rafferty were the emcees of *Package from Parker's*, a popular program that featured recorded music. The sponsor was the M. L. Parker Department Store, hence the name of the show. The two announcers seem to be enjoying a laugh, as the show was totally ad lib.

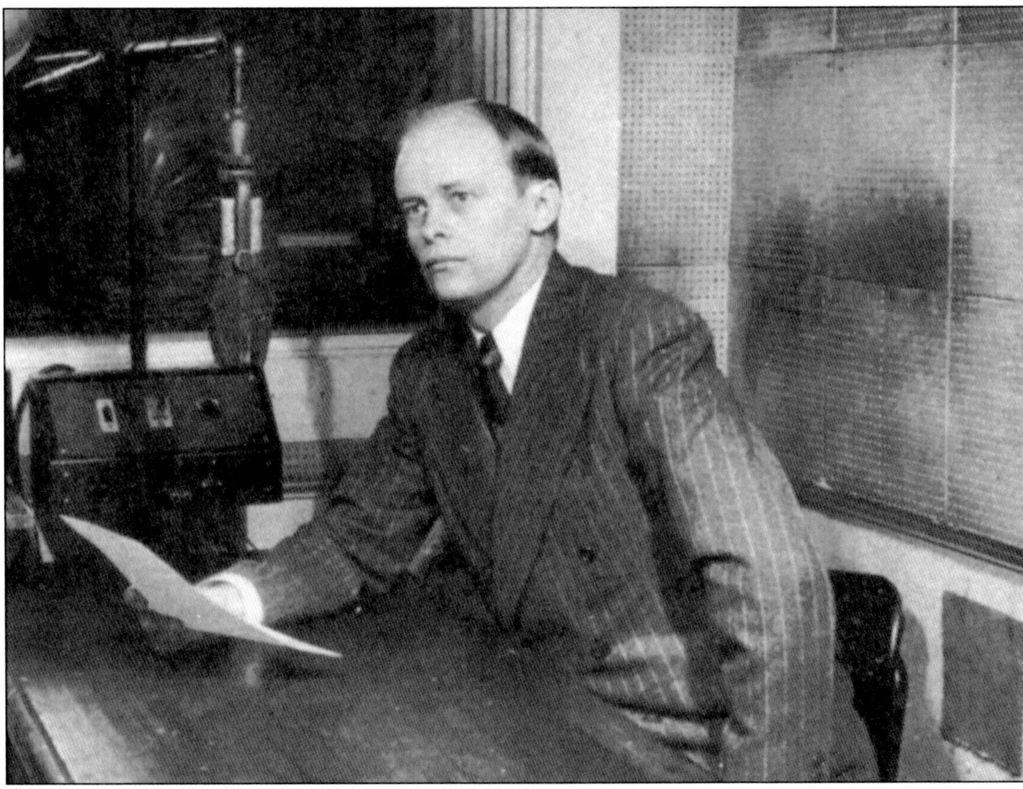

In addition to offering a wide variety of comedy, drama, and musical entertainment, WOC carried many hours of local, national, and international news programs per week. This 1947 photograph captures Bob Redeen, the station's news editor, during one of his daily news reports. Stock market reports, agricultural news, and direct broadcasts from the weather bureau were also part of WOC's daily schedule.

In this 1948 photograph, WOC announcer Dan Rafferty (left) and a group of unidentified actors demonstrate how a radio drama was presented, complete with sound effects. Today effects libraries can be found on records, CDs, or computers. In radio's earlier days, the sound effects had to be created live in the studio through the creativity and resourcefulness of engineers and actors. (Courtesy of Phil Roberts.)

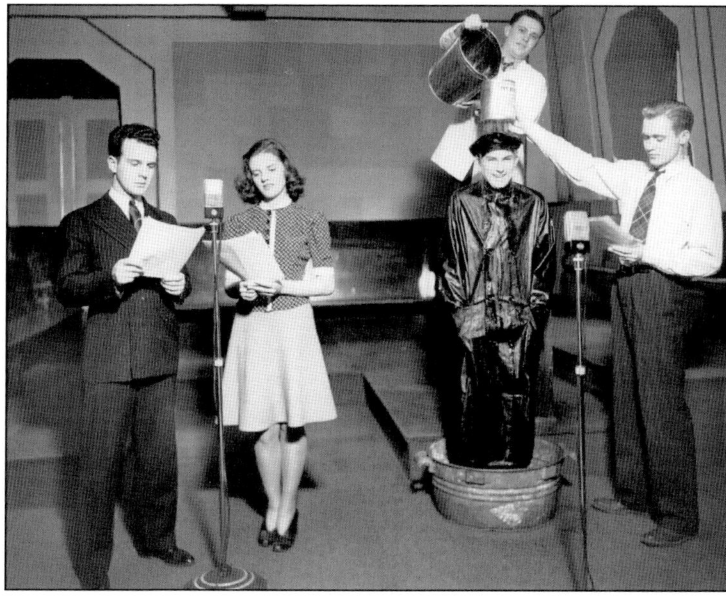

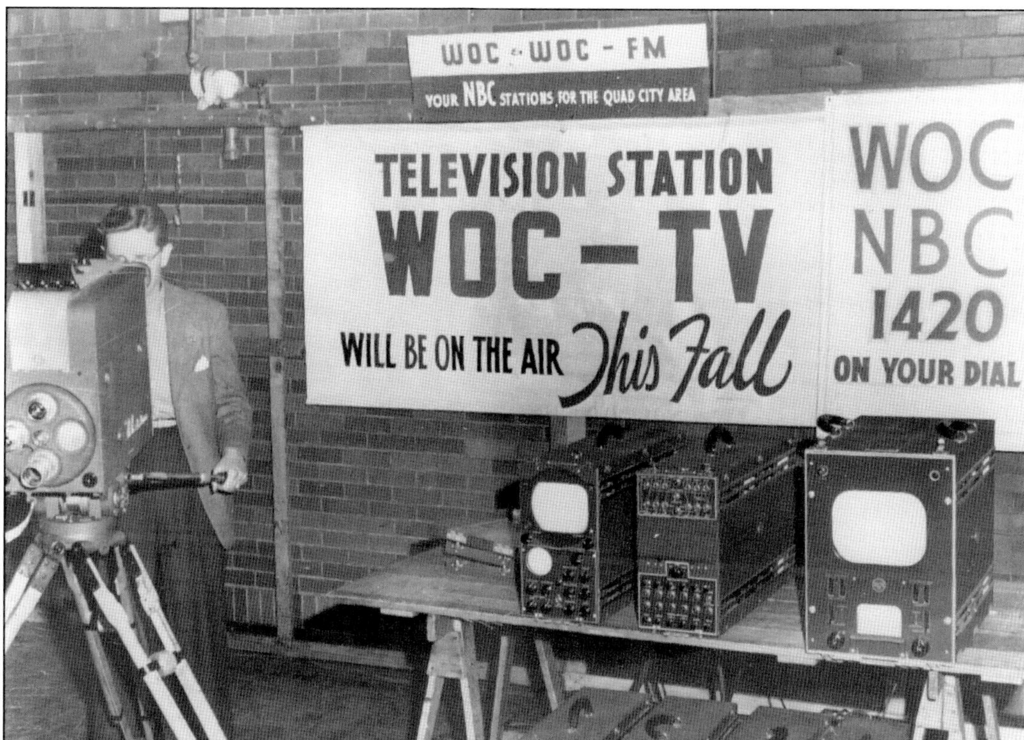

With television as an emerging medium, WOC took every opportunity to show the public what was coming. The station set up this display at various venues to inform the public that it was WOC-TV and would soon be on the air as the first television station in the Quad Cities. While it cannot be determined from this photograph, the station may have let people see themselves on camera. (Courtesy of KWQC-TV.)

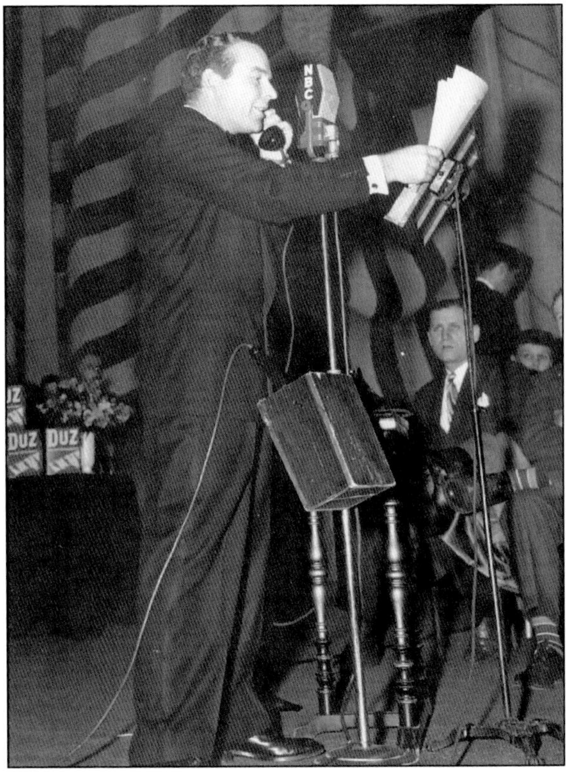

One of the most popular quiz shows on radio was *Truth or Consequences*, which starred Ralph Edwards and was carried by WOC. Contestants had to answer a zany question correctly in a very brief amount of time or face the "consequence," usually a funny or embarrassing stunt. As part of the Davenport Chamber of Commerce's Food and Home Show, Edwards and his program were brought to town for a week of performances. He would also air his two NBC network broadcasts from Davenport. In the photograph to the left, Edwards listens for his network cue to begin the program. In the photograph below, Edwards informs a contestant that she has not answered correctly and will now have to perform her "consequence." As a promotion for Edwards's appearance, WOC made him its general manager for the week. (Courtesy of John Flambo.)

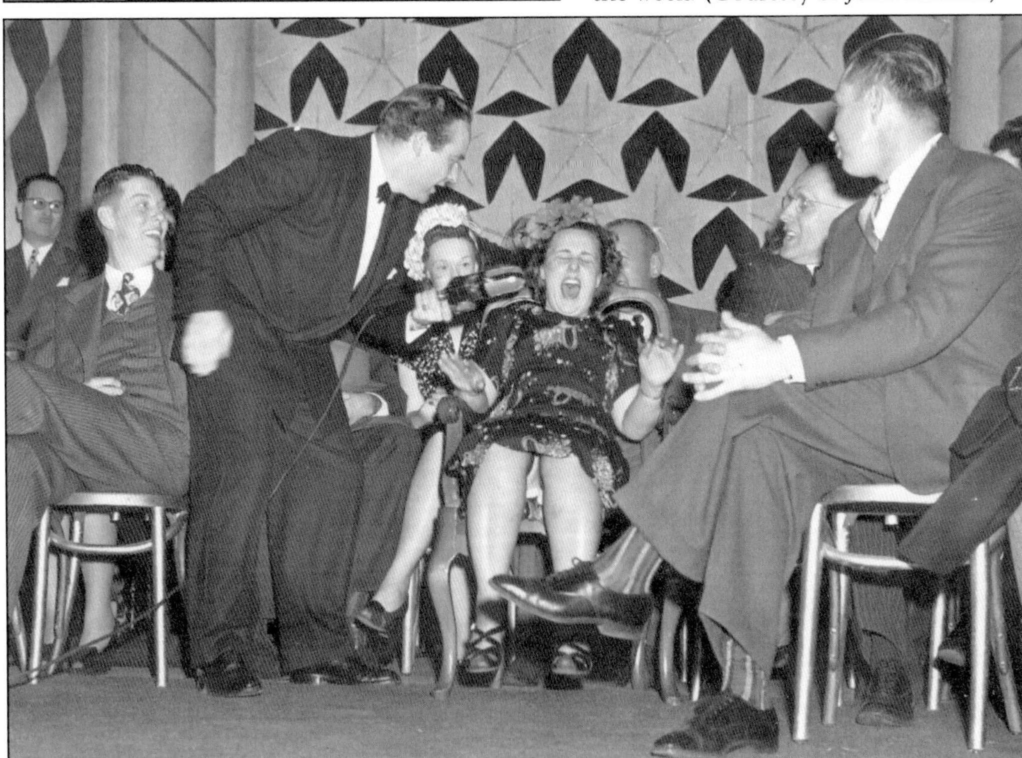

Three

Television Joins Radio

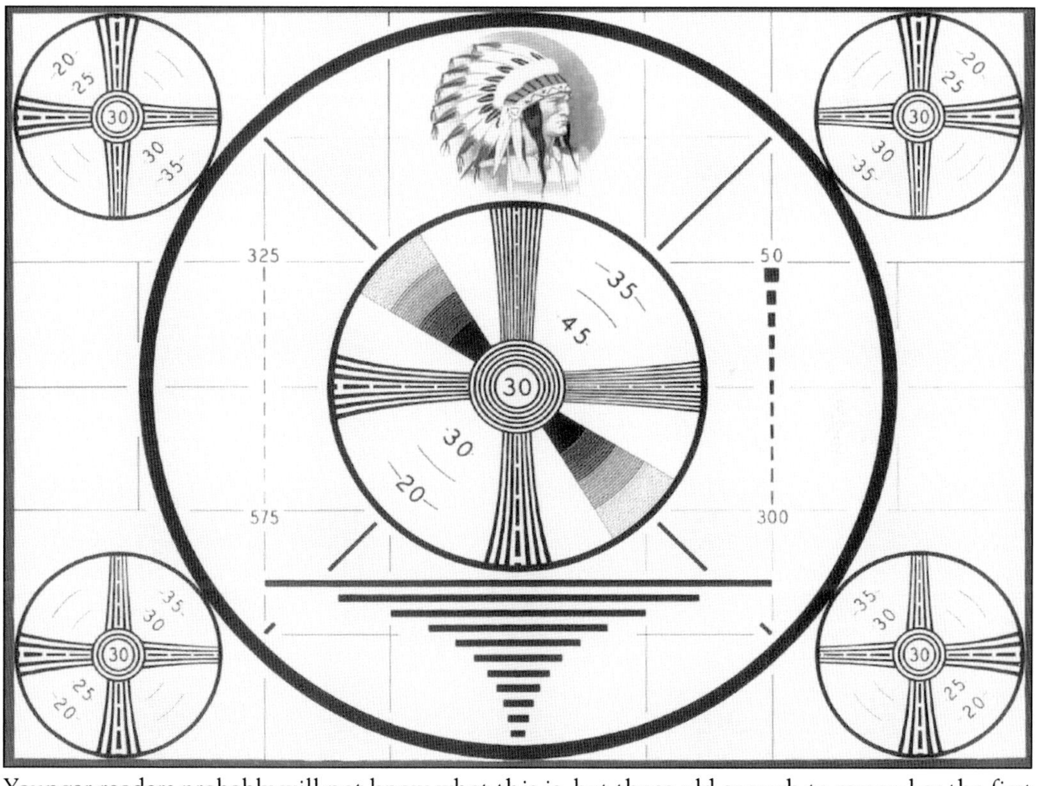

Younger readers probably will not know what this is, but those old enough to remember the first days of television do. This is called a test pattern. Early televisions had to have their picture constantly adjusted for clarity. Using controls on their televisions, viewers would "tune in" the picture when the set had warmed up. Would you believe people actually sat and watched the test pattern? (Courtesy of Chuck Pharis Video.)

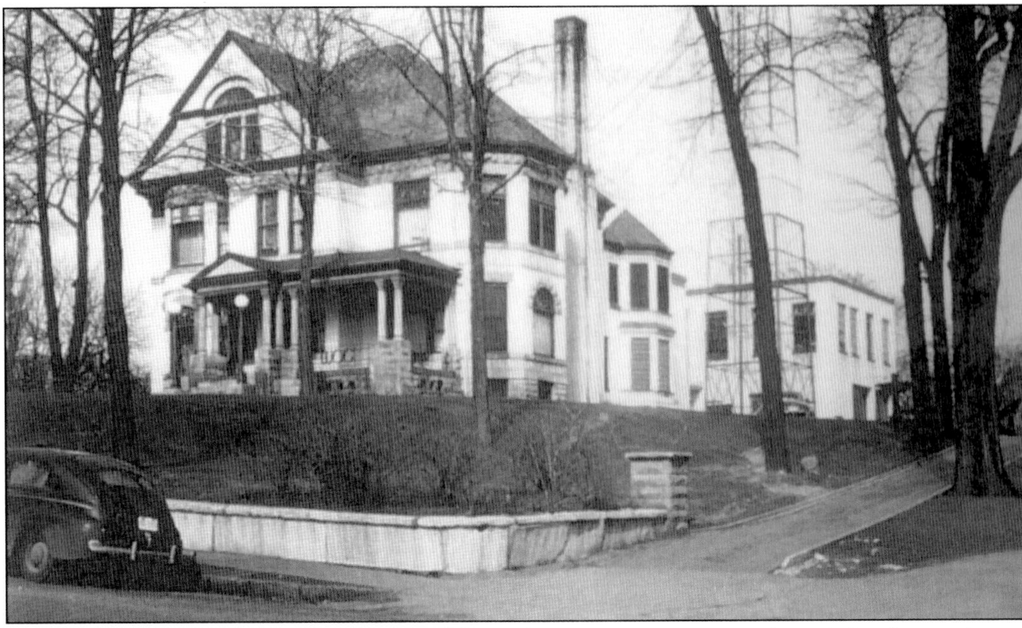

When WOC was given permission to build its television station, it purchased this former house, across the street from the Palmer School campus, to house both facilities. The interior was renovated into offices, control rooms, radio studios, and a small television studio. An annex was built at the rear of the property to house a larger television production studio and more office space. (Courtesy of Phil Roberts.)

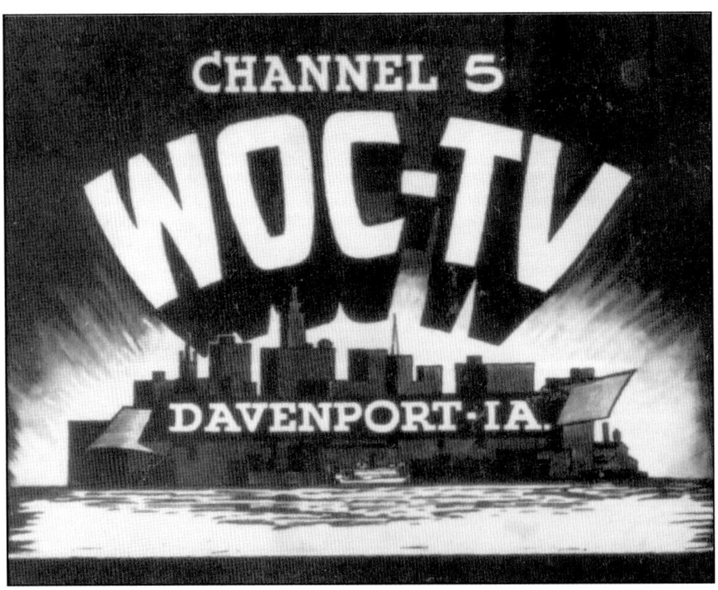

This is the original station identification slide, as drawn by WOC's staff artist Ken Wagner. The image portrays the sun rising over downtown Davenport with the Mississippi River in the foreground. It was a legal identification, as it listed channel number, call letters, and city of license. Wagner's artistic abilities were seen on a great variety of camera cards used for client advertisement graphics. (Courtesy of Ivan Owens.)

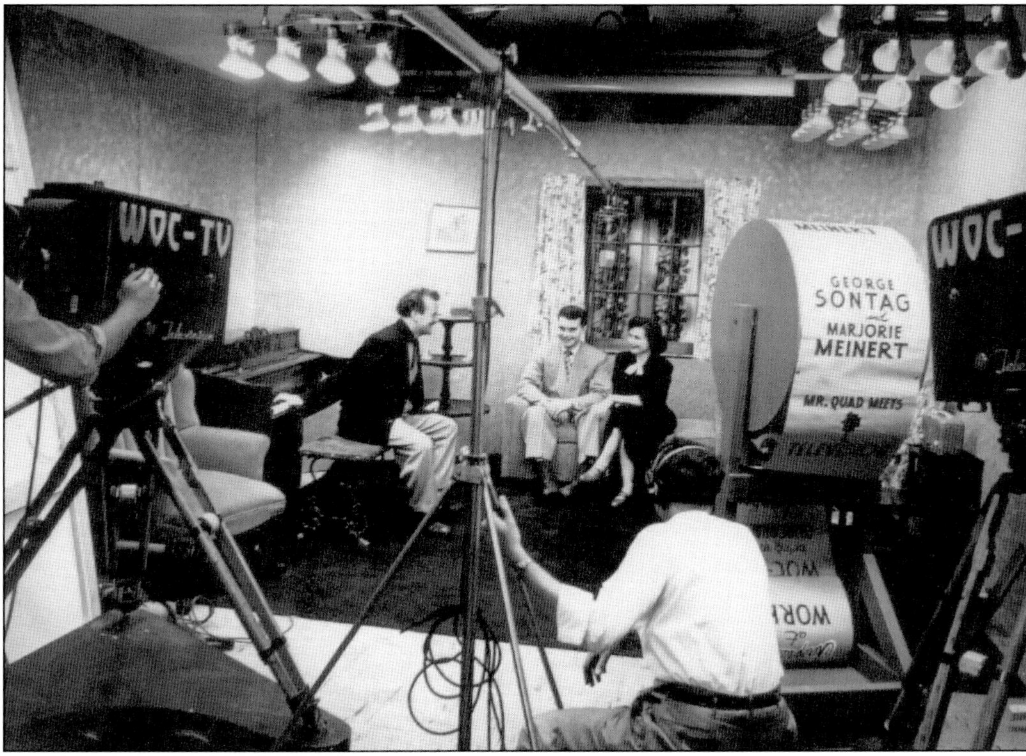

On October 31, 1949, WOC-TV would take to the air on channel five following weeks of technical and program rehearsals. George Sontag (left), Warren Vasen, and Marjorie Meinert are shown in a musical charade show rehearsal. The large roll of paper at the right had printed program titles and credits that were superimposed over an image on the television screen. Note the simple spotlights used for lighting. (Courtesy of Rich Birley.)

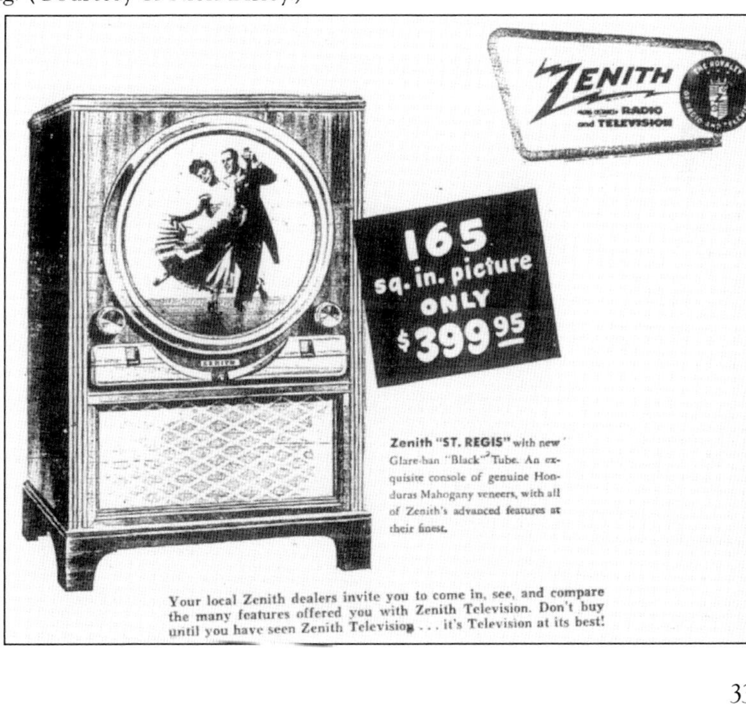

When WOC-TV first signed on the air, there were fewer than 400 television sets in the Quad Cities area. For several weeks before sign-on, advertisements similar to this one appeared in area newspapers on a daily basis. Within two weeks of channel five's inaugural broadcast, over 2,000 sets had been sold. At a time when a new stove cost $179, television sets remained a luxury that many could not afford.

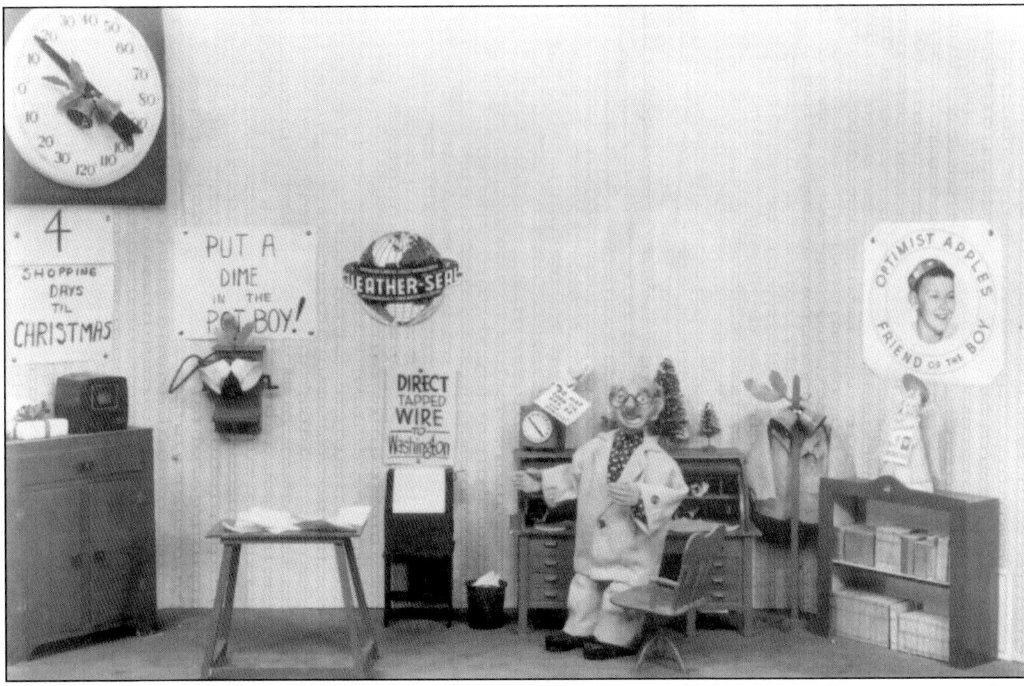

Talk about a rudimentary weather show! *Mr. Weatherwise* debuted the first day WOC-TV went on the air. The program was created to provide weather information with authority, yet with some humor. Ran Jensen was the voice of "Mr. Weatherwise," the puppet. Jensen would later become an on-camera weatherman at the station. The show's rather fitting sponsor was Weather-Seal, an aluminum storm door and window company. (Courtesy of KWQC-TV.)

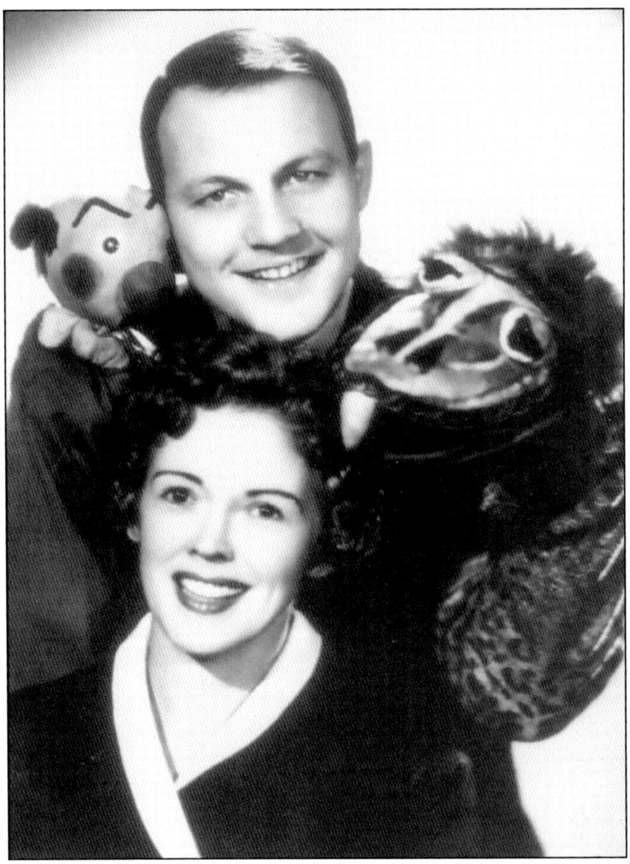

One of the first NBC programs that WOC-TV aired was *Kukla, Fran and Ollie*. Show creator Burr Tillstrom was the puppeteer and voice for Kukla, Ollie Dragon, and all the other puppet characters. La Porte City, Iowa, native Fran Allison was the voice of reason to the characters' foibles. The show was originally created for children but quickly became even more popular with adults. (Courtesy of Chicago Historical Society.)

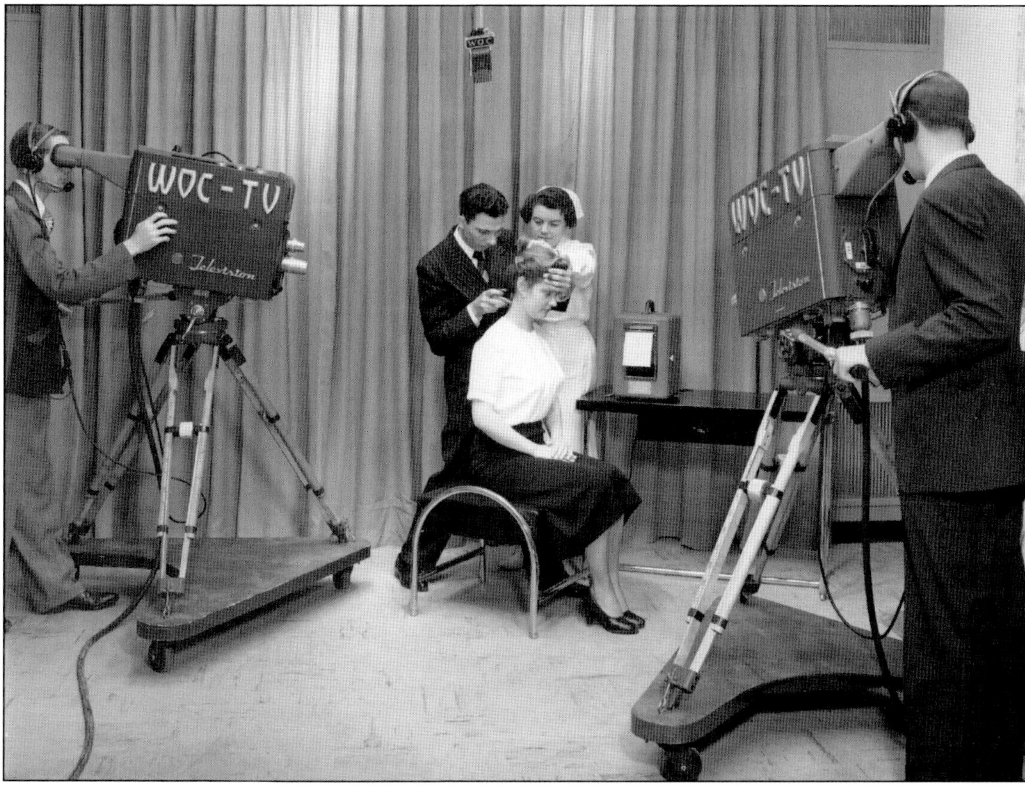

An early television program called *Chiropractic at Work* served to educate chiropractors and to inform and familiarize the general public with chiropractics as a viable, alternative form of treatment. In this 1950 photograph, an instructor from the Palmer School of Chiropractic demonstrates the use of a diagnostic aid called a nervoscope. (With permission of Palmer College of Chiropractic, Special Collections and Archives.)

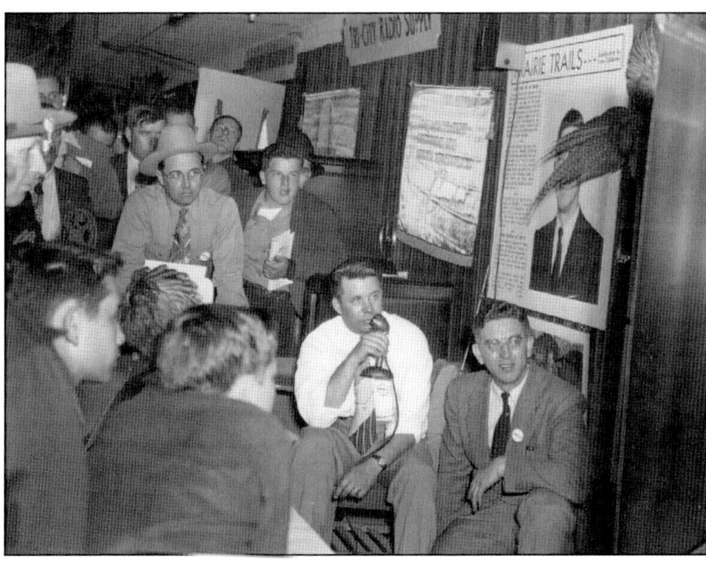

One of WOC-TVs early programs, and perhaps one of the first of its kind on television, was *Along the Outdoor Trails* with Porky and Ponce. Harry "Ponce" DeLeon (left, in hat and tie) and Orville "Porky" Meyers (with microphone) presented a weekly outdoor show. The program featured film of their hunting and fishing trips, products they used, and tips for the amateur angler or hunter. (Courtesy of Judith Carls.)

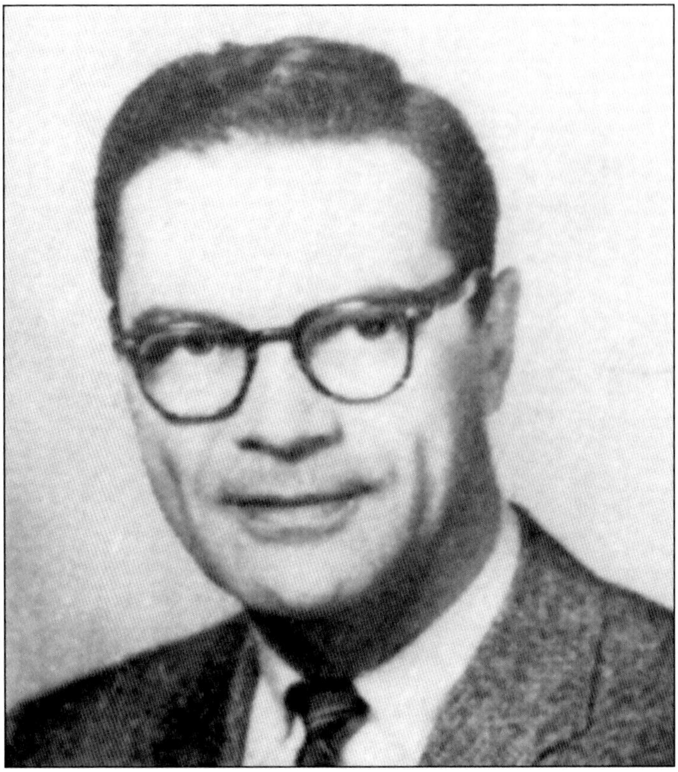

Bob Frank began his career at WOC in 1937 as a reporter and was one of the station's radio newscasters. When television took to the air, Frank became the news director and the newscaster viewers saw during the noontime and early evening news programs. His authoritative style of reporting served him well when he left the station to become head of public relations for insurance company Modern Woodmen of America.

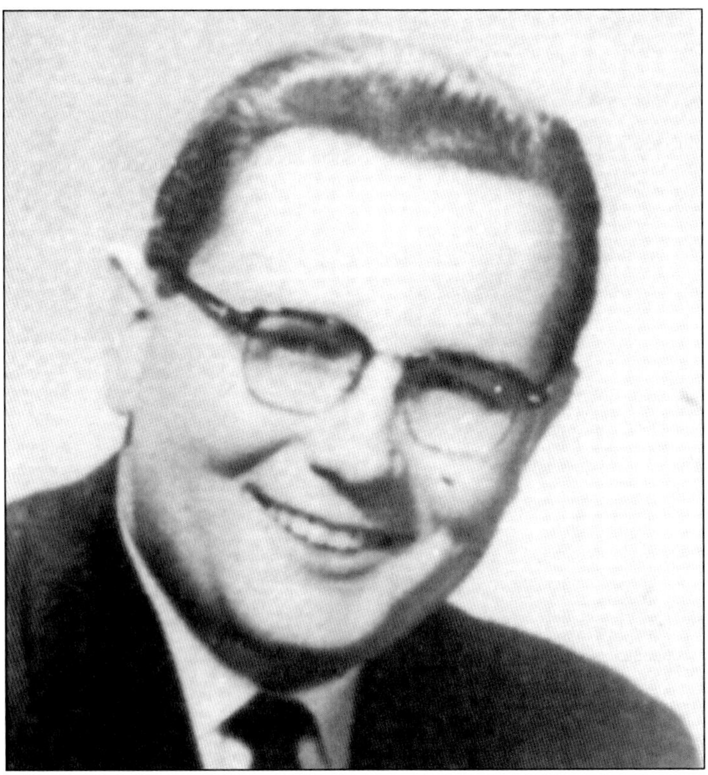

A well-known voice on both WOC radio and television was that of Bill Gress. He began at the station as a disc jockey in 1949 but soon moved into news. He later became director of public affairs. In that position, he was the host of *Call Bill Gress* on the radio and aired editorials each night on *Comment*. He is widely remembered for his interviews of state and national politicians.

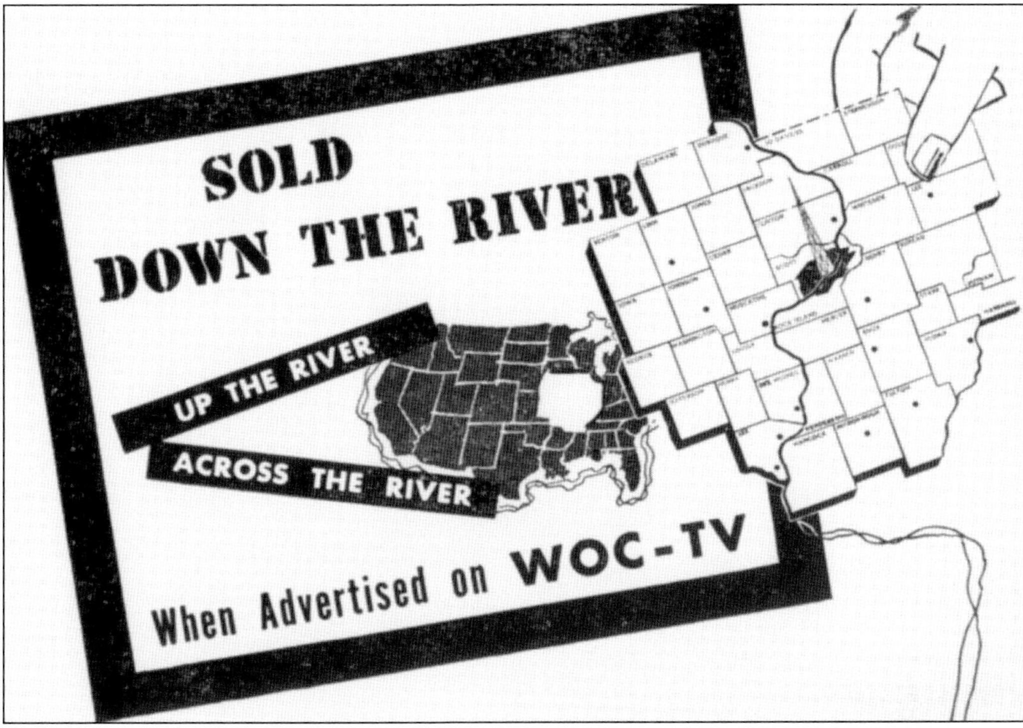

Commercial time is the only item that a television station has to sell. Without a revenue stream, stations could not operate, and viewers would not be able to watch the programs they enjoy. This advertisement from the early 1950s emphasizes WOC-TV's unique location and coverage. As the largest market between Chicago and Des Moines, and St. Louis and Minneapolis, it illustrates the station's local and regional advertising reach.

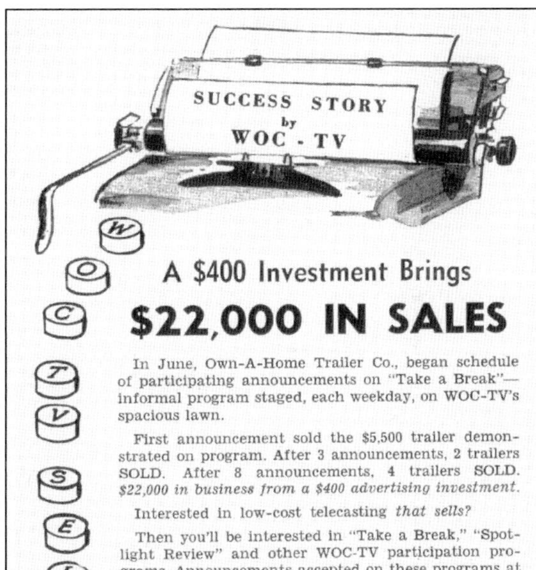

This advertisement appeared in several trade publications in 1952 to illustrate that advertising on WOC-TV brings results. Not only did the station bring results, it did so with just a small investment of money. Aimed at agencies' commercial time buyers, the advertisement's purpose was to persuade the agencies to place local and regional commercials on WOC-TV by giving testimony explaining how well viewers responded.

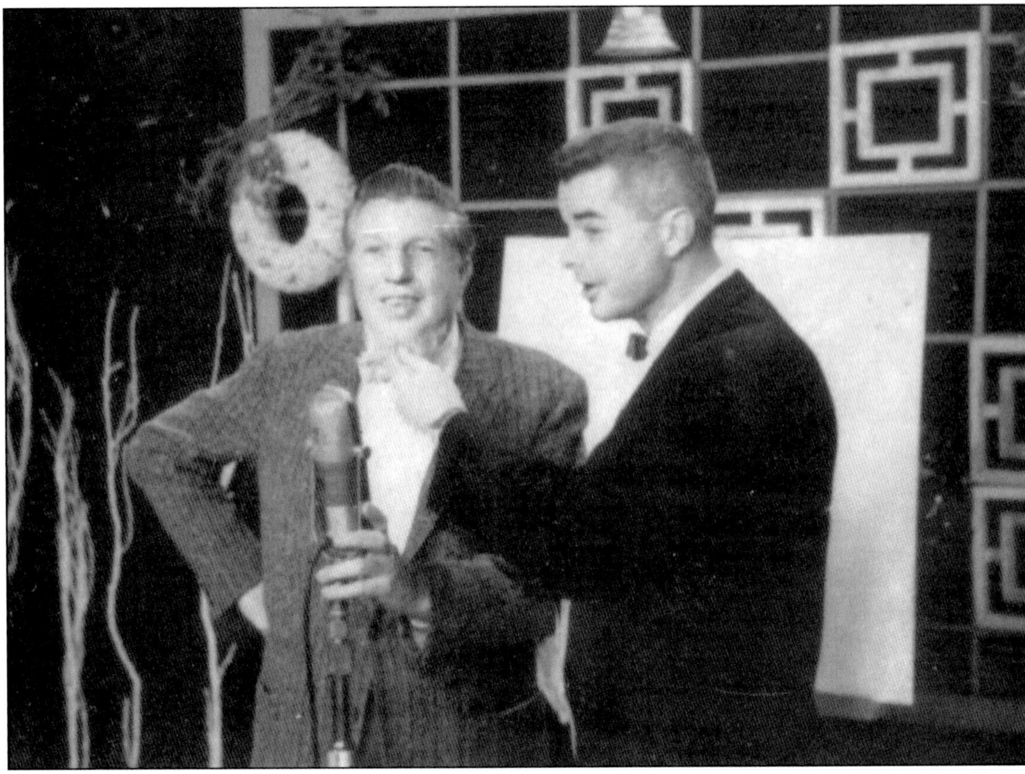

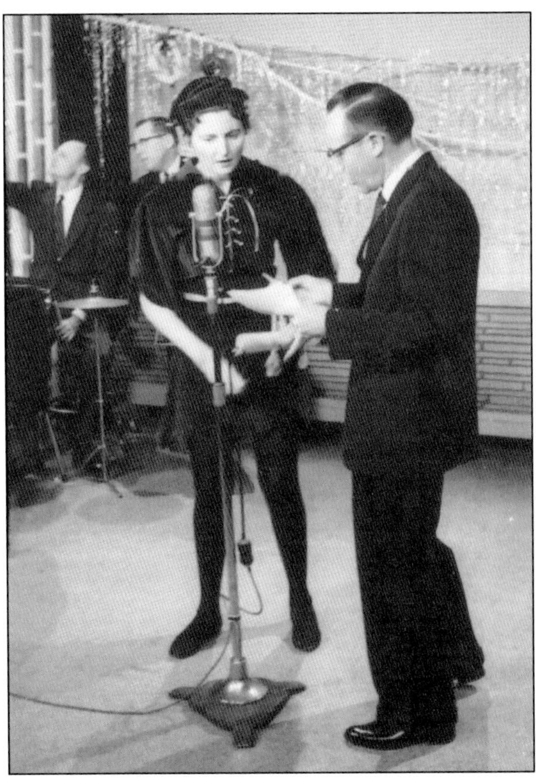

Late-night network programs were still in the distant future in the early 1950s, and stations filled time with whatever programming they could find. During the Christmas season, WOC-TV aired a weekly telethon-variety program for the Salvation Army called *Tree of Lights*. The show was a free-form mixture of local musical talent and skits. Ken Wagner (left) and Warren Vasen appeal to viewers for their pledges. (Courtesy of Anita Sundin.)

The *Tree of Lights* fund-raiser was a popular show for both the viewers and the staff of WOC radio and television. Local musical groups and soloists, including some members of the WOC staff, were featured performers, and they encouraged viewers to phone in pledges for the Salvation Army. "Elf" Anita Sundin and emcee Ran Jensen are announcing names of viewers who have made their pledges. (Courtesy of Anita Sundin.)

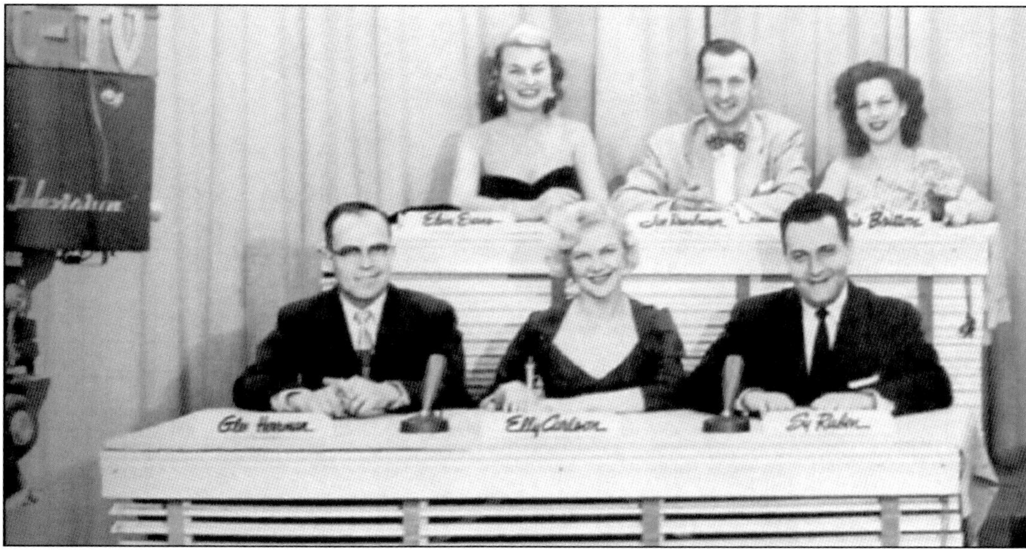

The local forerunner of *TV Guide* was *Tele-Views News*. *Tele-Views* sponsored the quiz show *If You Ask Me* during the early 1950s. Questions from the emcee and viewers were posed to a panel of local "experts." The panelist with the most correct answers won a prize. Pictured here are, from left to right, (first row) Glen Herman, Elly Carlson, and Sy Rabin; (second row) Elaine Evans, Joe Brandmeyer, and Lois Britton. (Courtesy of KWQC-TV.)

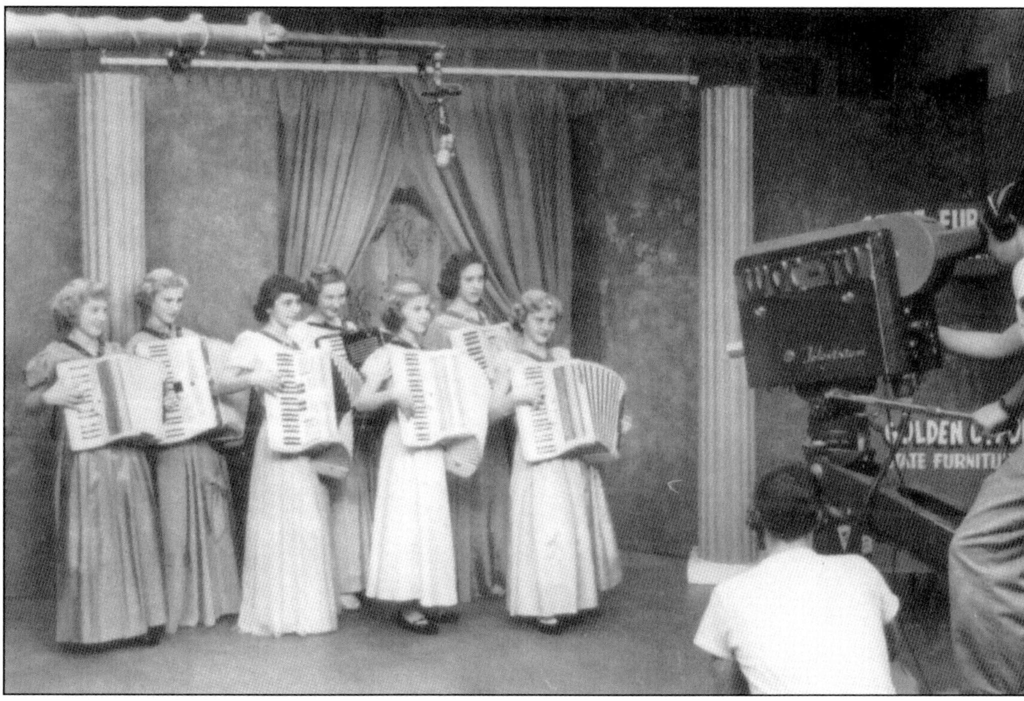

Styled after the nationally broadcast *Ted Mack's Original Amateur Hour*, WOC-TV's *Golden Opportunity* gave local talent the chance to perform and perhaps win an appearance on Mack's show. Each week's winning act would return the following week to compete again. If the act won three weeks in a row, it received the trip to New York. When Ted Mack went off the air, a cash prize was offered instead. (Copyright Moline Dispatch Publishing Company, used with permission.)

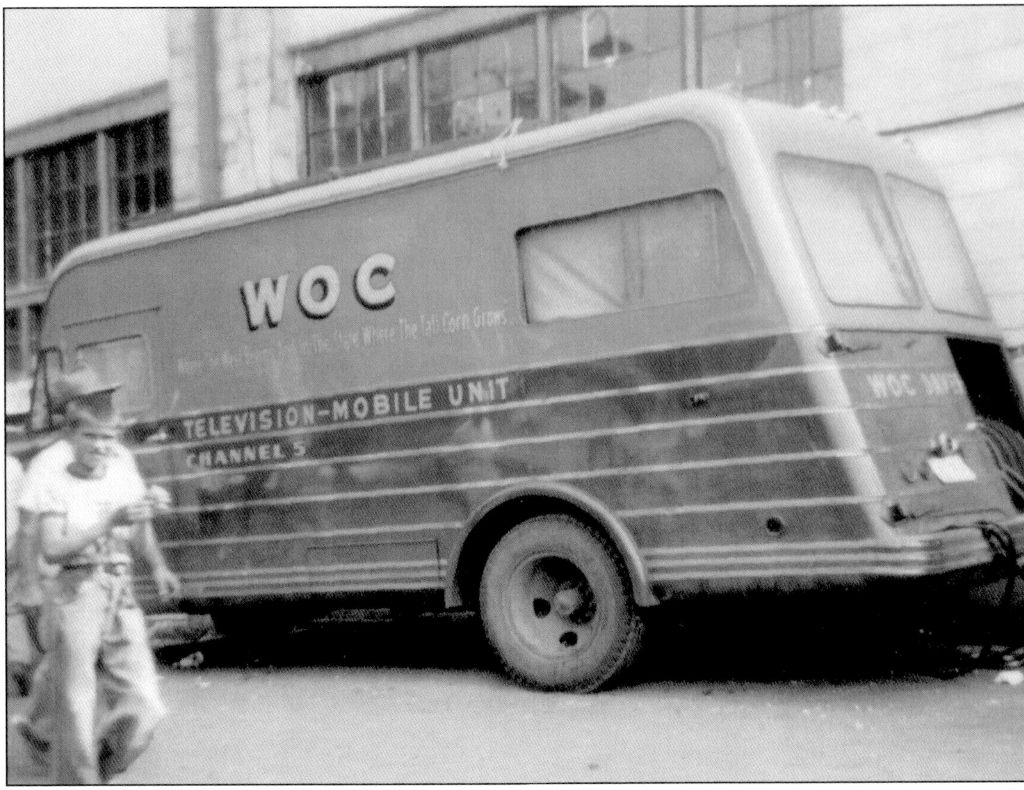

In addition to creating new television studios, WOC-TV also purchased this mobile unit for televising events away from the studio. The unit was self-contained with cameras, audio and video controls, cabling, and a microwave unit for sending the remote signal back to the station. As shown here, the unit is setting up for a week of broadcasts from under the grandstand at the Mississippi Valley Fair. (Courtesy of Ed Jones.)

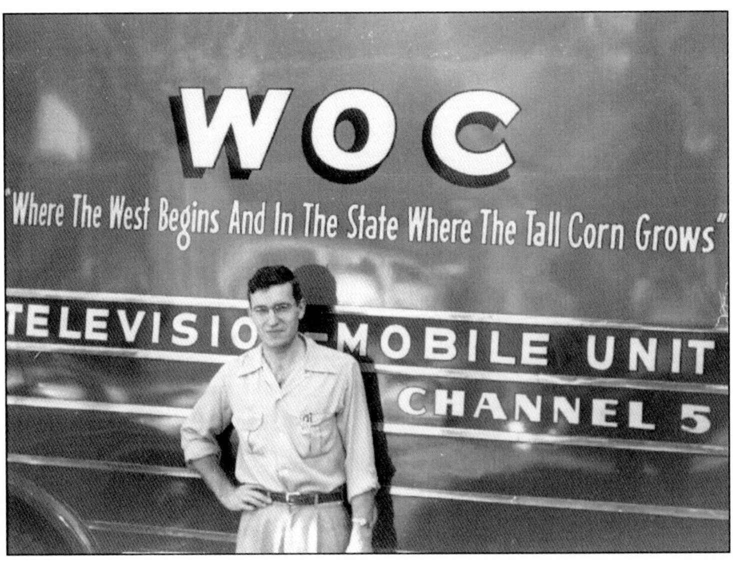

Engineer Stan Straight poses with the WOC-TV mobile unit in this early 1950s photograph. The station's motto, "Where the West Begins And In The State Where The Tall Corn Grows," was still being used to describe Davenport. It originated when WOC Radio signed on the air. WOC continued to use this unit until 1958, when it was sent to sister station WHO-TV in Des Moines. (Courtesy of Stan Straight.)

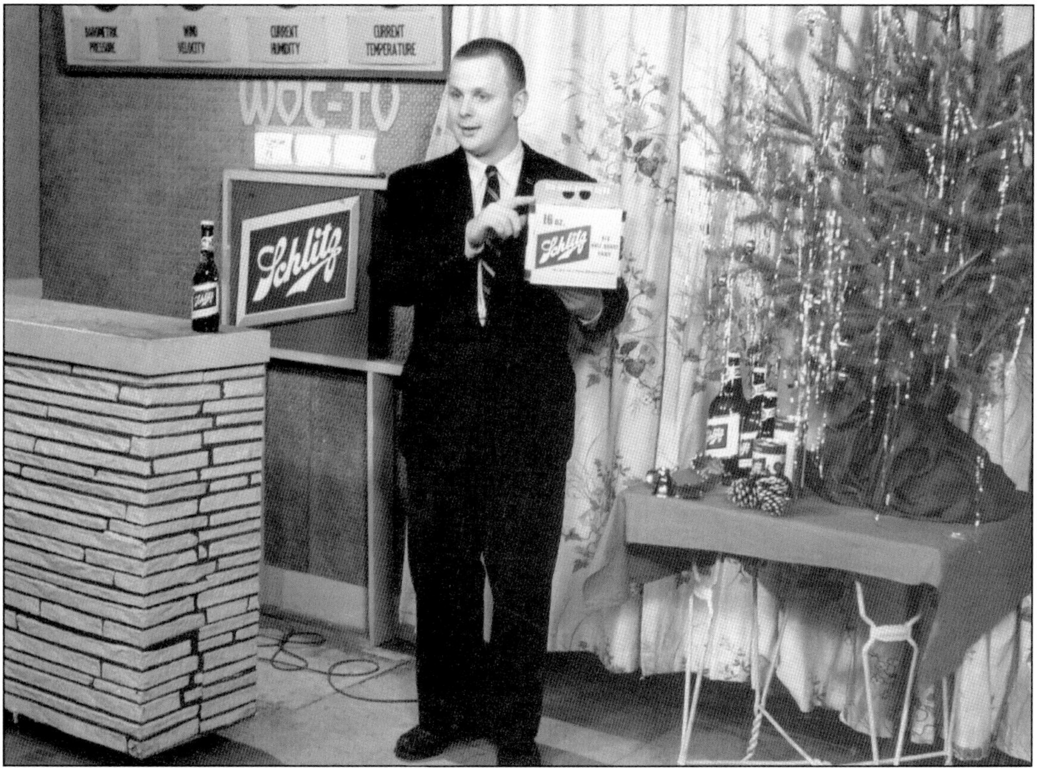

Announcers not only presented the weather or sports, but they also provided the commercial message. To shift emphasis, Ed Zack only had to step to his left out of one set and into another, decorated for Christmas. Evidently he was telling the audience to make sure they had plenty of beer on hand for their holiday guests. Pity the announcers who became tongue-tied pronouncing Schlitz Brewing Company. (Courtesy of Ed Zack.)

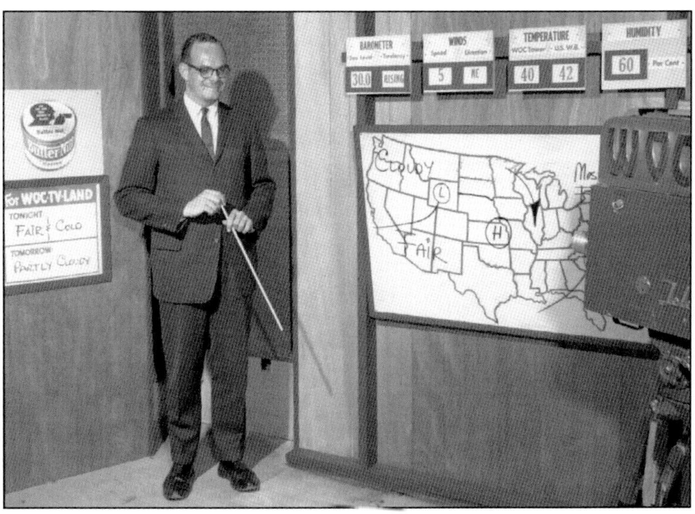

Definitely a step up from the original weather program on WOC-TV, but this is still not the type of weather set viewers have become accustomed to in current times. This early 1950s promotional photograph shows the primitive graphics that Bob Brown had to work with. Grease pencils and wooden pointers are now long gone, but this was the technology in the earlier days of television and a nice set as well.

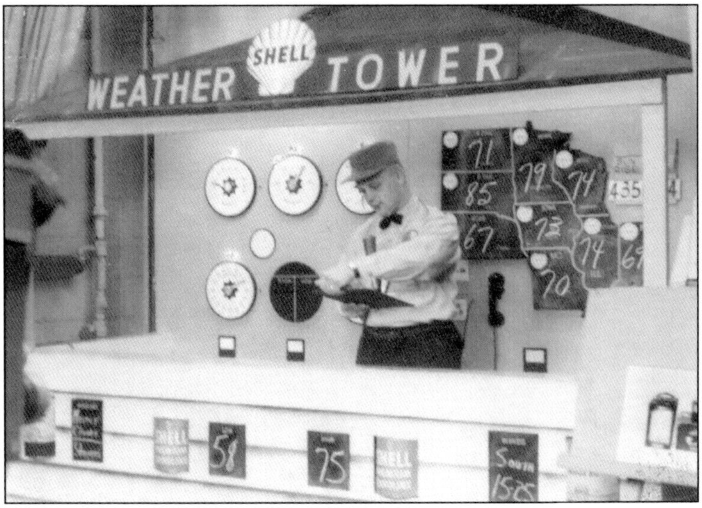

The *Shell Weather Tower* asked the viewer to believe that the weatherman was actually in a tower somewhere. WOC-TV announcer Ed Zack even had to wear a service station attendant's uniform. Those oilcans on the front of the set had slates on their back halves and were turned to show the current readings. The dials and gauges were only simulations and not directly linked to anything. (Courtesy of Ed Zack.)

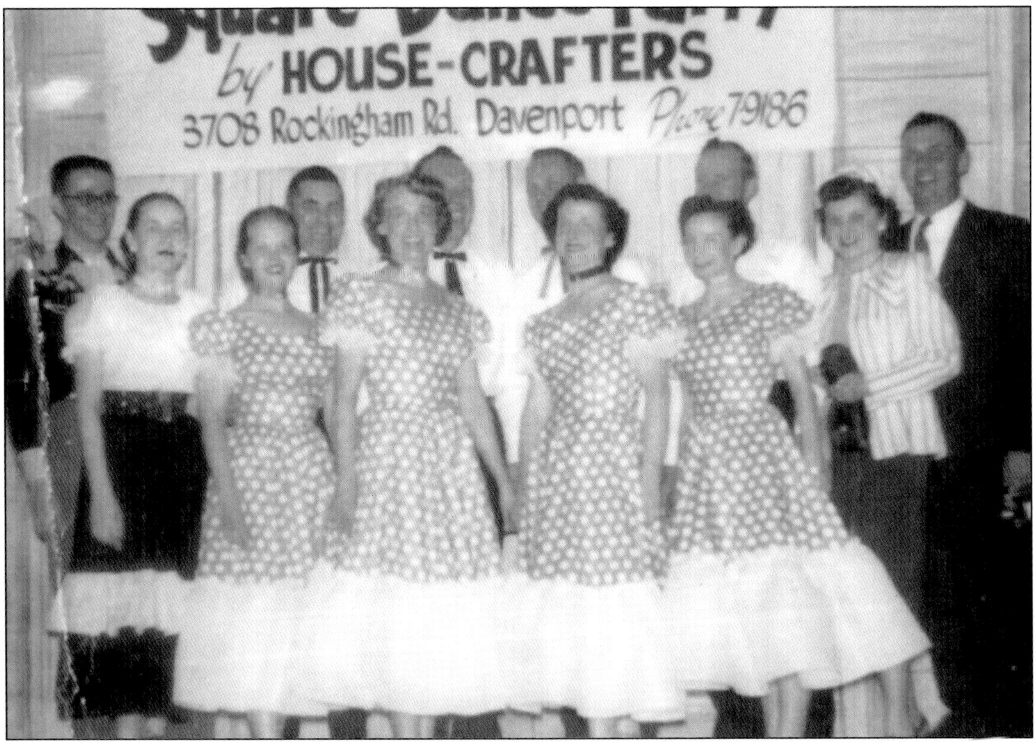

The weekly *Square Dance Party* on WOC-TV had a loyal audience in the mid-1950s. This particular week's dancers and callers were, from left to right, (first row) Ruth Hall, Bev Boettcher, Vivian Jamieson, Roseanne Bert, Jane Crouch, and Juanita Lyford; (second row) Jon Hall, Paul Boettcher, LaVern Jamieson, Vern Berg, Bill Crouch, and Gene Lyford. The set was the same one used on *Circle 6 Ranch*. (Courtesy of Ron and Linda Crouch.)

The most important piece of equipment needed to broadcast a signal was the transmitter. Without it, the pictures created in the studio went nowhere. This late 1949 photograph shows the RCA channel 5 transmitter and its control unit. The photograph was used in special newspaper sections that introduced the medium of television to the Quad Cities and showed off WOC-TV's new broadcasting equipment.

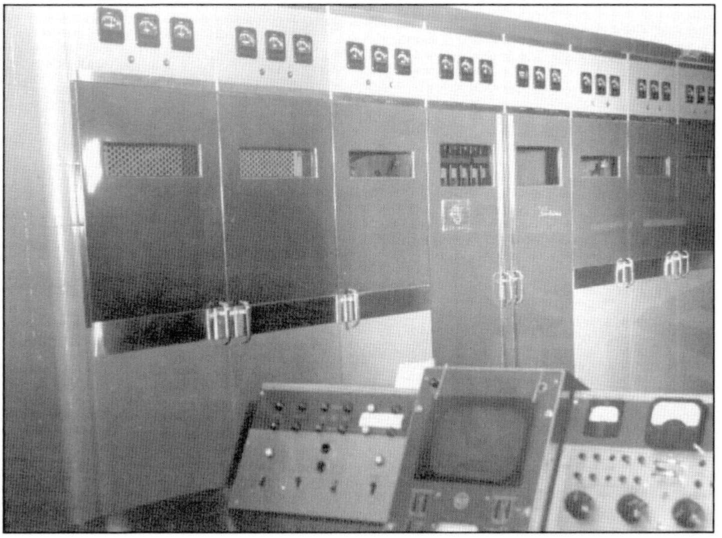

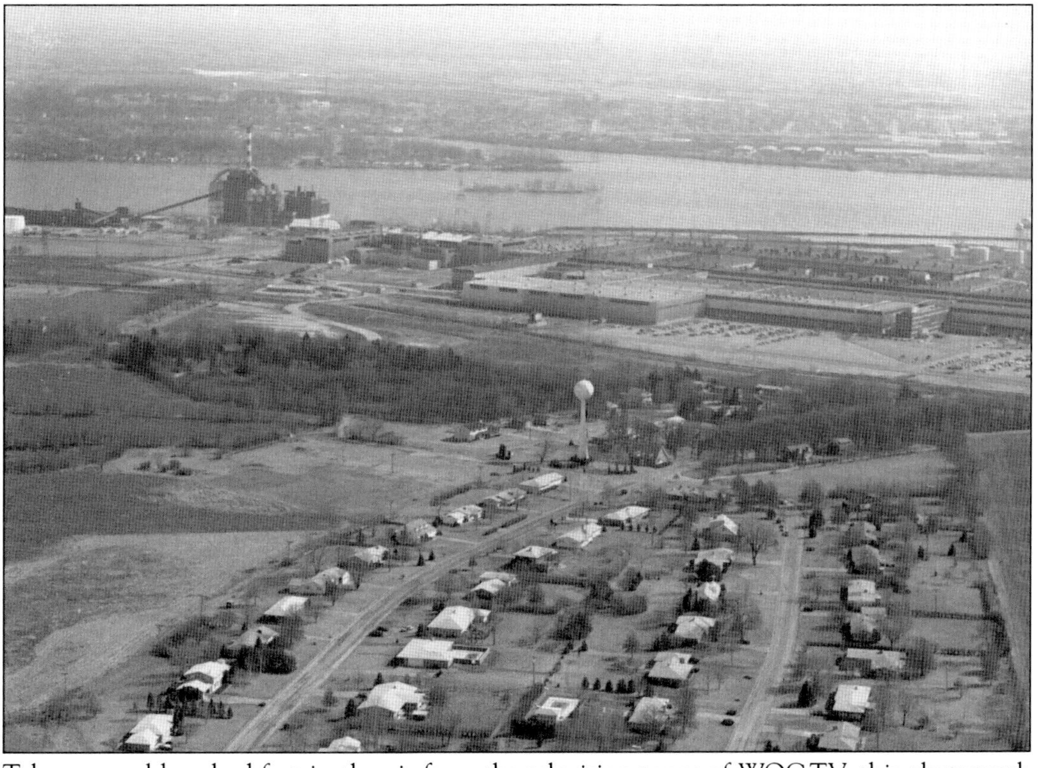

Taken several hundred feet in the air from the television tower of WOC-TV, this photograph gives a good view of the early Riverdale housing development and the Alcoa plant. To the left of Alcoa is the Riverside Generating Station. Across the Mississippi River are Campbell's Island and the East Moline shoreline. The dark line in the center of the photograph is one of the tower's guy-wires. (Courtesy of KWQC-TV.)

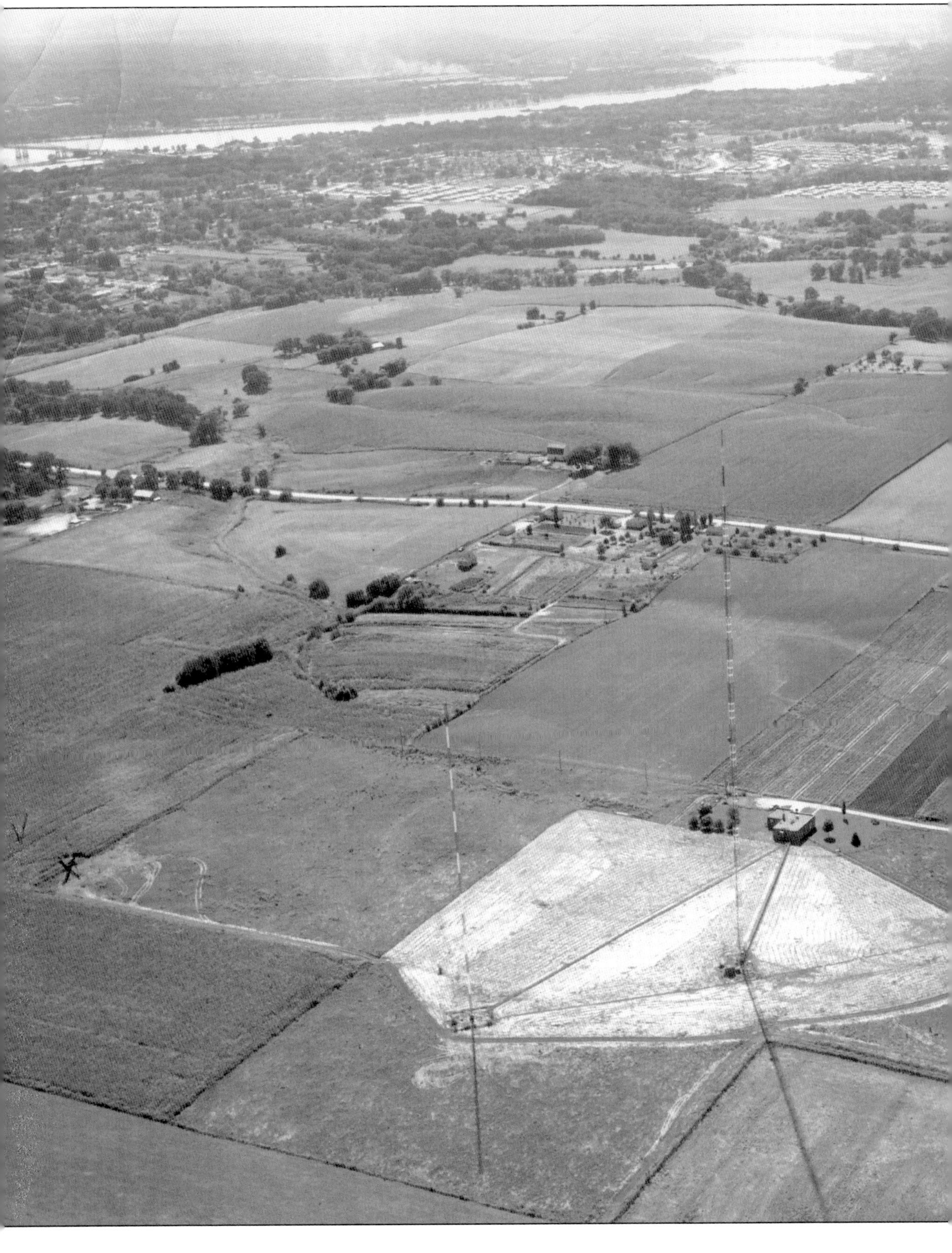

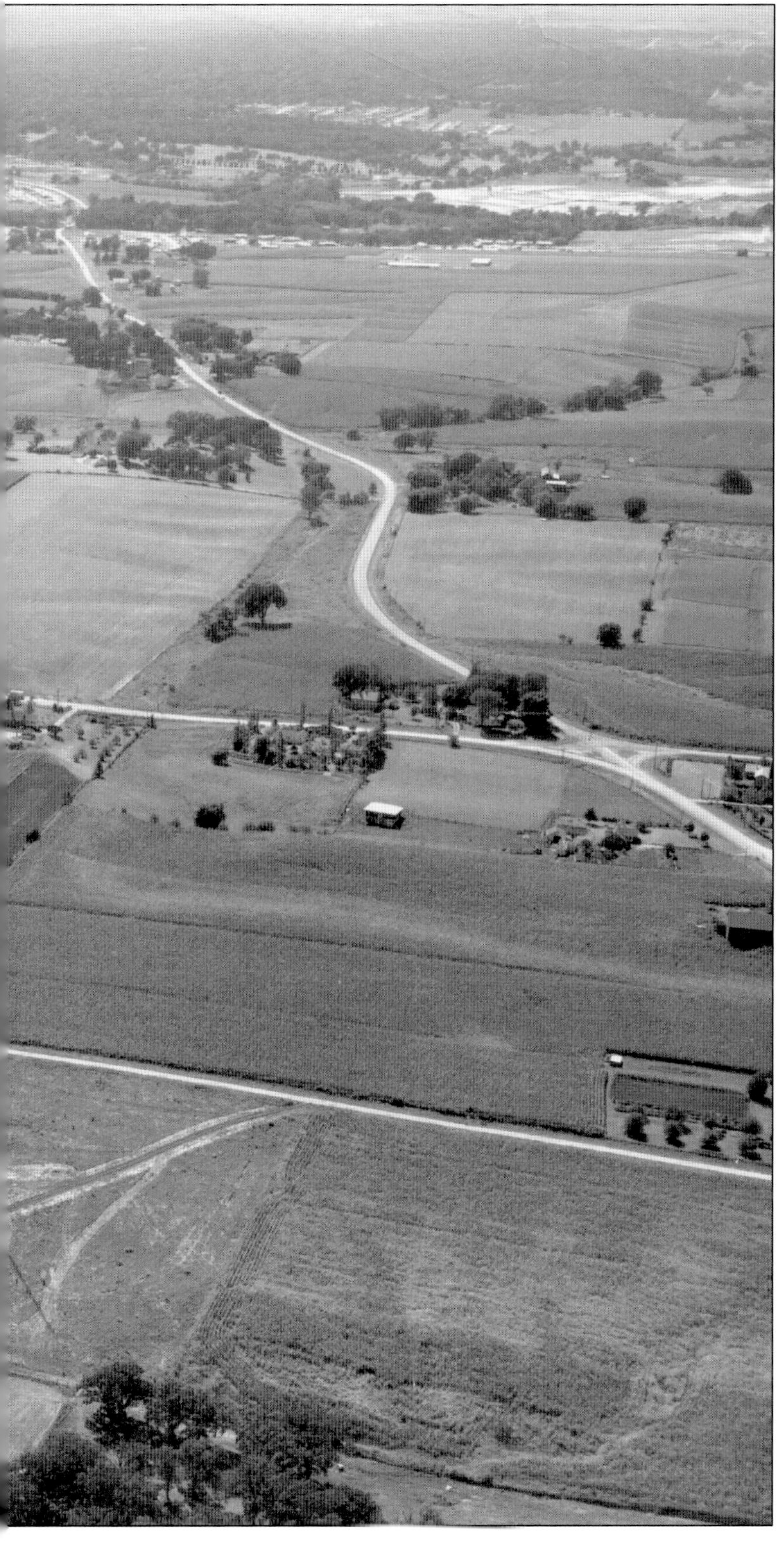

This 1954 photograph looks west over the WOC stations' transmitter and tower site in Bettendorf, Iowa. Three towers are used to direct WOC radio's signal, as a different signal pattern is used during the nighttime hours. WOC-TV's transmitting tower was mounted on top of the center radio tower. While this site was once considered far out in the country, farmland has given way to housing, schools, shopping centers, and other business development. Palmer Hills Golf Course is now in the upper center of this photograph. Devil's Glenn Road is seen in the center and joins up with Middle Road on the right. In the upper right, just below the line of trees, the two grass runways and hangers of the former Bettendorf Airport can be seen.

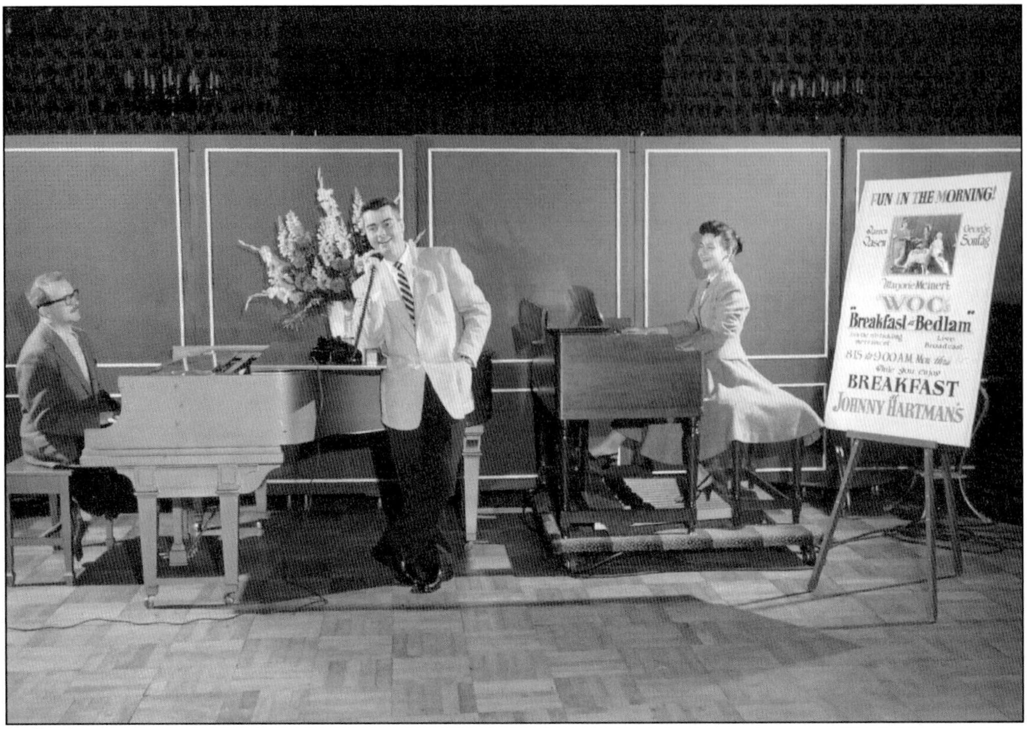

Breakfast in Bedlam was a daily live broadcast from Johnny Hartman's restaurant during the early 1950s on WOC. Airing Monday through Saturday from 8:15 to 9:00 a.m., the trio of George Sontag (left), Warren Vasen, and Marjorie Meinert provided music, comedy, and silly phone calls to the radio listeners at home, while patrons enjoyed breakfast at the restaurant. (Courtesy of KWQC-TV.)

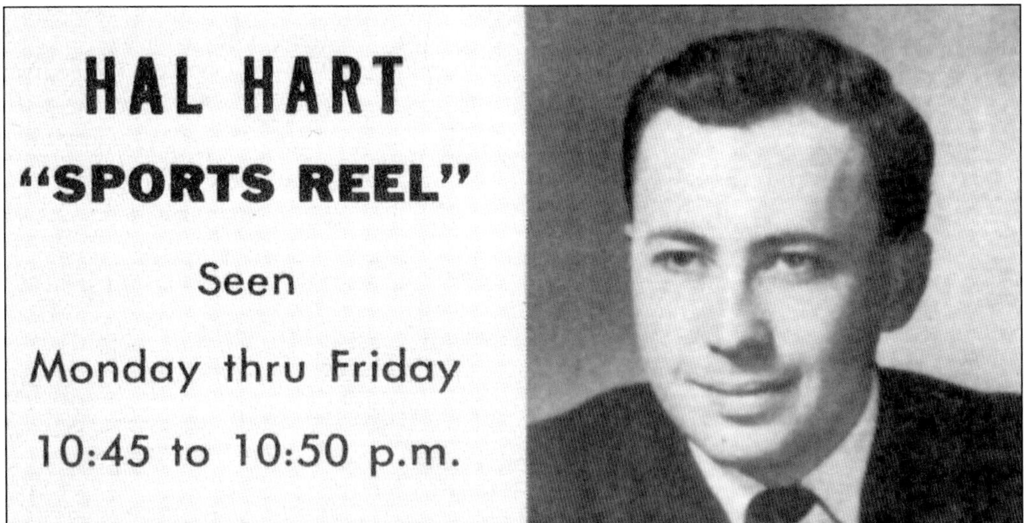

Hal Hart was not only heard on the radio but was seen on WOC-TV's *Sports Reel*. While all sports news was important in the early 1950s, local sports scores and stories captured the most interest of local viewers. Hart also called the action of the high school football and basketball games that were televised live using the station's mobile unit.

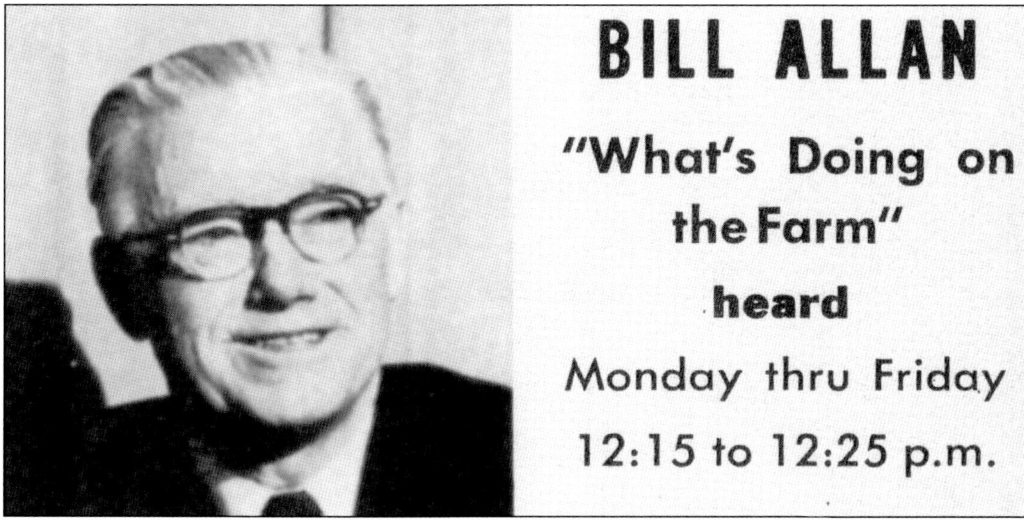

Farm market reports and news were important at WOC Radio from its beginning, and the station has employed several agricultural business reporters over the years. Bill Allan was the national sales manager of Ralston-Purina Company. Upon his retirement from that firm, he joined WOC. His reports included livestock and grain prices and news that farmers found important to their livelihoods in the early 1950s.

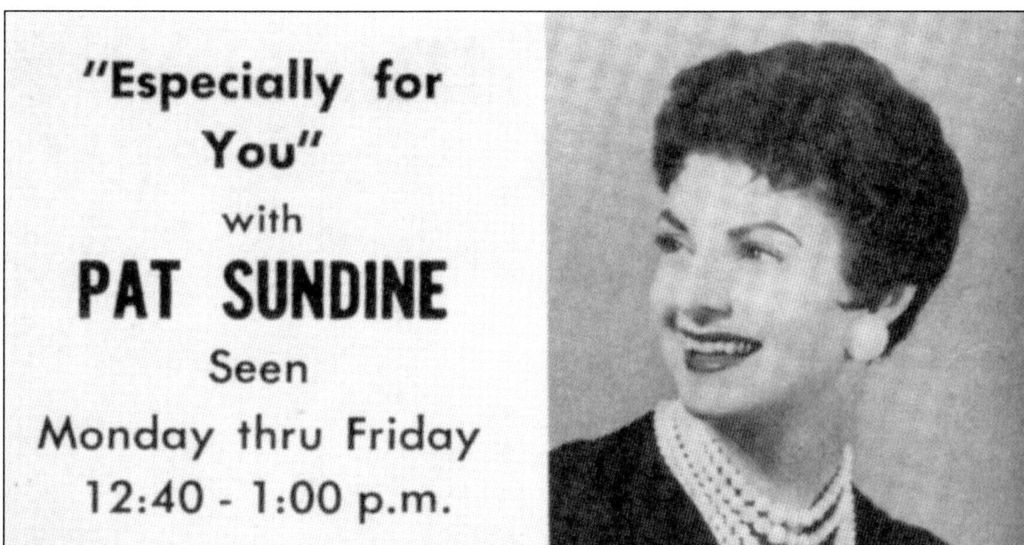

Undoubtedly the "queen" of WOC was Pat Sundine. She had her own phone show on the radio, was seen in countless live and recorded commercials, and spent 16 years as hostess of WOC-TV's *Especially for You*. She felt it was her duty to inform, and that she did. Countless interviews with interesting people and many segments on gardening, fashion, baking, and household hints made the show one of the most popular on the station.

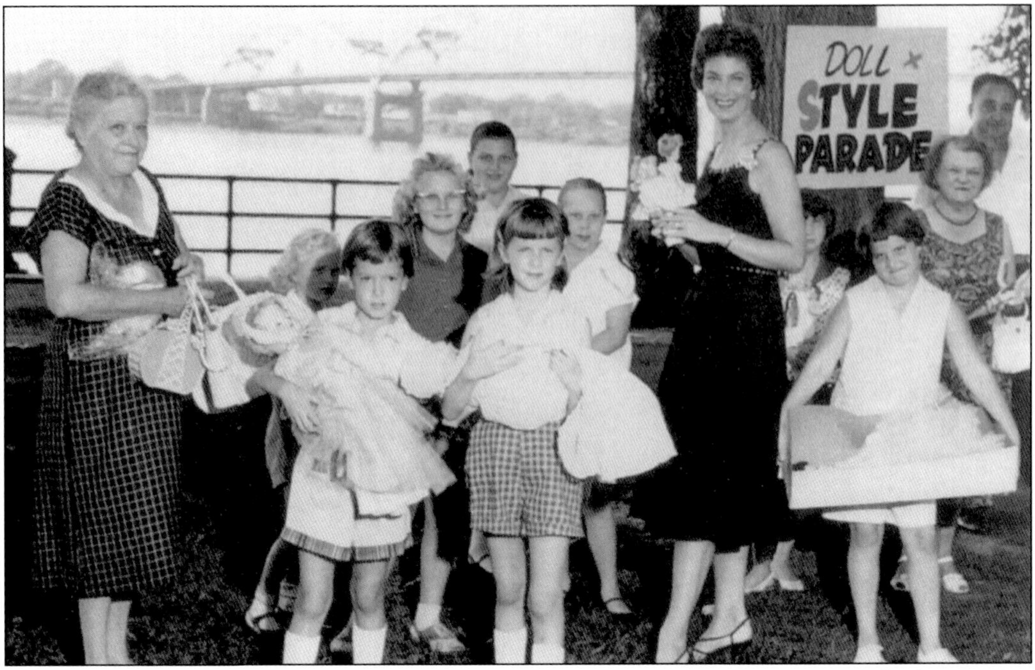

The popularity of *Especially for You* brought gals of all ages out for an appearance by hostess Pat Sundine. Whether it was a department store or grocery store, the crowds gathered. This group of mothers and daughters turned out to see a program promotion for a style show of dolls in the late 1950s. The location was Davenport's LeClaire Park. (Courtesy of KWQC-TV.)

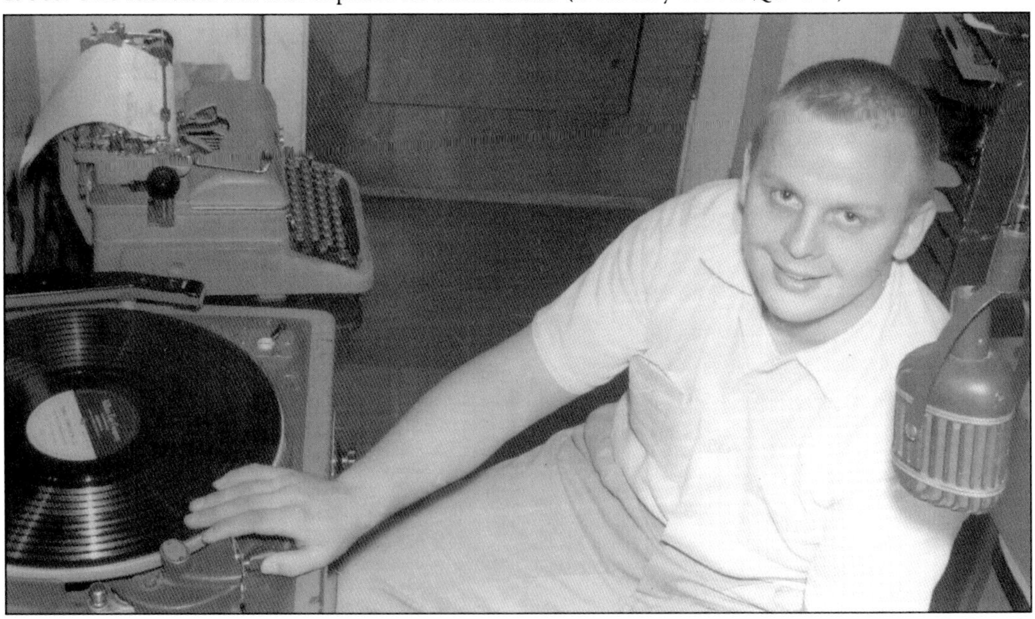

Ed Zack's career at WOC started with the position of staff radio announcer and ended with television program director. In between, he served as radio-television sports director and radio program director. This mid-1950s photograph captures Zack fulfilling his position as the "morning mayor" of Quad Cities radio. He also served as one of the emcees of WOC-TV's short-lived version of *American Bandstand*. (Courtesy of Ed Zack.)

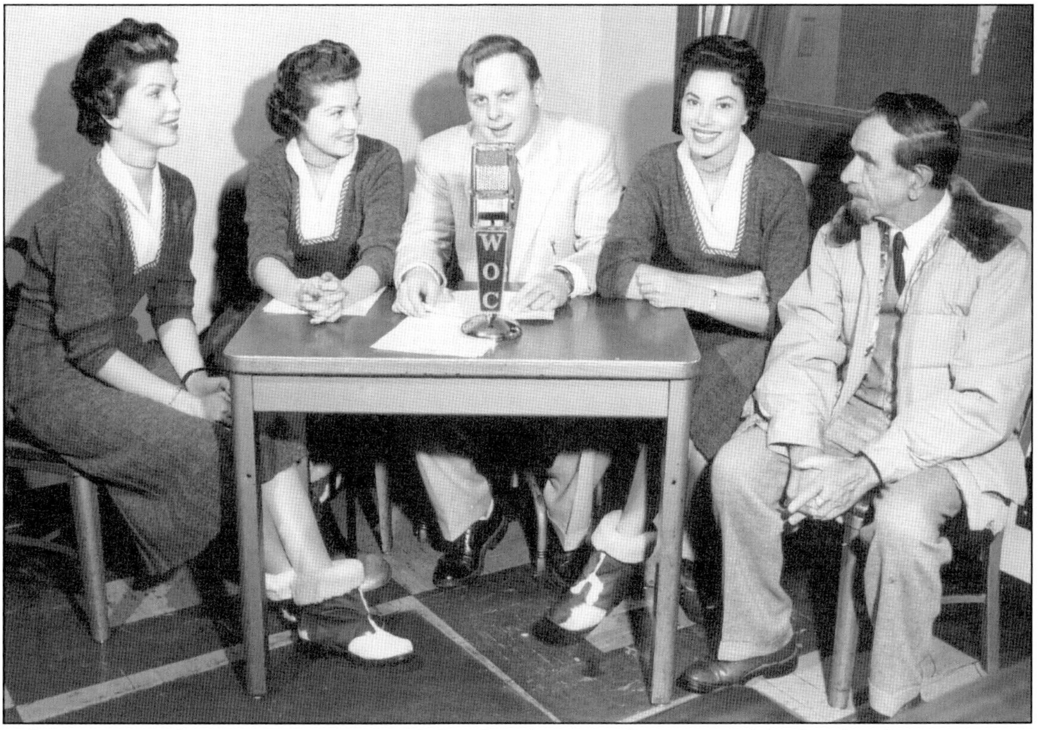

Whenever popular entertainers visited the Quad Cities, they stopped by local radio stations to promote their appearance. In 1956, the McGuire Sisters were in town for a week of performances at the Quad City Automobile Dealers' automobile show at the Rock Island Armory. The trio took time to stop by WOC Radio for an interview with Ed Zack (center) and station owner Dr. B. J. Palmer. (Courtesy of Ed Zack.)

One of the early syndicated Westerns televised by channel 6 was the *Range Rider*. The show was produced and sold by Flying A Productions, a company owned by cowboy star Gene Autry. Jock Mahoney (left) and Dick Jones starred in the production. The show had special interest to area viewers as Mahoney was raised in Davenport and had been an outstanding athlete at Davenport High School and the University of Iowa.

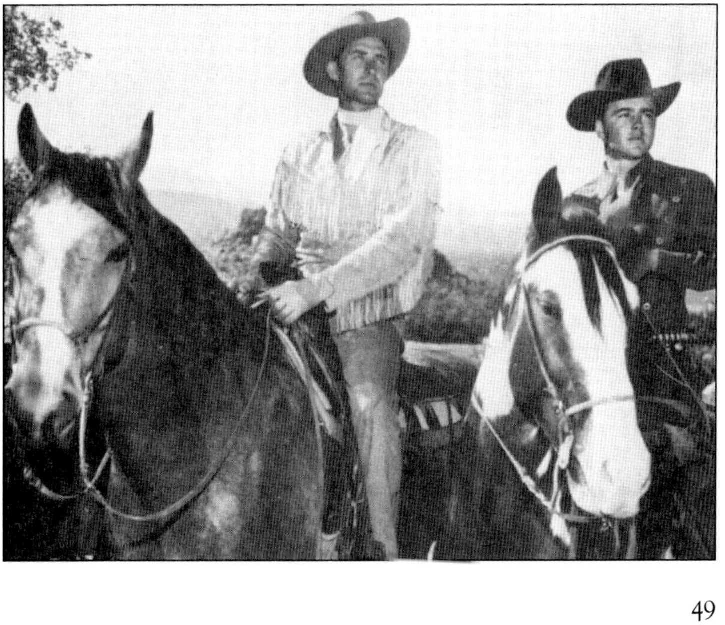

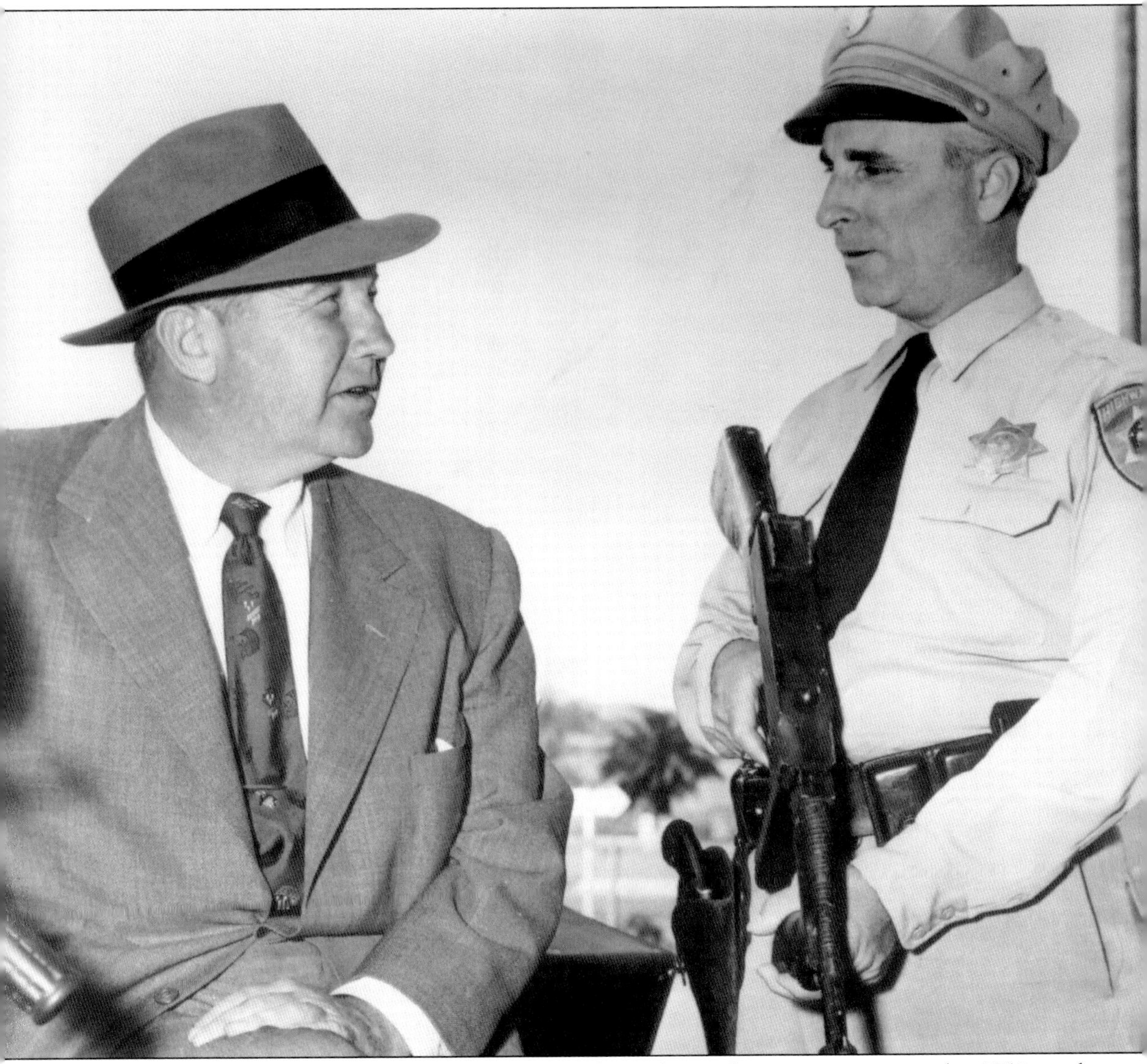

Television networks did not fill an entire broadcast day with programming in the 1950s and early 1960s the way they do today. That meant that stations had to fill the time with local live productions or shows purchased from program syndicators. Syndicators produced first-run programs but bypassed the networks and sold the shows directly to local sponsors and stations. Desilu and National Telefilms were several of the larger firms, but the largest was Ziv Television. Ziv produced shows like *Whirlybirds*, *Sea Hunt*, and *Highway Patrol*. WOC-TV ran all of these shows, but by far the most popular was *Highway Patrol* starring Broderick Crawford (left). Crawford had a long career in motion pictures and in 1950 won the Oscar for best actor in *All the King's Men*. In the early 1950s, he was Hollywood's favorite tough guy lead, and he was one of the biggest film stars to make the move to television. In *Highway Patrol*, Crawford played Chief Dan Mathews, head of an unnamed state's highway police. The show featured plenty of speeding patrol cars and screaming sirens. (Courtesy of Kelly Crawford.)

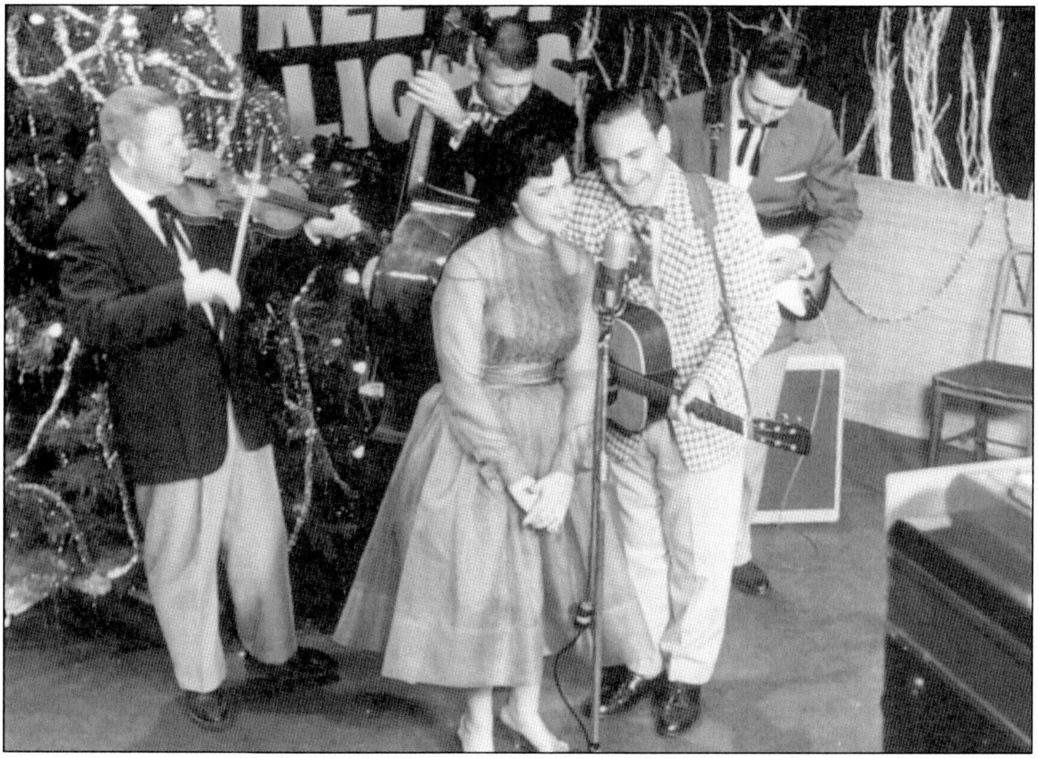

Wes Holly first appeared on WOC-TV's *Tree of Lights* benefit program in 1955. Shown here with his then-wife, Joy, and his band, The Rhythm Ranchers, Holly went on to host two cartoon programs and *The Wes Holly Show*, a barn dance program. Holly was a popular performer at channel 6 until he left in 1960 to work in Nashville, perform on the Grand Ole Opry, and record. (Courtesy of KWQC-TV.)

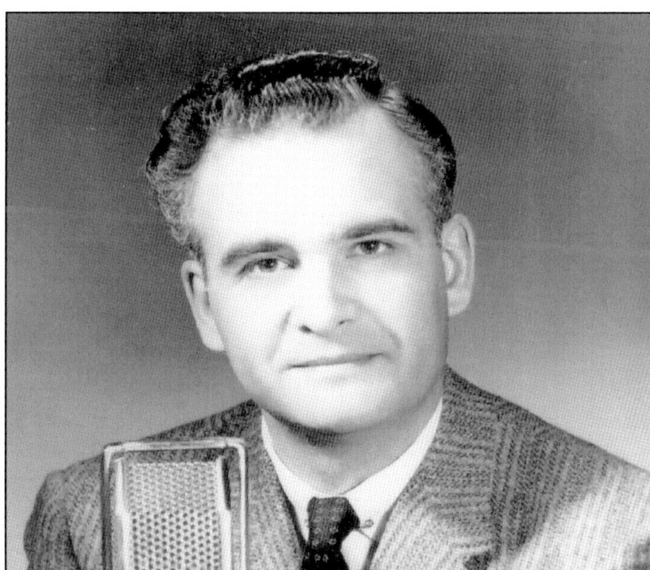

One of the more familiar voices heard on WOC Radio was that of Bob Allard. His smooth delivery was heard on many different programs, including an hour each evening that featured international music. While many might remember him as television's "Cactus Jim," he is probably most remembered for his late-night telephone call-in show *Contact WOC*. Show subjects may have been provocative, but Allard's guests and callers were always interesting.

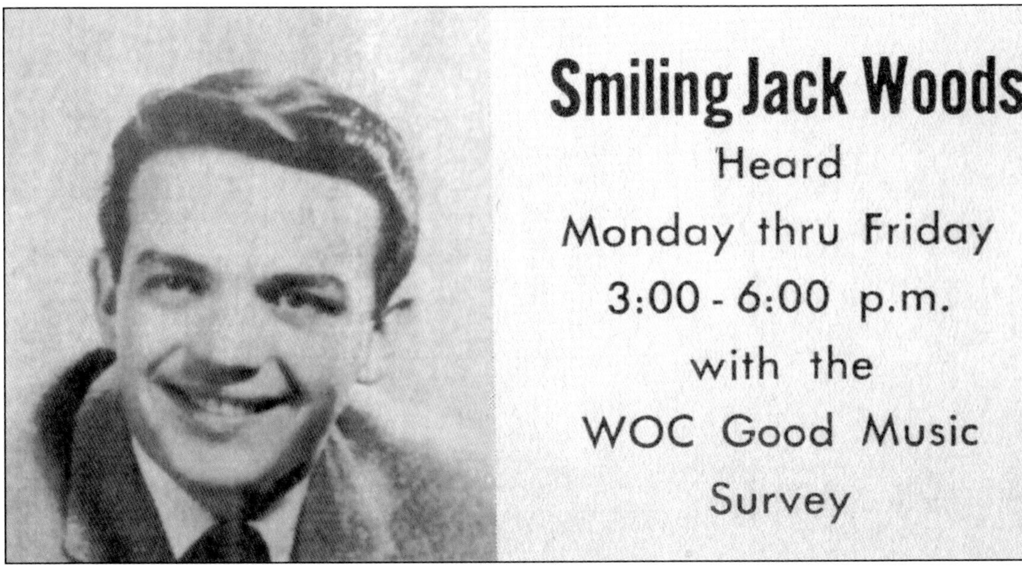

Jack Woods began his career at WOC in 1958 as a sign-on announcer and board operator on radio and as a booth announcer in television. He also substituted for other announcers. WOC switched from adult standards to rock-and-roll for a short period of time, and Woods really clicked in the afternoon drive-time slot. Ed Zack and Woods were also the popular emcees of a teen dance show on WOC-TV.

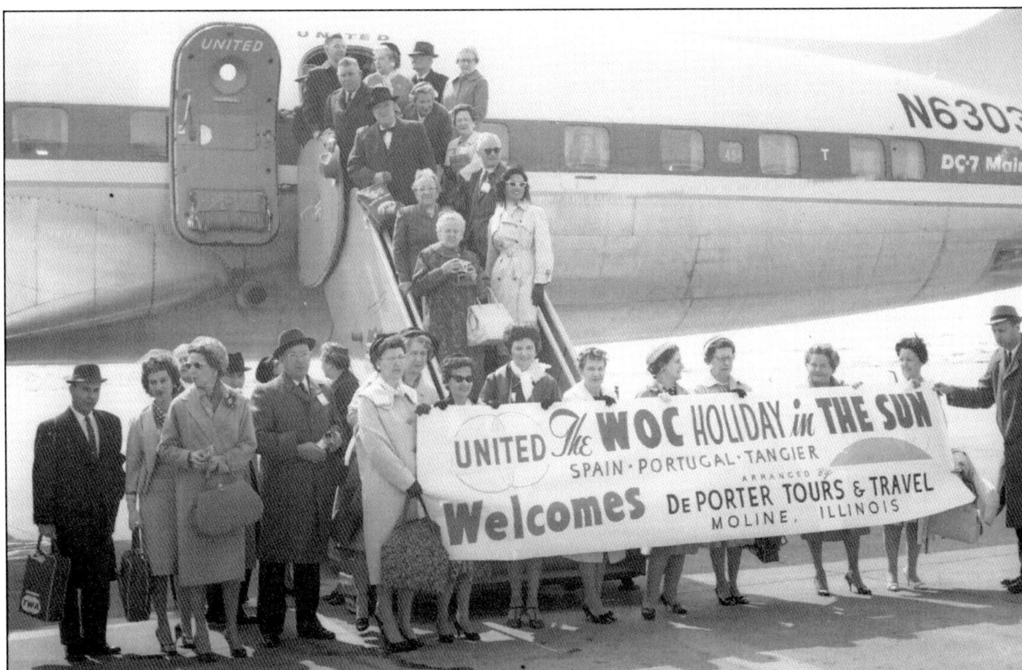

It was not unusual for broadcasting stations to promote themselves with station-sponsored tours, and WOC was no exception. In this 1961 photograph, participants in the "Holiday in the Sun" tour of Spain, Portugal, and Tangiers pose before boarding their plane at the Quad City Airport. Interestingly, tour operator Walt Cornelis (far right) is the father of current channel 6 sports director Thom Cornelis. (Courtesy of Anita Sundin.)

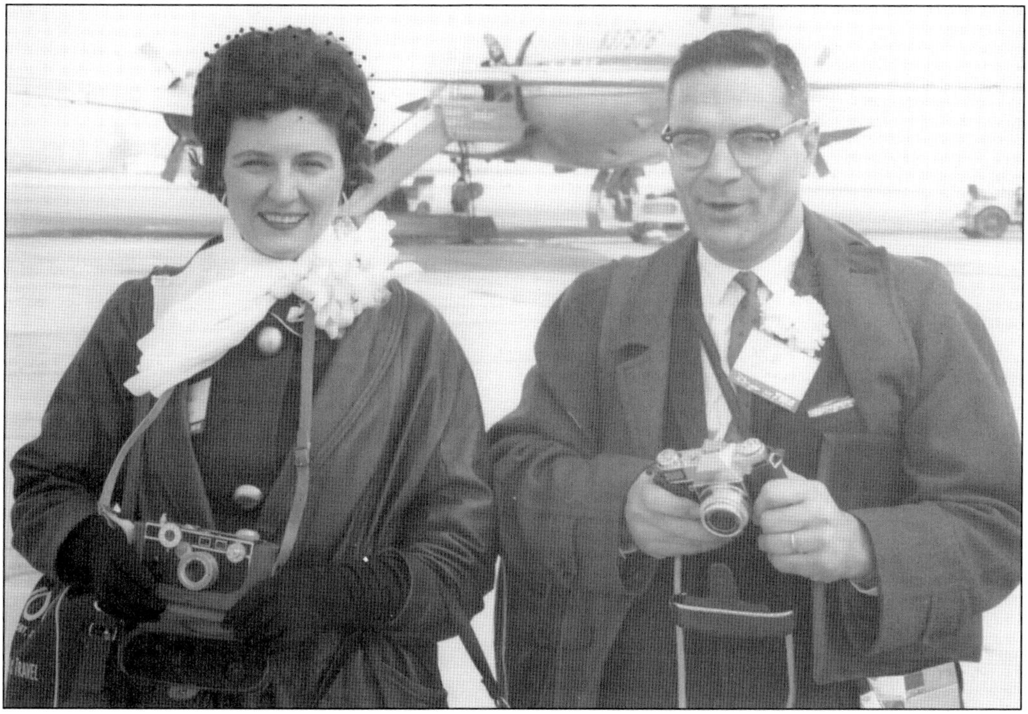

Hosting the "Tour in the Sun" adventure were station personality Anita Sundin and news director Bob Frank. The presence of notable station personnel provided a draw for promoting and selling the tour. Newsman Don Rhyne always gives credit to this trip for his employment at the station, as Frank was told he could not go unless he filled an opening in the news department. (Courtesy of Anita Sundin.)

Evidently Tangiers can be cold and rainy, as this photograph taken in one of the local marketplaces seems to bear witness. This was one of the stops on the 17-day "Holiday in the Sun" tour that allowed participants the opportunity of shopping for souvenirs. It is interesting to note that travelers dressed a little more formally in the early 1960s than they do today. (Courtesy of Anita Sundin.)

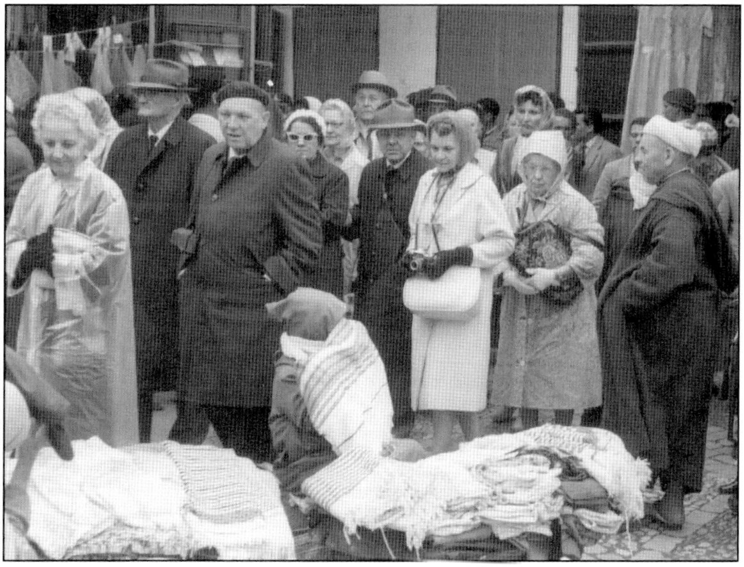

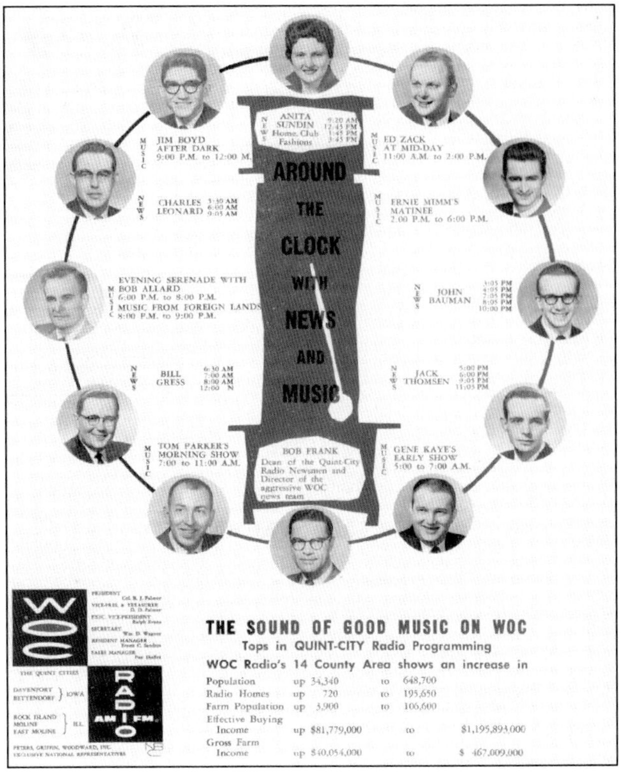

This promotional sheet sent to advertising agencies emphasized WOC's around-the-clock news and good music schedule during the early 1960s. Pictured clockwise from the top are Anita Sundin, announcer; Ed Zack, announcer; Ernie Mimms, announcer; John Bauman, news; Jack Thompson, news; Gene Kay, announcer; Bob Frank, news; Tom Parker, announcer; Bill Gress, news; Bob Allard, announcer; Charles Leonard, news; and Jim Boyd, announcer.

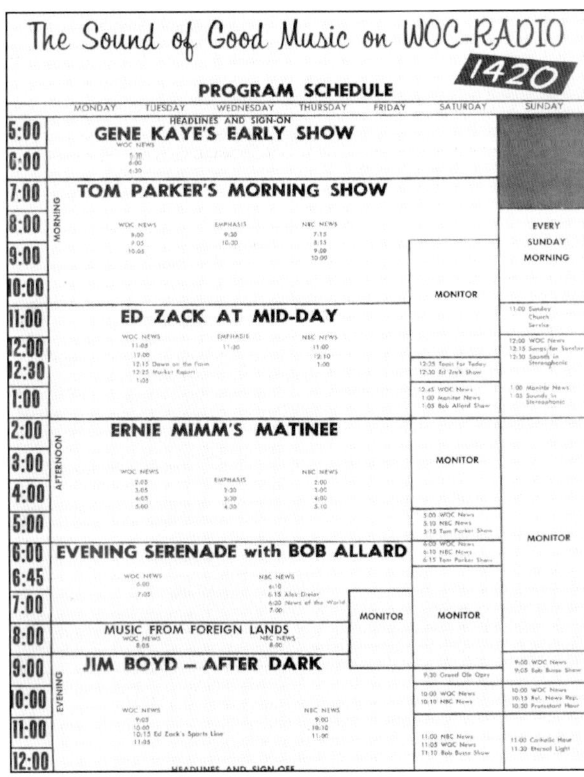

The WOC Radio program schedule is pictured as it appeared in the late 1950s. The majority of the weekend schedule was public service and the NBC network's *Monitor*. *Monitor* offered a mix of news, comedy, sports, music, and celebrity interviews. The segments were hosted by well-known names in broadcasting, entertainment, and journalism. In addition to *Monitor* and various religious programming, an instrumental music show called *Every Sunday Morning* was extremely popular.

Following *Highway Patrol's* popular four-year run on channel 6, the station purchased another Ziv Television syndicated series titled *Sea Hunt*. The show starred Lloyd Bridges as an ex-Navy skin diver and aired for four years, beginning in 1958. Bridges dealt with all forms of underwater villains and helped salvage boats, missiles, and sunken treasure. The show's popularity was probably responsible for many viewers taking up scuba diving.

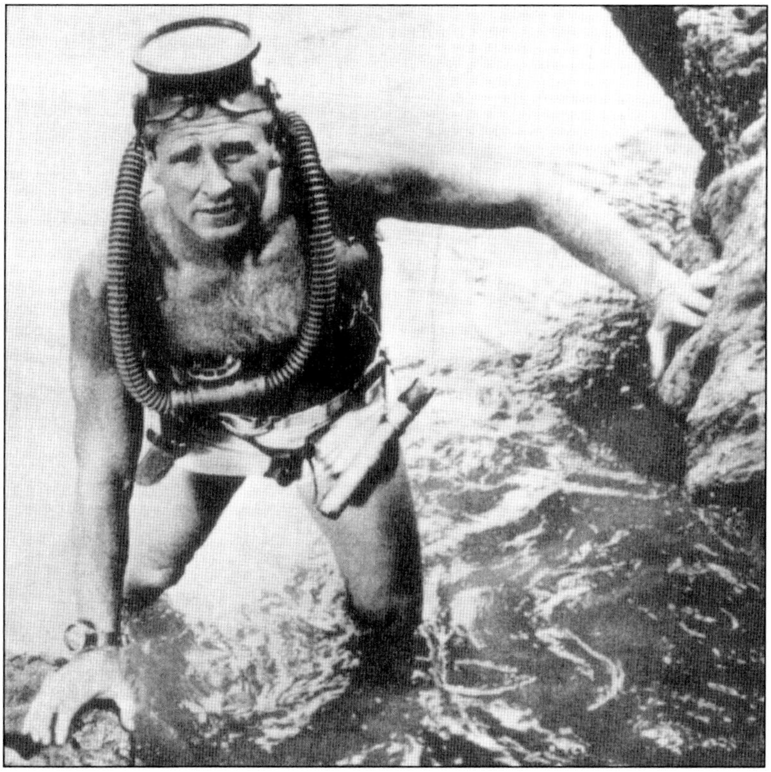

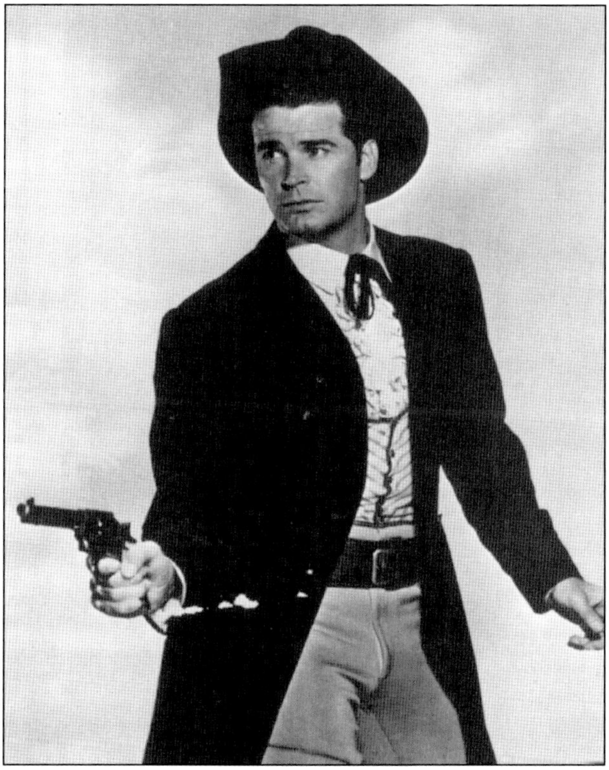

Although a primary affiliate of NBC, WOC-TV also televised programs normally aired on the ABC network. As ABC did not yet have a network affiliate in the area, it would pay prime-time rates to have its programming seen. *Maverick*, starring James Garner, was one of several ABC programs that aired on WOC-TV. When Moline's WQAD-TV signed on in 1963, that practice came to an end.

WOC WOC-FM DAVENPORT, IOWA

DAY FRIDAY DATE 5/10/63 PAGE NO. 3

ORIGIN	TYPE	CLASS
ST: Studio	LS: Local Sustaining	1—Entertainment
RC: Record	LC: Local Commercial	2—Religious
NDT: Net Delay Tape	NS: Net Sustaining	3—Agricultural
T: Tape	NC: Net Commercial	4—Education
CT: Cartridge Tape	SP: Sponsored Pgm.	5—News
SPT: Special Tape	PT: Participating Pgm.	6—Commentary
ET: Transcription	LF: Local Free Anncmt.	7—Discussion
R: Remote	CA: Courtesy Anncmt.	8—Political
N: NBC	P: Promo. Anncmt.	
X: Transmitter	V: Sp. Pgm. Annct.	

OPERATORS ON O

DAILY PROGRAM LOG

SCHEDULED BROADCAST TIME	ACTUAL BROADCAST TIME	ORIGIN	CLASS	PGM. OR SPOT TITLE and SPONSOR
:22AM		ST-RC	1	THE MORNING SHOW
		CT		Vademecum Prod. (30 sec)
		CT		Champion Spark Plugs (Min) CT 1
		CT		Ford Dealers-DAV DIST (Min) 2292 Cut 6
		CT		Firestone Store (30 sec)
		CT		Skelly Keotane (Min)
:29:50		ST		Sta Ident
:30		SPT	6	BILL GRESS COMMENT
:35		ST-RC	1	THE MORNING SHOW
		CT		Champion Spark Plugs (Min) CT 1

From its first days of broadcasting, WOC kept records of electrical consumption, voltage, current, tube values, and other items related to signal transmissions. These records, known as "logs," were taken every half hour. WOC also kept records of the exact start and stop times of its programs. When commercial announcements were allowed to be sold, WOC also logged their start and stop times. Stations across the United States soon adopted this logging practice. Later the FCC actually required stations to do this. Transmitter logs served as proof to the government that the equipment was operating correctly. Program logs provided proof that a client's scheduled commercial actually aired. This program log from 1963 illustrates an eight-minute segment of programming. It tells the announcer which commercials and programs are to run between 8:22 and 8:30 a.m. Note that the recorded commercial announcements take up four out of eight minutes. That does not leave much time for music or a typical morning show announcer's patter. (Courtesy of Phil Roberts.)

Four

The Broadcast Centre

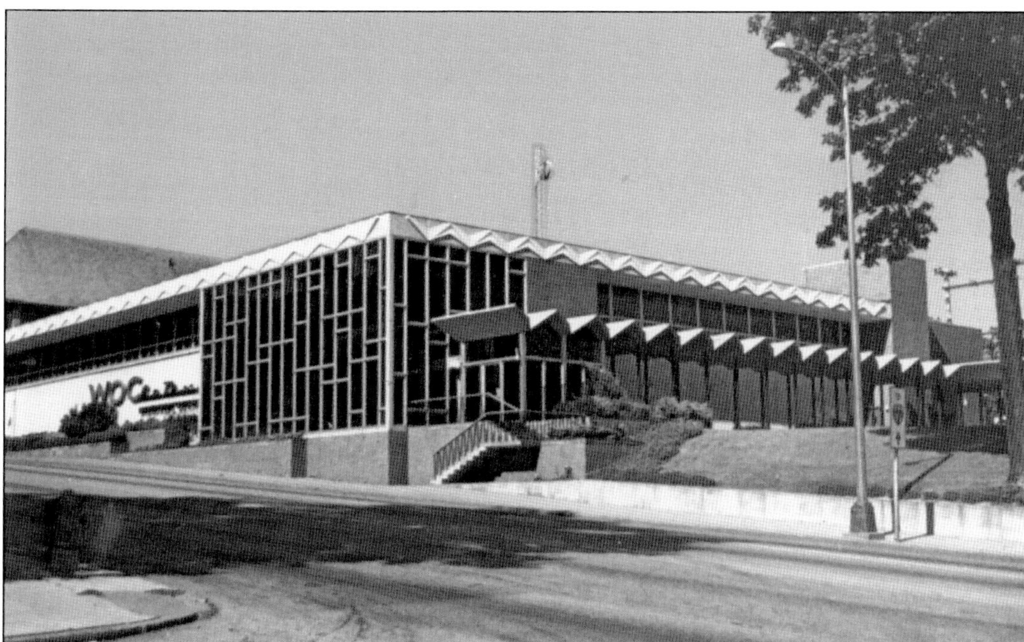

In 1963, the WOC stations moved into their new home just north of the old studios. Dubbed the WOC Broadcast Centre, it was equipped with the latest in broadcast equipment. The building was a model of efficiency and capability. Designers made provisions for growth and the eventual full-color operation. The station's former building was leveled, but the studio annex was kept for storage of equipment and station vehicles.

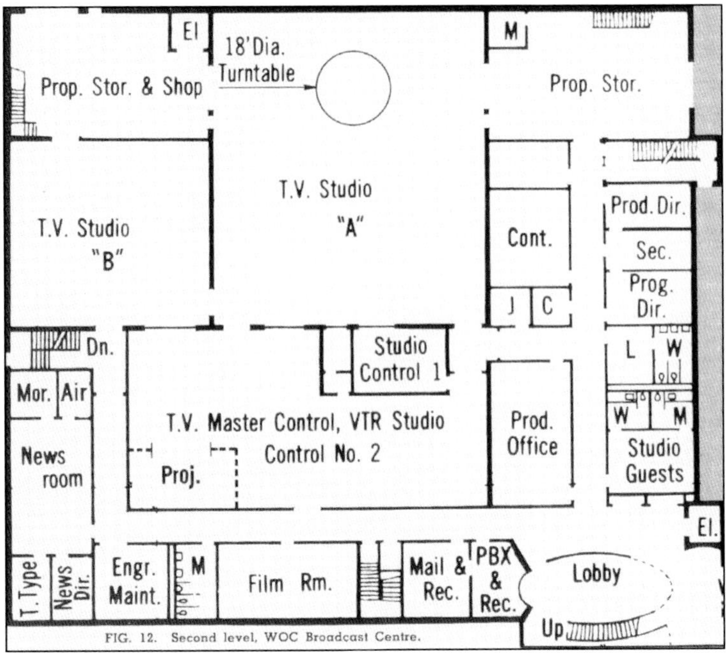

FIG. 12. Second level, WOC Broadcast Centre.

Pictured are floor plans for the first (above) and second floors of the new broadcast center. As the renderings illustrate, the second floor contained the radio studios and the majority of the sales and business offices. When WOC-FM became KIIK-FM, its studios were built in what was originally the staff conference room in the lower left of the rendering. Television studios, news, the film departments, production offices, and engineering equipment and control rooms occupied the first floor. The biggest feature was the 18-foot turntable in studio A. Automobiles could be driven through prop storage on the right, into studio A, and then out again through the prop storage area on the left. For years, a local automobile dealership used this feature to display used vehicles during its sponsorship of the Sunday night movie. (Courtesy of *RCA Broadcast News*.)

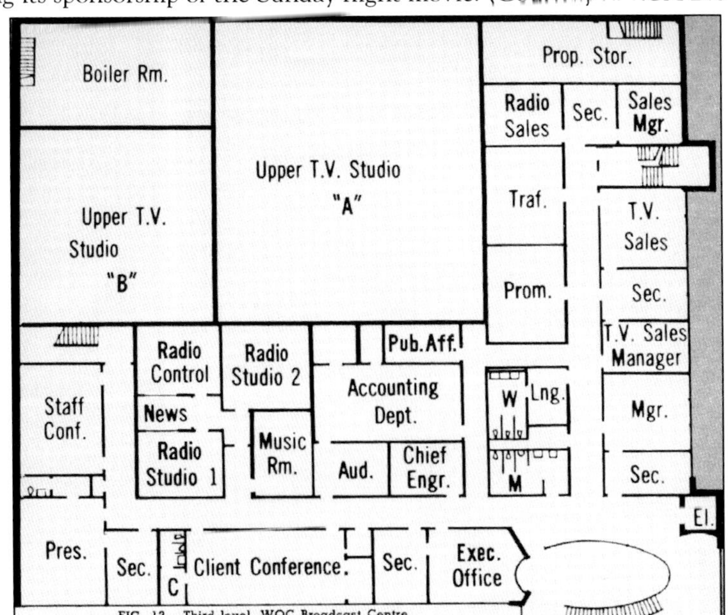

FIG. 13. Third level, WOC Broadcast Centre.

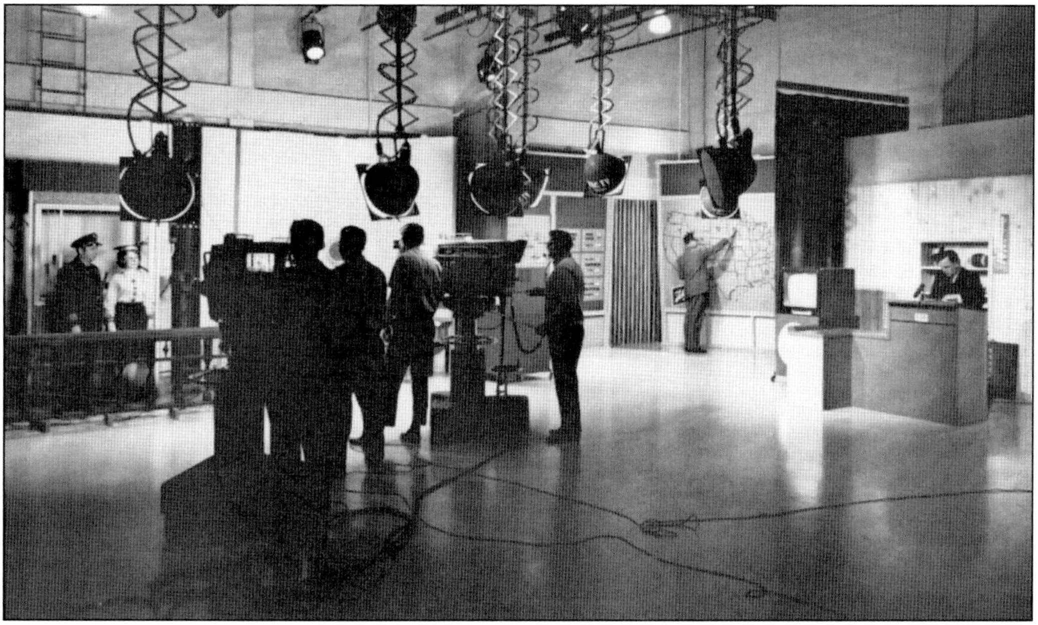

Studio B, the smaller of WOC's two studios, contained all the permanent sets with the exception of the *Especially for You* set. The *Cartoon Showboat* pilothouse is at the extreme left. Next to it is the showboat's "galley," which was used for guest interviews. Weather and sports sets can be seen on the right. The news set cannot be seen in this photograph. (Courtesy of *RCA Broadcast News*.)

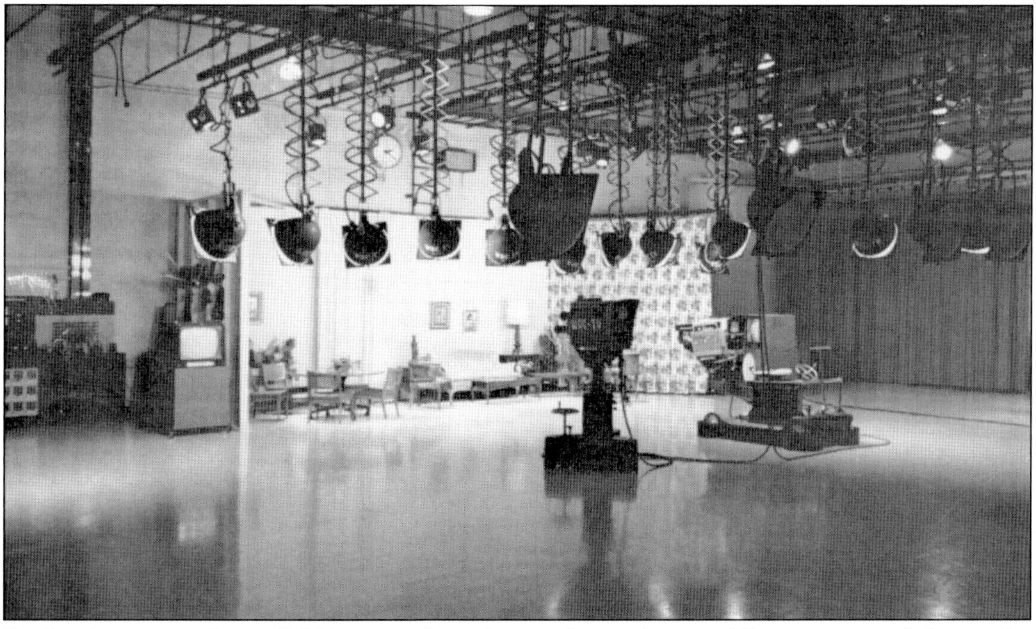

Studio A contained over 5,000 square feet of space for production. The station used this studio for commercials and recording large groups, such as choirs and orchestras. It also contained the permanent set for *Especially for You*. Note the lighting grids with their adjustable spotlights. Cameras needed a lot of light and even more when the station installed color cameras. (Courtesy of *RCA Broadcast News*.)

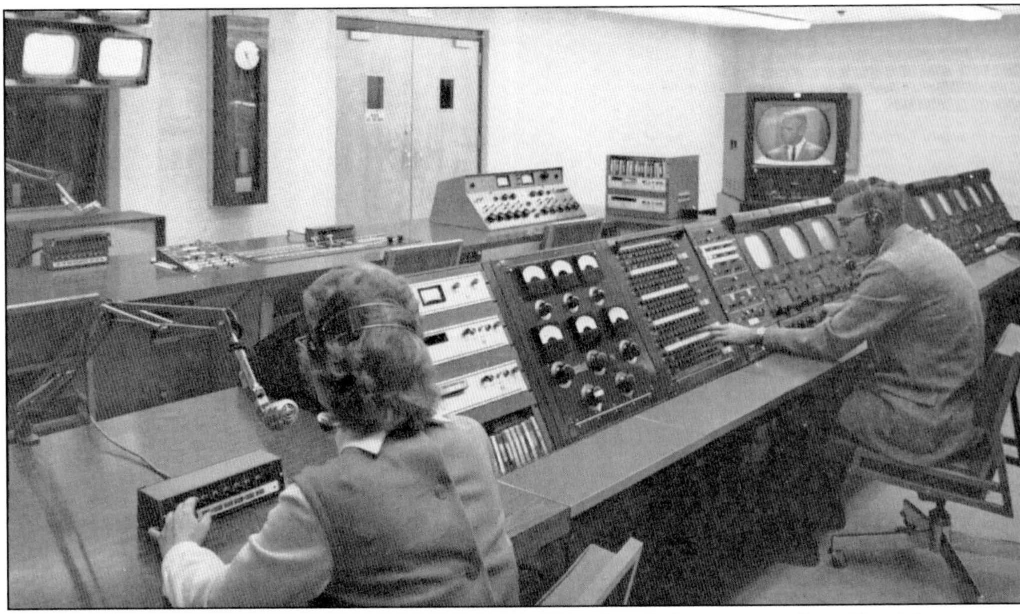

Mary Bullard (left) gives the directions for a station break, while engineer Stan Straight operates the master switcher. This back row controls the function and flow of all audio and video signals. The front row is used for live production from Studio B, the smaller of WOC-TVs two studios. The director sits to the left, the video switcher in the center, and the audio operator on the right. (Courtesy of *RCA Broadcast News.*)

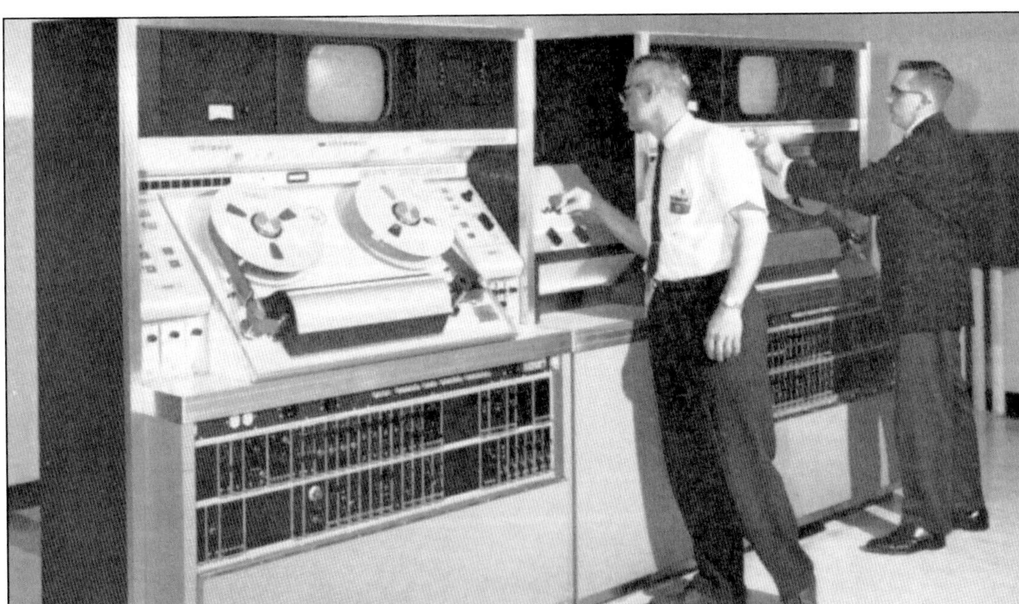

The invention of videotape was a great step forward for television. Programs and commercials could be recorded and played back immediately and with all the clarity of a "live" performance. John Seran (left) and Bill McCutcheon are shown setting up WOC-TV's new videotape machines for a program recording session. These machines used two-inch videotape, while later models would eventually use much smaller width tape. (Courtesy of *RCA Broadcast News.*)

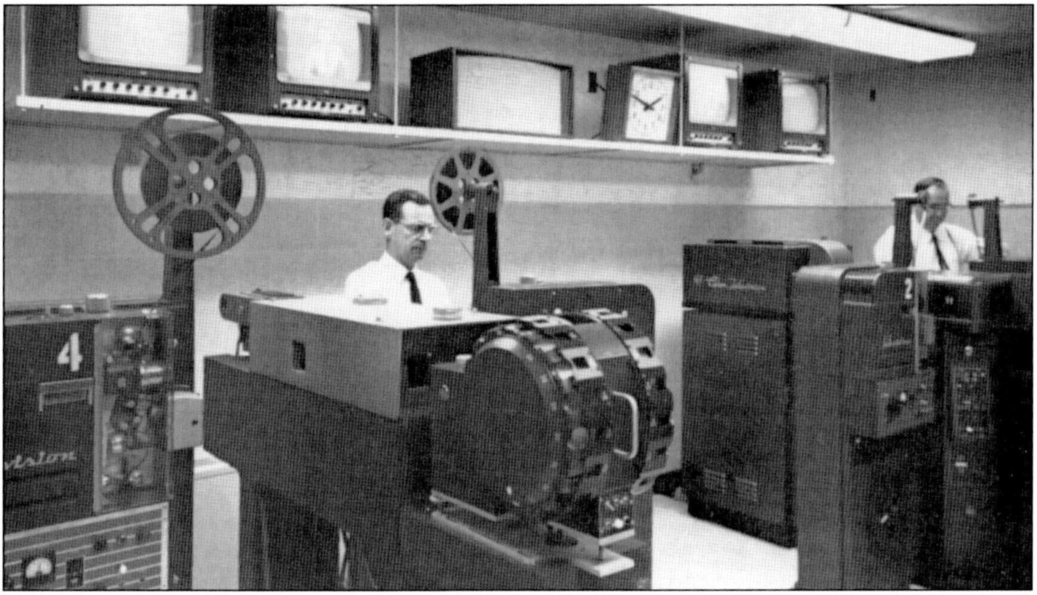

While videotape was becoming more prevalent in the 1960s, the movies, cartoons, and many commercials were still provided on film. Al Starkweather (left) and Gus Wendt are seen threading the film projectors. The cameras are located between the projectors. The units on the left handled black and white film only. Those on the right could project both color and black-and-white film and slides. (Courtesy of *RCA Broadcast News*.)

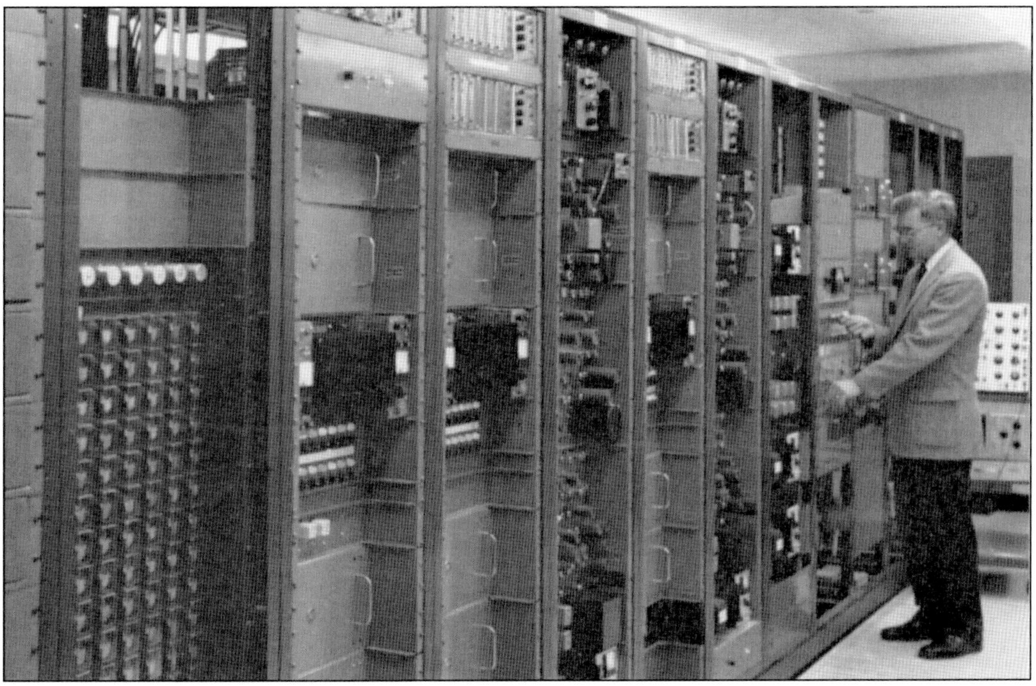

These racks hold just some of the power supplies, relays, switchers, tubes, and distribution amplifiers that send the sounds and pictures from the studio equipment out to the transmitter. There is another rack of equipment just like this behind the one shown here. Engineer Stan Straight had the duty of repairing whatever went wrong with this equipment. (Courtesy of *RCA Broadcast News*.)

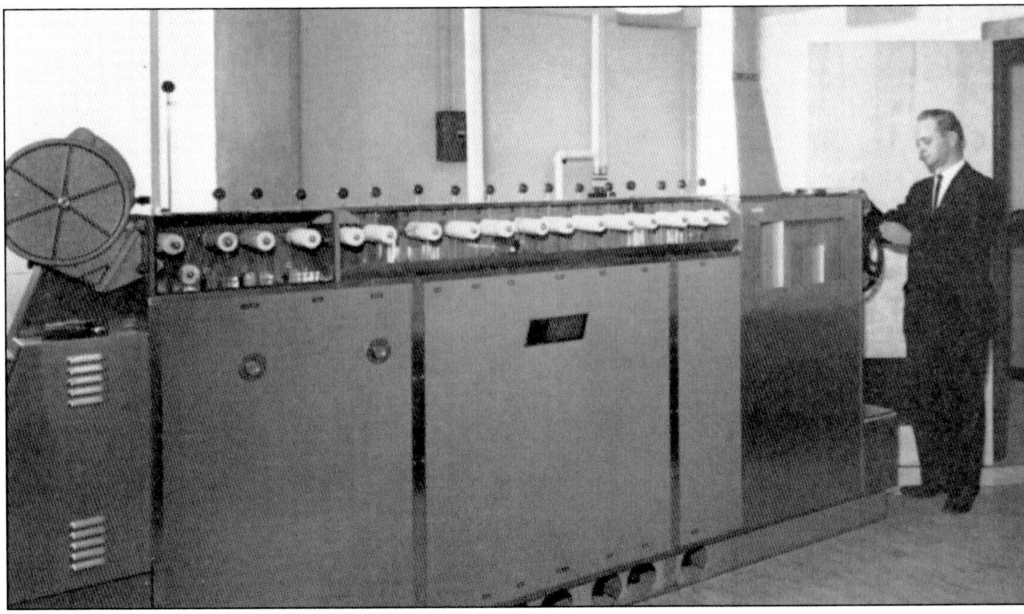

Before video cameras became small enough to carry by hand, news and sports reports were captured on film. Enough time had to be allowed after shooting for the film to be developed. Max Lindberg operates the news department's 16mm processor. Exposed film enters from the left, travels through the tanks of developing chemicals, and exits on the right, ready for editing. (Courtesy of *RCA Broadcast News*.)

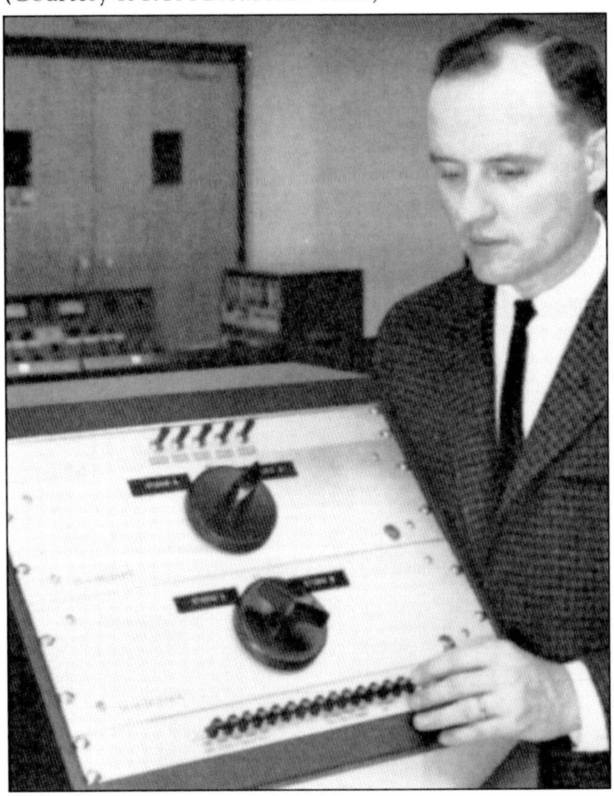

Dave Hauser, WOC-TV's chief engineer, was responsible for designing and overseeing the construction and installation of the new television facilities. He is shown here with the projection room delegation control. The two large switches assigned operating functions of the film and slide projectors to any one of three control positions. The smaller switches are part of the building's monitoring system. (Courtesy of *RCA Broadcast News*.)

Ernie Mimms cues up a record in the Broadcast Centre's AM radio studio. To the right of the reel tape recorders are the tape cartridge playback machines and the rack of cartridges that contained many of the commercial messages. On the other side of the window was a small booth that could be used by the newsman or a program guest. (Courtesy of *RCA Broadcast News*.)

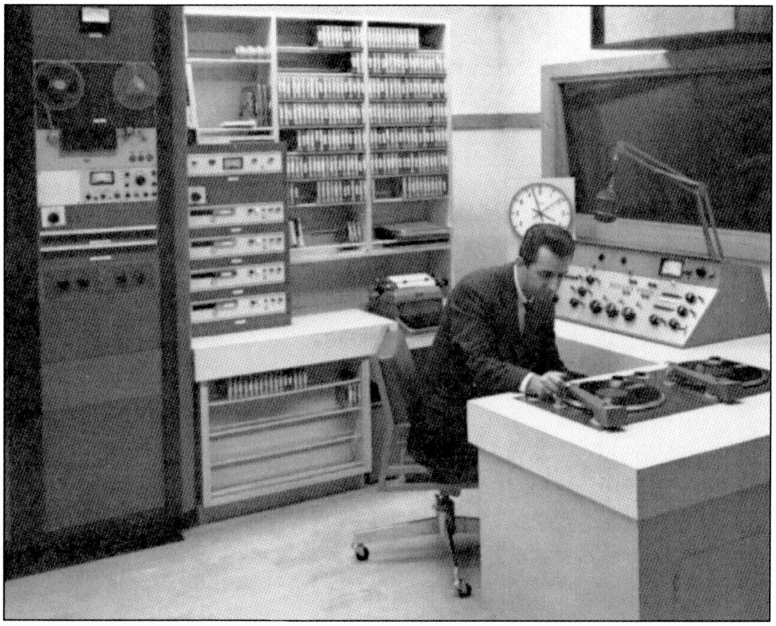

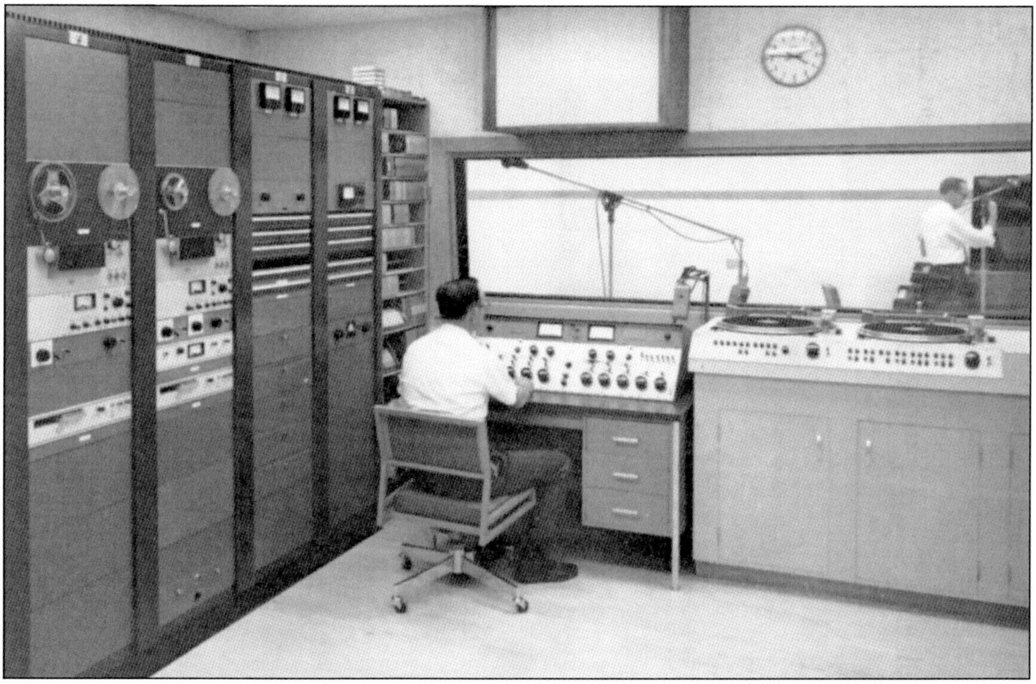

This is WOC Radio's master control and production studio. Coy Bullard (left), who would later become the WOC stations' director of engineering, and Bill Smith are setting up for a recording session. Below the turntables are remote start switches for any tape machine in the production or AM studio. This was also the spot where the audio signals were sent to the transmitter via telephone lines. (Courtesy of *RCA Broadcast News*.)

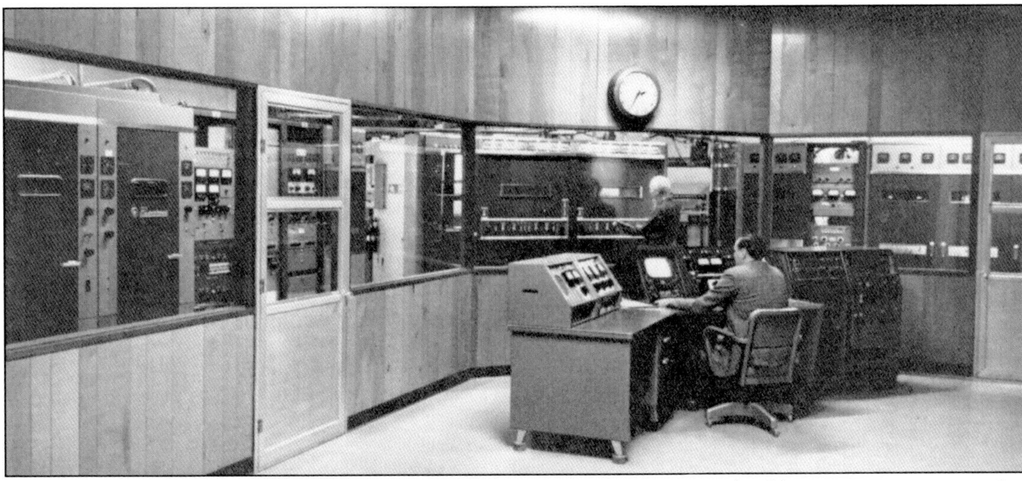

In 1961, a new television tower was erected, and a new transmitter building was constructed at the Bettendorf tower site. In the center of the room are the master control units for each of the transmitters. Behind the glass are the transmitters; AM radio (left), television (center), and FM radio (right), along with associated control and monitoring units for each. (Courtesy of *RCA Broadcast News*.)

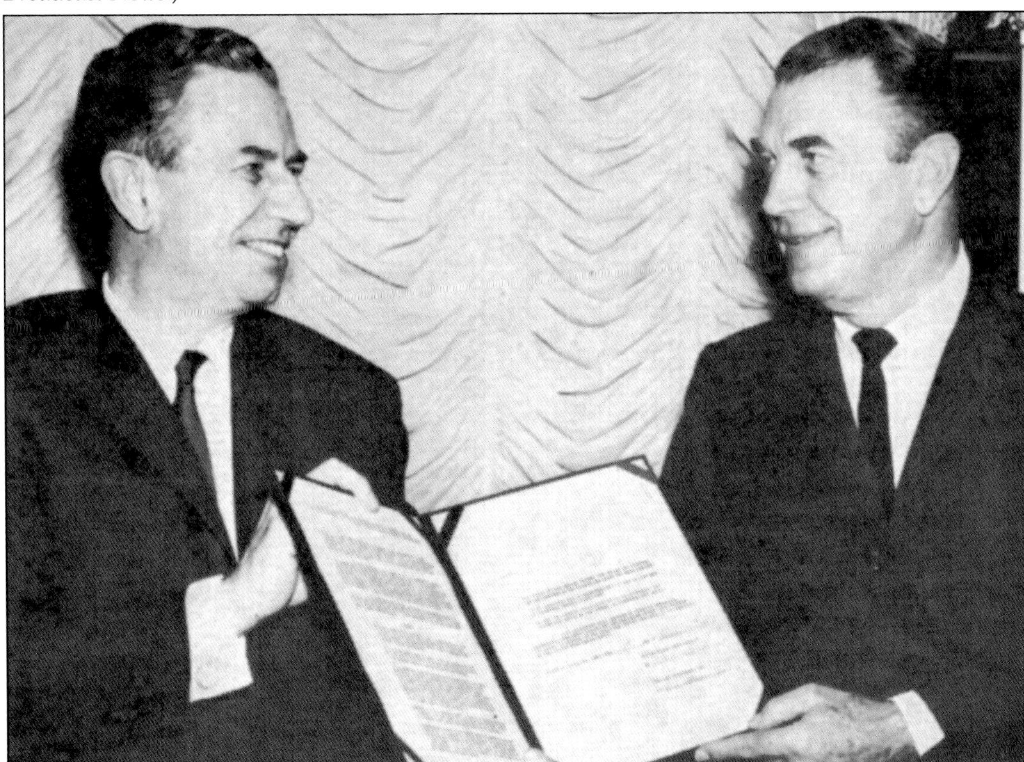

In 1932, WOC became the first client of Peters, Griffin, Woodward, Inc., a national sales agency that represented broadcasting stations in major cities. The firm's president, H. Preston Peters (left), presented Dr. David Palmer with the original contract for Tri-City Broadcasting Company during a week of open house festivities for WOC's Broadcast Centre. David Palmer's signature was on that contract. (Courtesy of *RCA Broadcast News*.)

Fireworks promoted WOC's new facilities and provided a great station promotion that lasted for 10 years. Beginning in 1964, channel 6 staged a huge two-night display over the Mississippi River each summer to thank viewers for their loyalty. A barge would anchor between Moline and Bettendorf the first night and between Davenport and Rock Island the next evening. Thousands lined the shores for the 45-minute show. (Courtesy of Ivan Owens.)

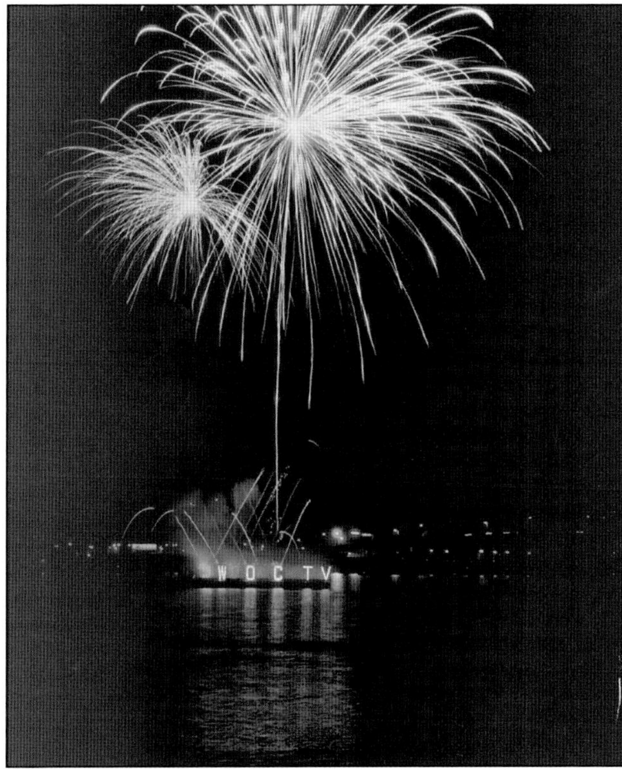

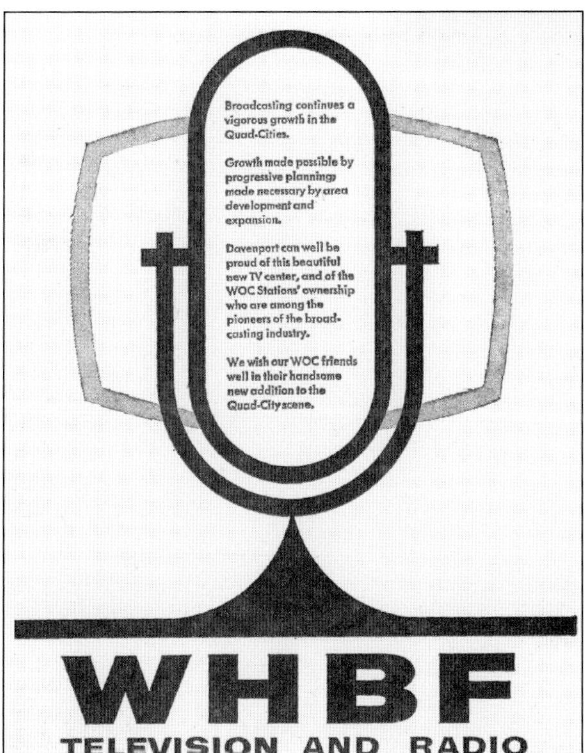

While the WHBF stations in Rock Island were in direct competition with WOC, it did not stop them from saluting the WOC stations on the new Broadcast Centre. Competition between stations was a little different in the late 1950s and early 1960s. If equipment failed and put a station off the air, another station would usually step up and loan equipment that would put it back on the air.

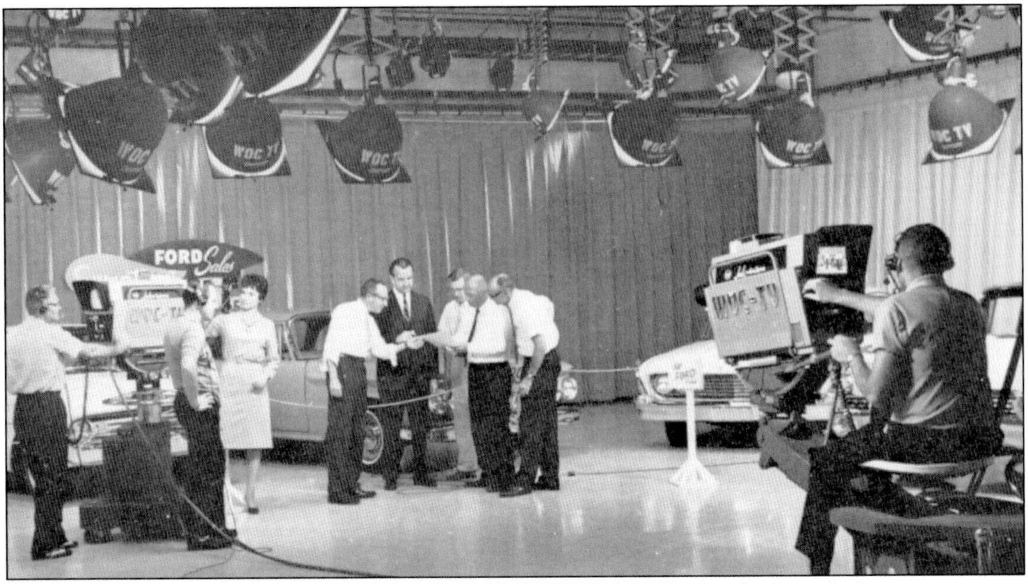

The preparation of videotaping a commercial took a large group of individuals, including cameramen, copywriter, director, lighting director, technical director, sales representative, and the talent or spokesperson. This commercial would be one of three shown during the Sunday night movie presentation sponsored by Sumption Ford Sales. WOC-TV's large production studio featured an 18-foot turntable that was perfect for highlighting an automobile's fine lines and styling. (Courtesy of *RCA Broadcast News.*)

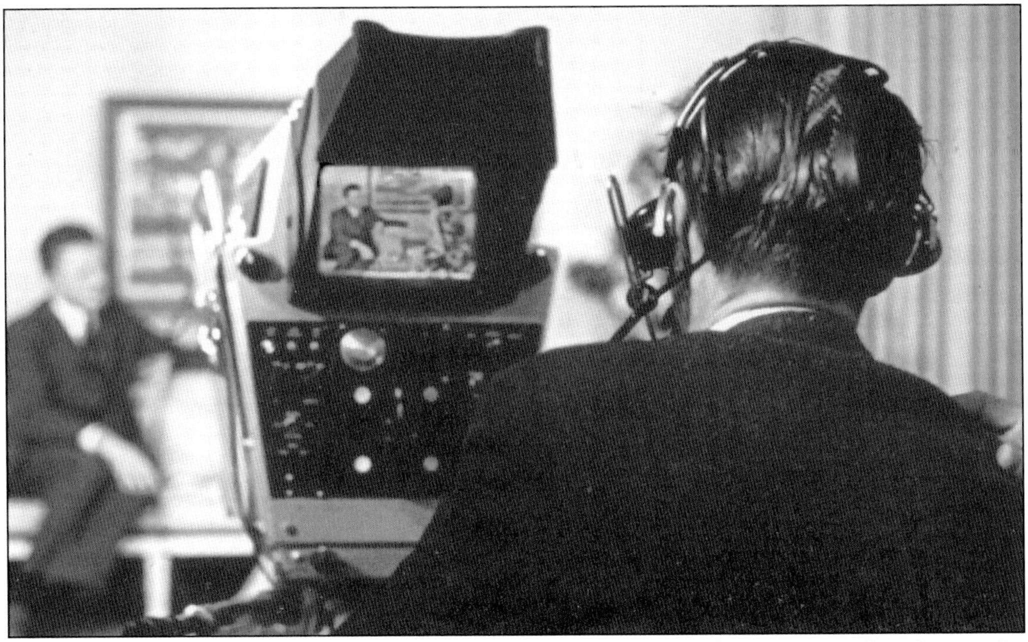

This is the view from behind the camera as engineer Max Roth frames a two-shot during the production of *Especially for You*. This camera was not equipped with a zoom lens. A handle at the back of the camera allowed the cameraman to rotate the lenses for different focal lengths, depending upon the wishes of the director. The small lights on either side of the viewfinder indicate when the camera is on the air. (Courtesy of *RCA Broadcast News.*)

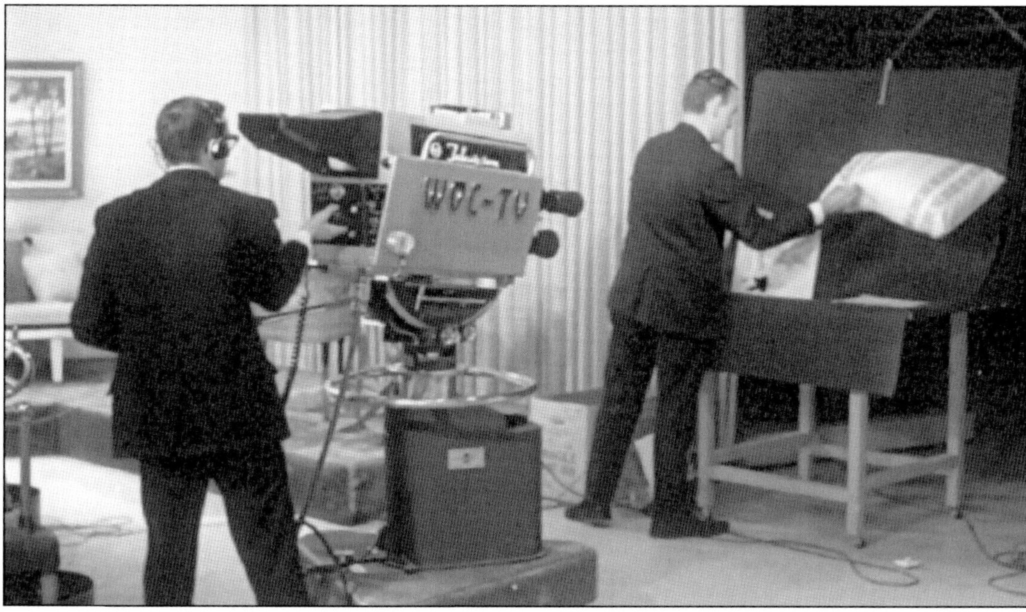

Live television requires many fast setups between the on-air shots. Cameraman Bill McCutcheon and stage manager Ivan Owens make a fast change of a visual display used during an *Especially for You* segment. McCutcheon's hand is on the lens turret control and is most likely changing to a lens that will allow for a close-up view of the display. (Courtesy of *RCA Broadcast News*.)

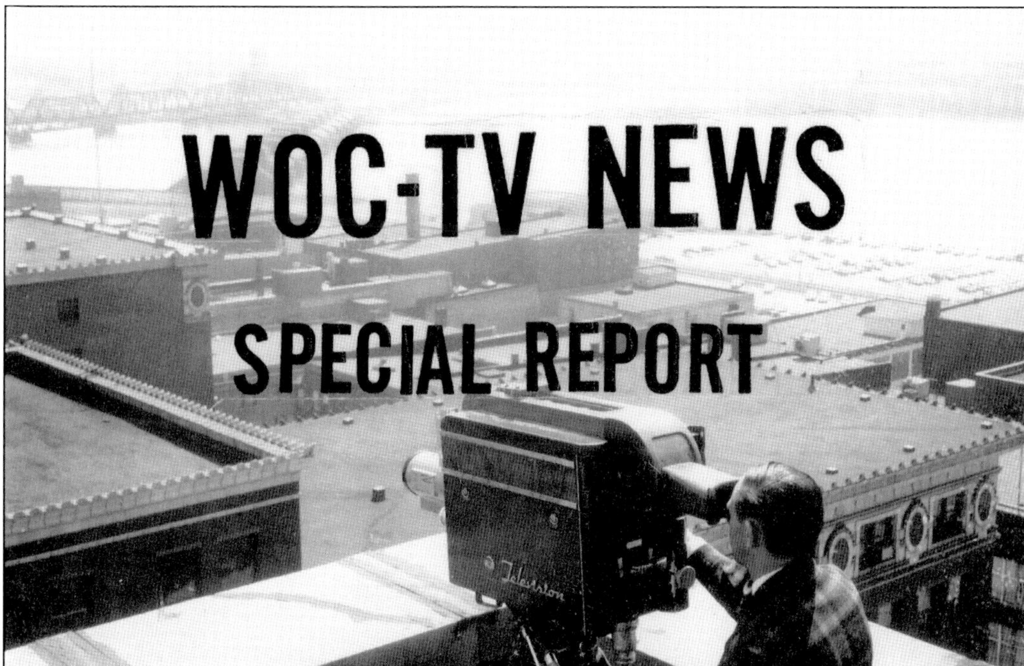

In 1965, the "flood of the century" rolled down the Mississippi River. The flood's crest of 23 feet was the highest ever recorded to that point. WOC-TV put a camera on the roof of the Davenport Bank and Trust building to give viewers a look at the devastation caused to the downtown area. NBC also received a video feed for use on its network news. (Courtesy of Ivan Owens.)

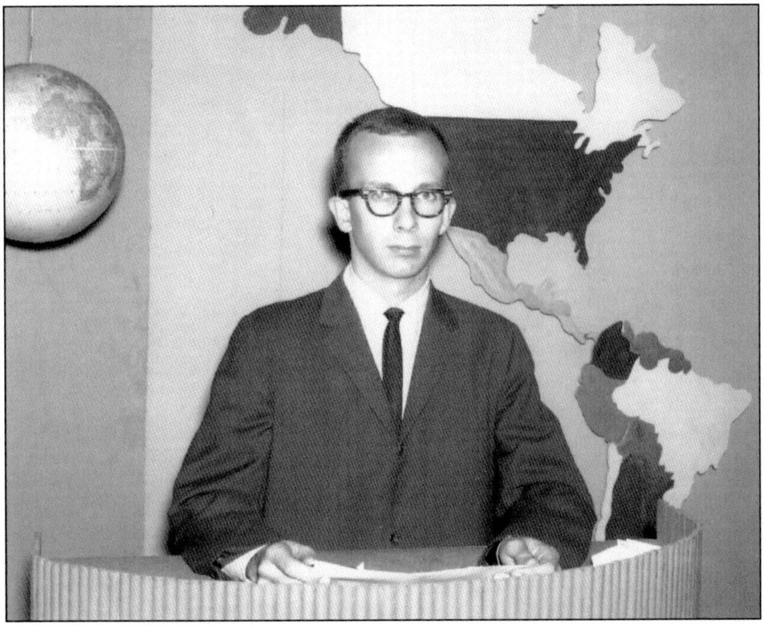

A young-looking John Bauman delivered the news from this rather simple set in the early 1960s. This set was most likely used for either *Today Show* local news cut-ins or for the Sunday morning news that had the newsman doing weather and sports as well. The globe hangs from fishing line. One might wonder how many times Bauman walked into that globe. (Courtesy of KWQC-TV.)

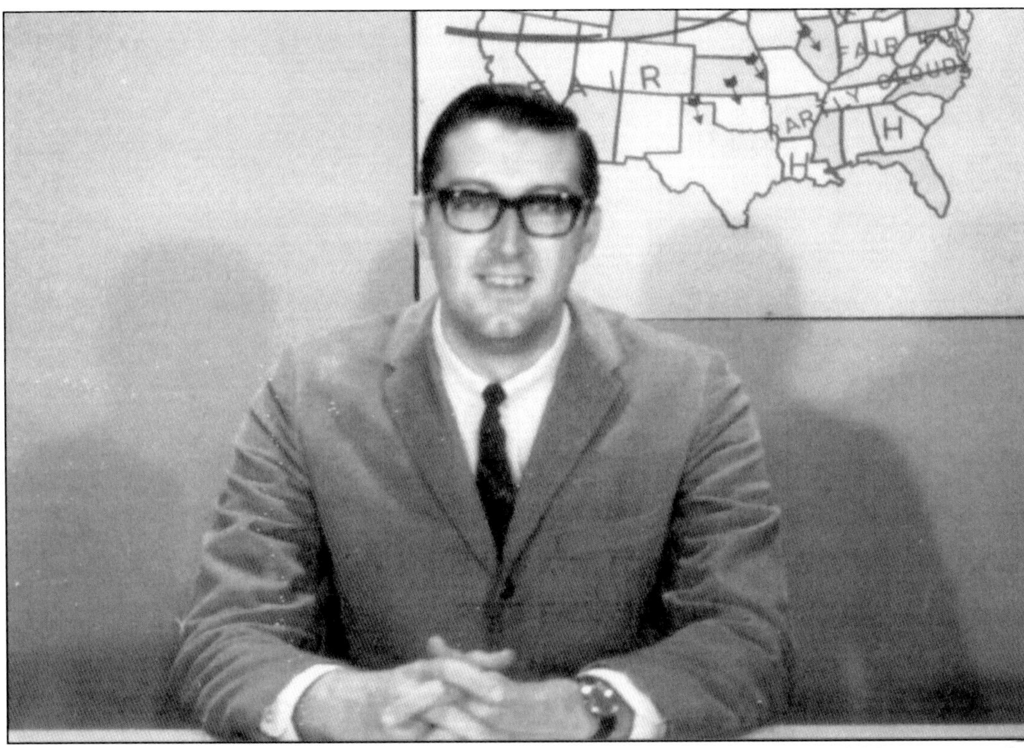

Charles King was the weatherman on the early evening newscast in the mid-1960s. Note the rather simple weather map. It used magnetic letters and symbols to denote conditions and weather fronts; a far cry from the computer graphics used today. King was also the afternoon host on WOC Radio. The announcing staff could make extra money, a talent fee, for filling positions and hosting on channel 6. (Courtesy of KWQC-TV.)

WOC announcers Don Warren (left), Tom Parker, and Doug Dahlgren pull music for their record shows. During the mid-1960s, Warren signed the station on in the morning, Parker hosted a midday show, and Dahlgren was the afternoon drive-time host. Warren also served as "Captain Don" on WOC-TV's *Cartoon Showboat*. Warren would later join WHO and Dahlgren moved on to WCFL in Chicago. (Courtesy of KWQC-TV.)

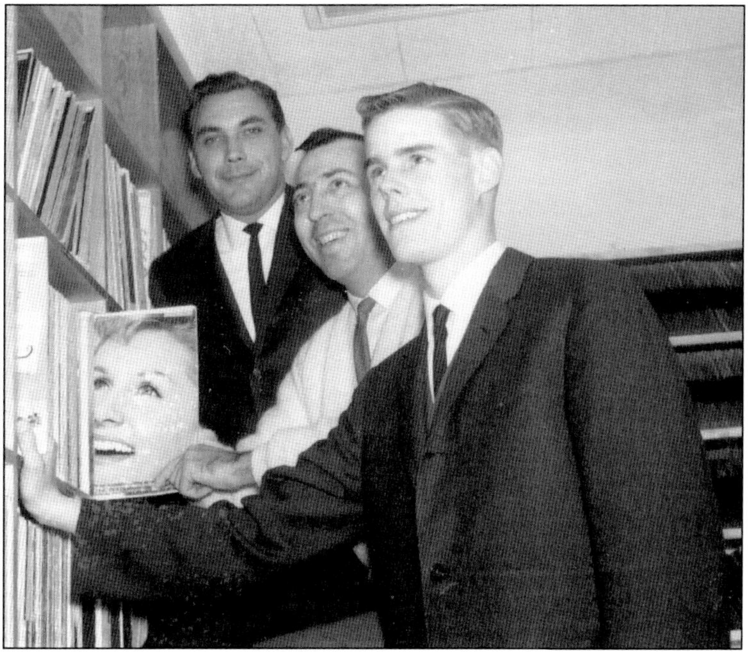

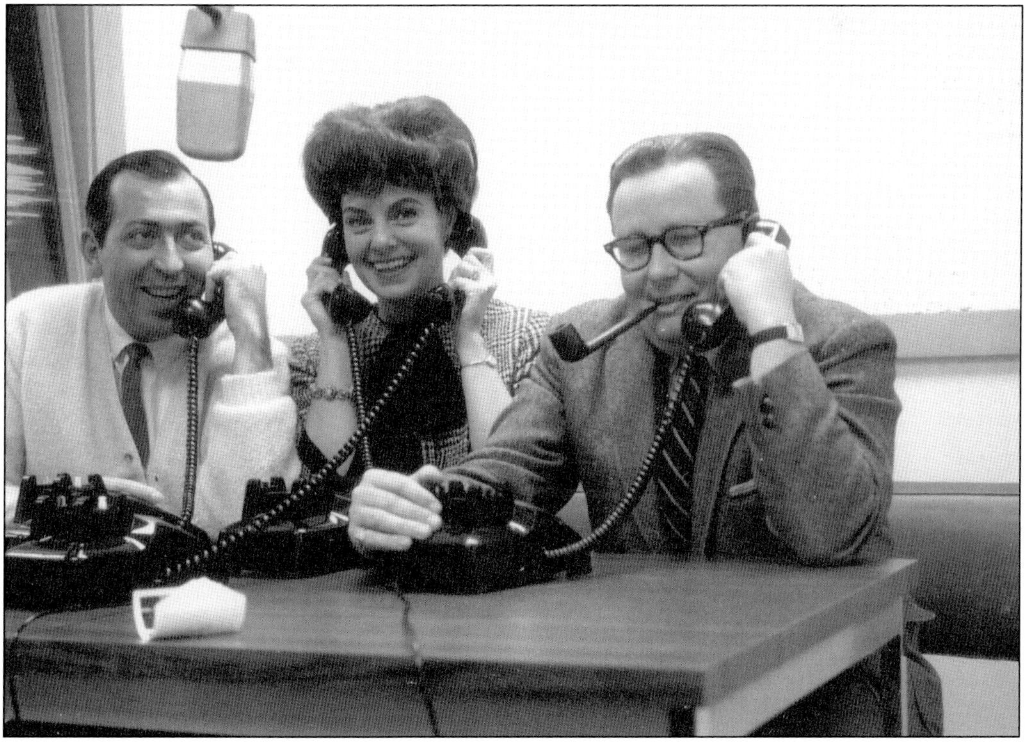

In the mid-1960s, WOC had three telephone call-in shows on the air. Tom Parker (left) hosted *TP's Trading Post* each morning. Callers could chat with Pat Sundine regarding women's topics on *Phone Forum* in the early afternoon. Bill Gress had the phone to his ear for an hour just before noon, on *Call Bill Gress*, where any topic might be fair game. (Courtesy of KWQC-TV.)

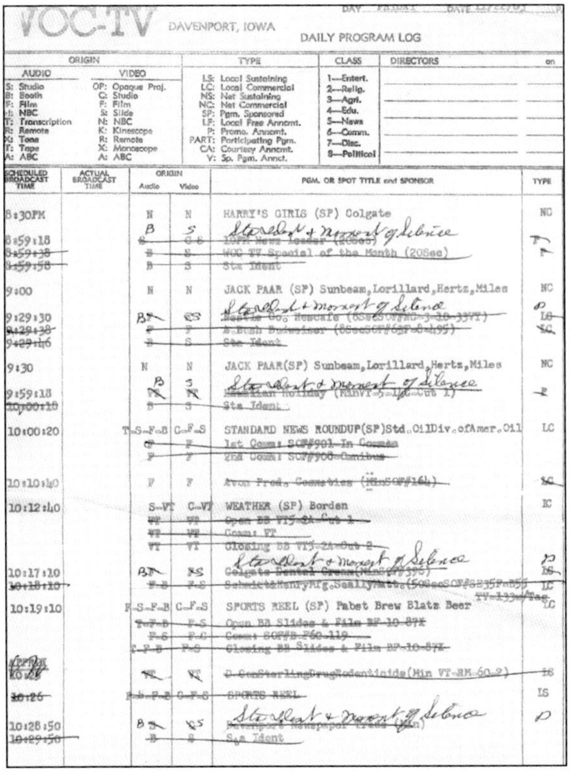

WOC-TV DAVENPORT, IOWA

DAILY PROGRAM LOG

ORIGIN AUDIO	ORIGIN VIDEO	TYPE	CLASS	DIRECTORS
S: Studio	OP: Opaque Proj.	LS: Local Sustaining	1—Entert.	
B: Booth	C: Studio	LC: Local Commercial	2—Relig.	
F: Film	F: Film	NS: Net Sustaining	3—Agri.	
N: NBC	S: Slide	NC: Net Commercial	4—Edu.	
T: Transcription	N: NBC	SP: Pgm. Sponsored	5—News	
R: Remote	K: Kinescope	LF: Local Free Anncmt.	6—Comm.	
X: Tone	R: Remote	P: Promo. Anncmt.	7—Disc.	
T: Tape	X: Monoscope	PART: Participating Pgm.	8—Political	
A: ABC	A: ABC	CA: Courtesy Anncmt.		
		V: Sp. Pgm. Annct.		

SCHEDULED BROADCAST TIME	ACTUAL BROADCAST TIME	ORIGIN Audio	ORIGIN Video	PGM. OR SPOT TITLE and SPONSOR	TYPE
8:30PM		N	N	HARRY'S GIRLS (SP) Colgate	NC
8:59:18		B	S	Sta Ident + moment of Silence	
9:00		N	N	JACK PAAR (SP) Sunbeam, Lorillard, Hertz, Miles	NC
9:29:30		B	S	Sta Ident + moment of Silence	
9:30		N	N	JACK PAAR(SP) Sunbeam, Lorillard, Hertz, Miles	NC
9:59:18		B	S	Sta Ident + moment of Silence	
10:00:20		T-S-F-B	C-F-S	STANDARD NEWS ROUNDUP(SP) Std. Oil Div. of Amer. Oil	LC
10:10:40		F	F	~~Avon Prod. Cosmetics~~	
10:12:40		S-VT	C-VT	WEATHER (SP) Borden	LC
10:17:10		B	S	Sta Ident + moment of Silence	
10:19:10		F-S-F-B	C-F-S	SPORTS REEL (SP) Pabst Brew Blatz Beer	LC
~~10:26~~				~~SPORTS REEL~~	LS
10:28:50		B	S	Sta Ident + moment of Silence	
~~10:29:50~~		~~B~~	~~S~~	~~Sta Ident~~	

Upon the assassination of Pres. John Kennedy, all regular programming came to a halt nationwide. Commercials were cancelled. Radio stations, regardless of format, played classical music. Television stations stayed with network coverage. This image is a two-hour segment of WOC-TV's program log for November 23, 1964. At each half-hour break, the log notes "station identification and moment of silence." Network programs were replaced by news coverage. (Courtesy of Wally Boller.)

The television director is not only responsible with what camera shots to put on the air but also what the set and props should look like. Ed Jones, the director for *Especially for You*, is balancing the floral arrangements for just the right look on-air. Jones was also responsible for assigning the directors and talent and the scheduling of all production recording sessions. (Courtesy of Anita Sundin.)

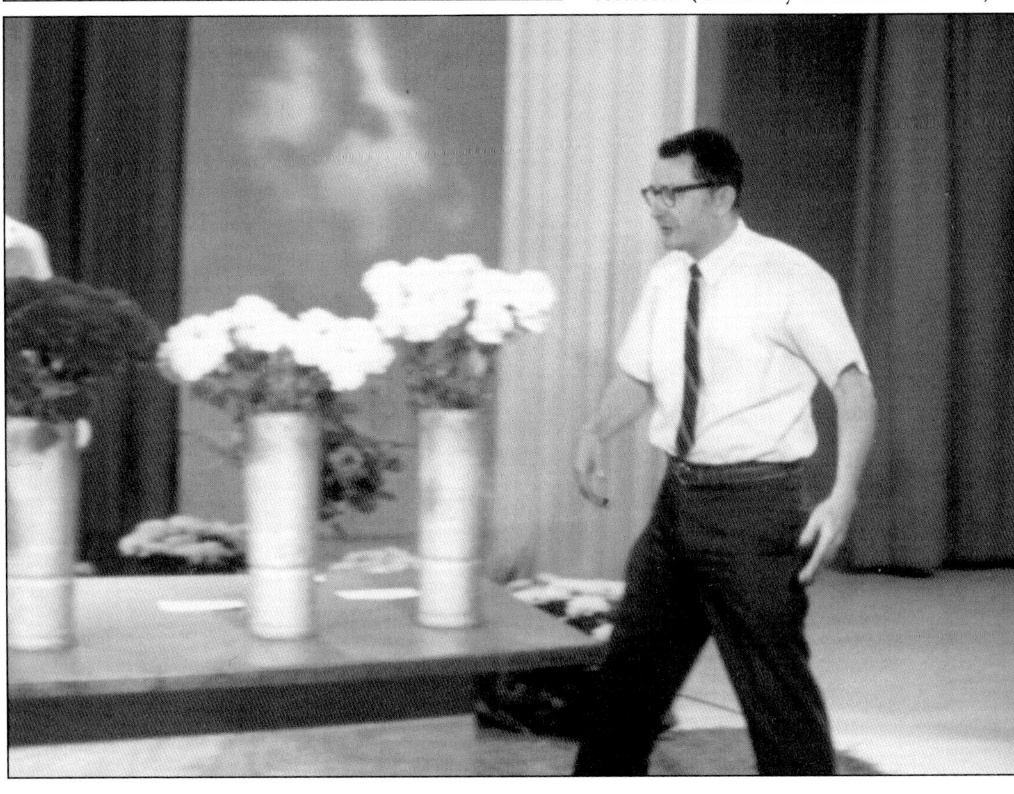

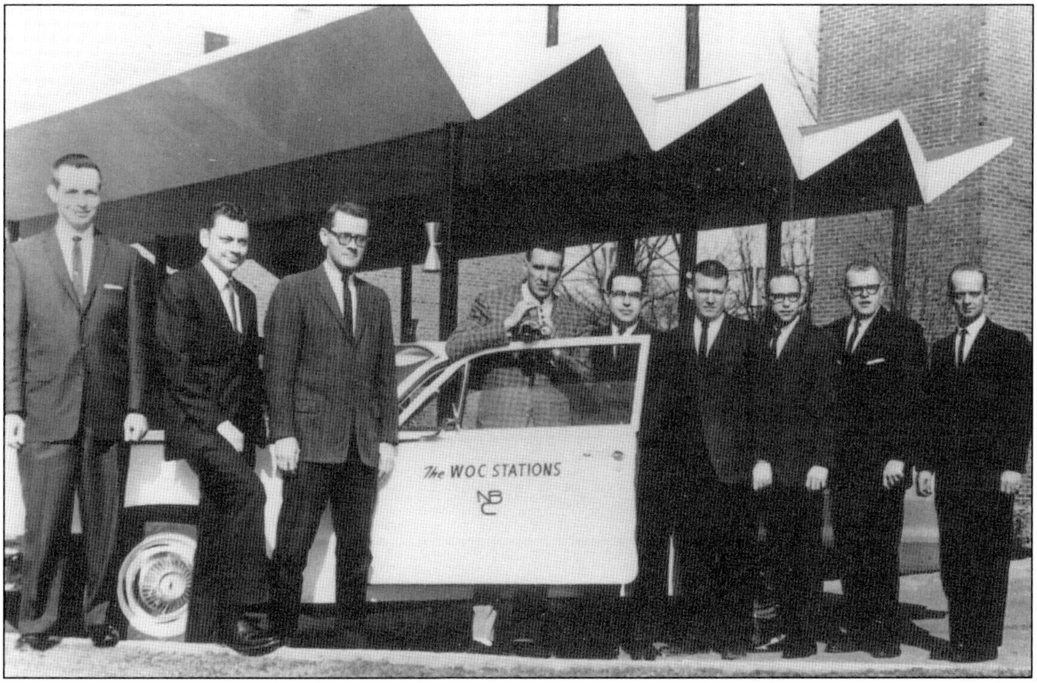

As both a radio and television station, WOC could employ a large group of reporters to cover the important stories of the day. Members of the 1963 news department are, from left to right, Jack Thomsen, Jerry Jorgensen, Don Rhyne, Justus Smith, Charles Leonard, Don McGonegle, Dick Scott, Phil Fleming, and Max Lindberg. Rhyne noted, "We looked like G-men in this picture, and we thought we were." (Courtesy of Don Rhyne.)

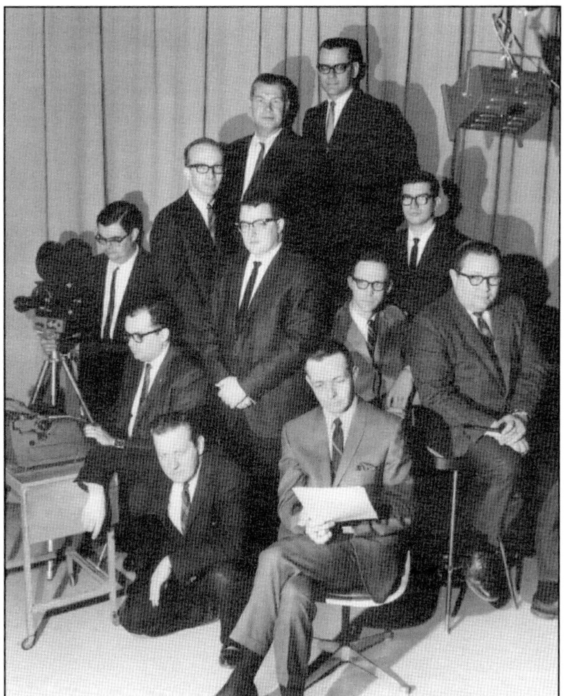

A promotional photograph taken in 1966 shows some changes in the news department. Members now included are, from left to right, (first row) Chuck Roberts, George Johnson, and Jack Thomsen; (second row) Al Carter, Bob Kay, Dick Scott, and Bill Gress; (third row) John Bauman, Don McGonegle, Don Rhyne, and Tom Hecht. (Courtesy of Don Rhyne.)

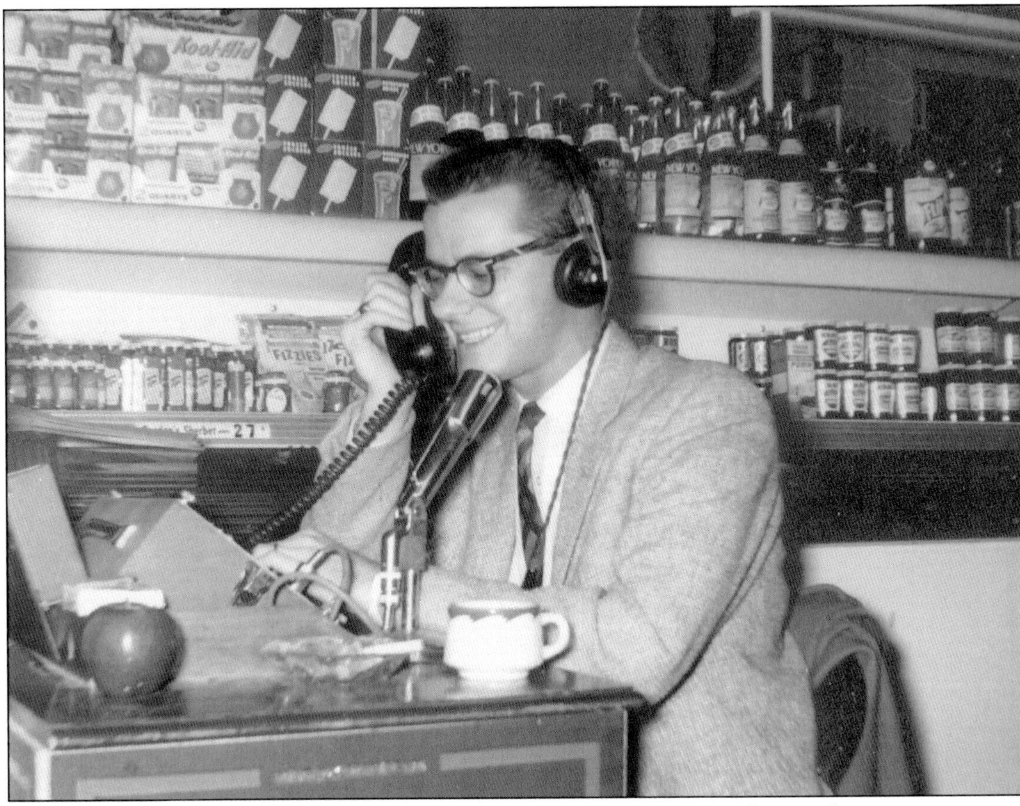

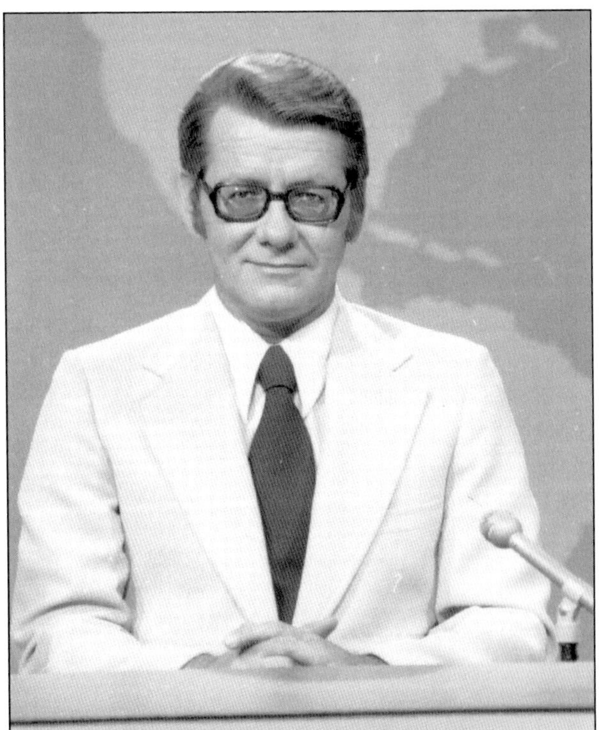

Newsmen do not always start as newsmen. Longtime WOC-TV news anchor Don Rhyne was once the morning deejay and program director at KCLN in Clinton, Iowa. Shown in the above photograph, Rhyne is hosting KCLN's weekly remote broadcast from the Paetz Super Value grocery store. In 1961, a competing Clinton radio station suggested Rhyne for an opening in the WOC news department. Rhyne followed up on that opening at the right moment, as WOC news director Bob Frank was told he could not go on a station-sponsored trip to Spain unless he filled the open position. The day before the trip was scheduled to depart, Rhyne was hired. That started a long career that ended after 15 years as WOC-TV's principle news anchorman. (Courtesy of Don Rhyne.)

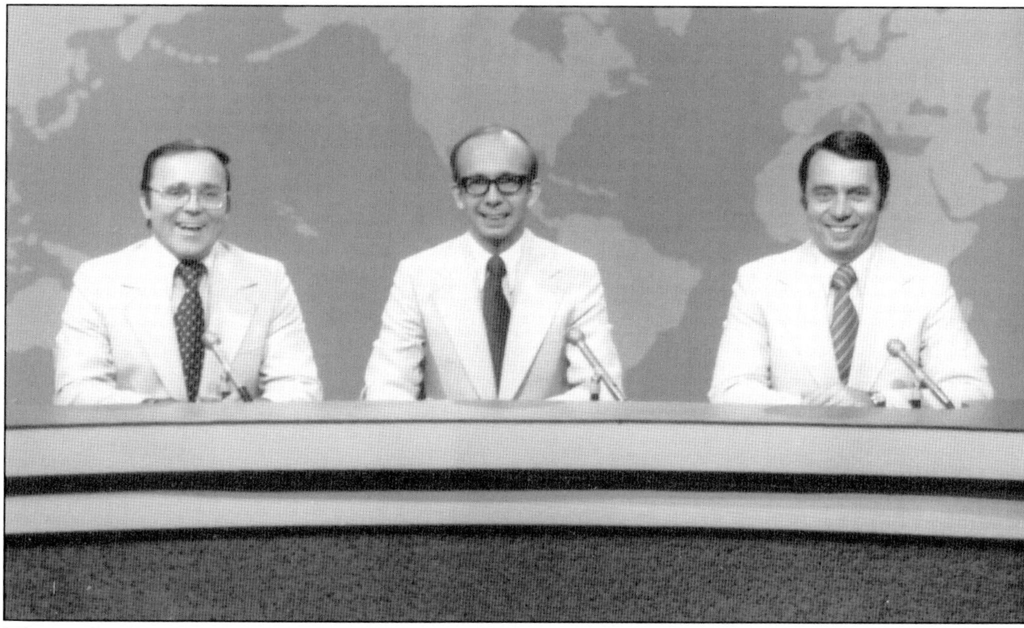

The early evening newscast in the mid-1970s was called the *Channel 6 Six O'clock Edition*. It featured, from left to right, weatherman Bill Bailey, news anchor John Bauman, and sportscaster Wally Boller. This was just one of many news sets used over the years. Sets were modified or changed to coincide with each new fall television season and to give a fresh look to the program. (Courtesy of Don Rhyne.)

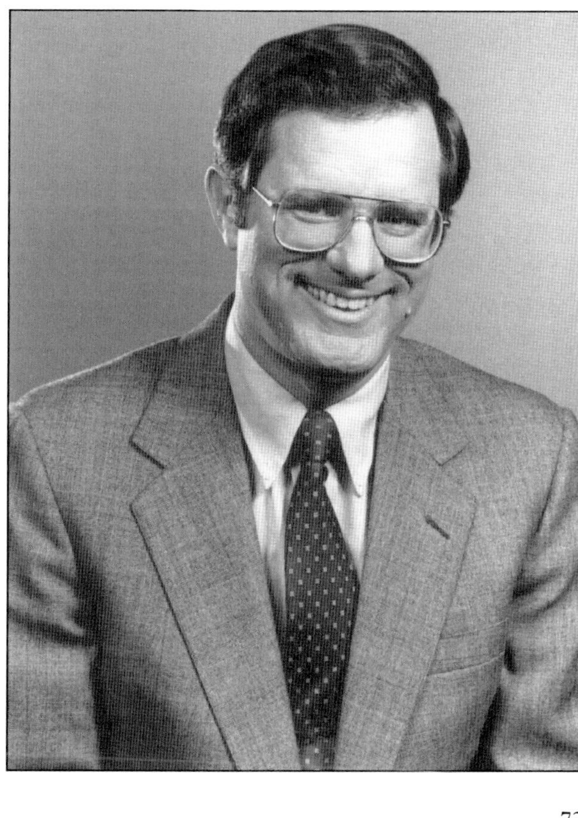

John Collins started at WOC while in college. After serving in the U.S. Air Force, he returned as an evening announcer. When the station's music format changed to news and talk, he was heard on the afternoon news. In the early 1980s, Collins became the primary weatherman on WOC-TV. He gave viewers concise information about weather formation in general and delivered accurate forecasts for viewers to plan their day.

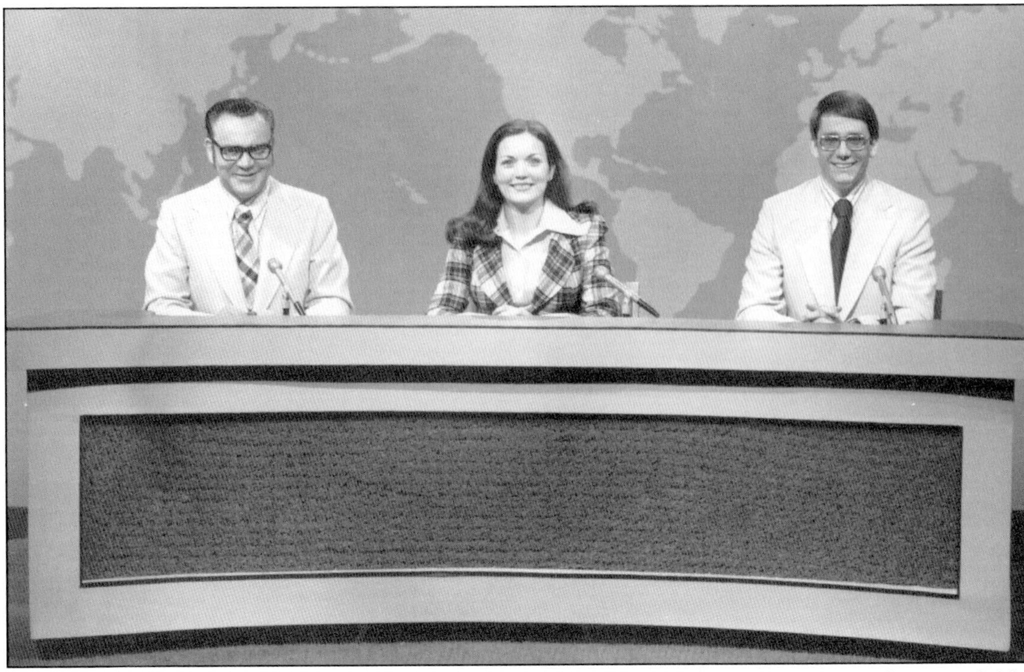

The Saturday *Channel 6 Ten O'clock Edition* anchors in the mid-1970s were weatherman Mike Blair (left), news anchor Kathy McFarland, and sports reporter John Danner. McFarland was the first WOC-TV female reporter to be utilized as a news anchorperson. This style news set was used for nearly a dozen years. Its blue background allowed for easy chroma keying of visuals to accompany a news or sports story. (Courtesy of Don Rhyne.)

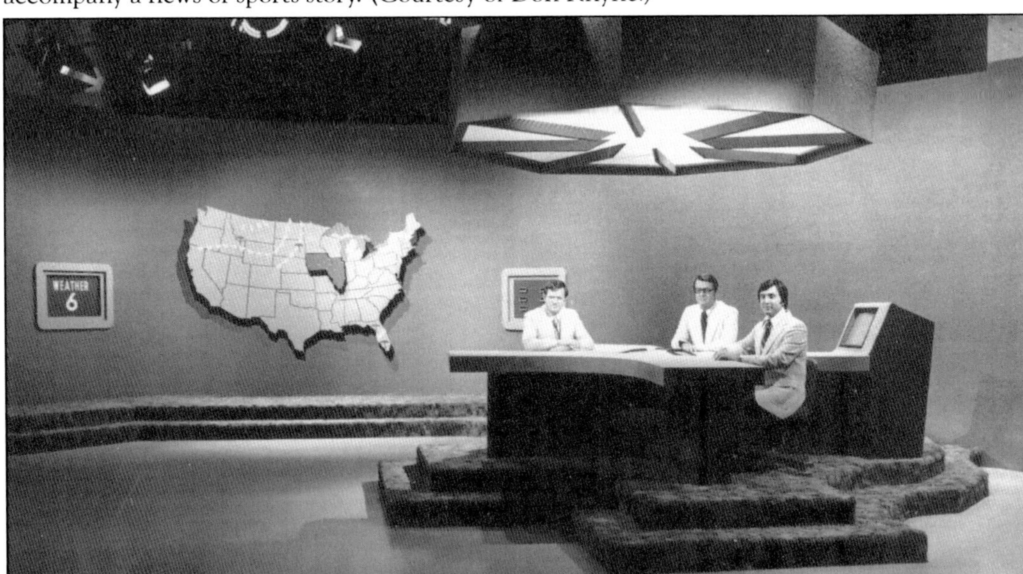

This striking version of the news set made its appearance in about 1980. It allowed the weatherman full use of the large U.S. map. News and sports visuals appeared on the monitor between the news and sports anchors. The *Channel 6 Ten O'clock Edition* reporting team are, from left to right, weatherman John Collins, news anchor Don Rhyne, and sportscaster John Popovich. (Courtesy of Don Rhyne.)

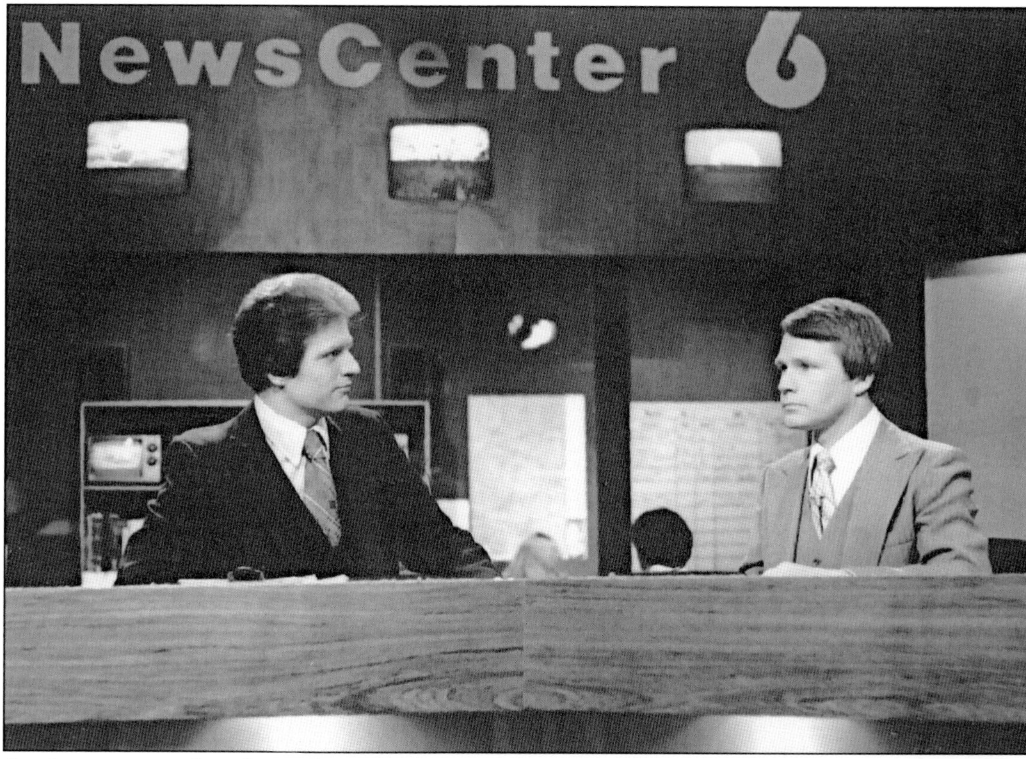

A television trend in the early 1980s was to have a station's newsroom become the studio. To cut down on noise, yet achieve the desired effect, WOC-TV separated the studio from the newsroom with glass partitions. With the completion of this new set, the *Channel 6 Noon Edition* became known as *Newscenter 6 at Noon* and was anchored by Rick McGuire (left) and Jim Malmberg. (Courtesy of Rick McGuire.)

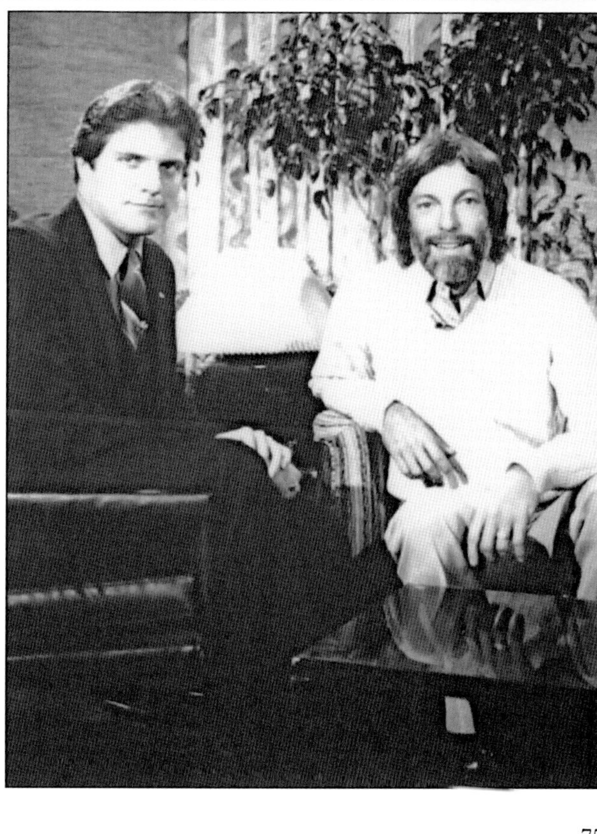

KIIK-FM announcer Rick McGuire (left) was not only heard in morning drive time, but was also seen on the *Noon Edition* newscast. Part of McGuire's responsibility for the show was human-interest stories and capturing interviews with news makers and celebrities who appeared in the area. He is shown here with stage and screen performer Richard Chamberlain, who had been the star of television's *Dr. Kildare* in the 1960s. (Courtesy of Rick McGuire.)

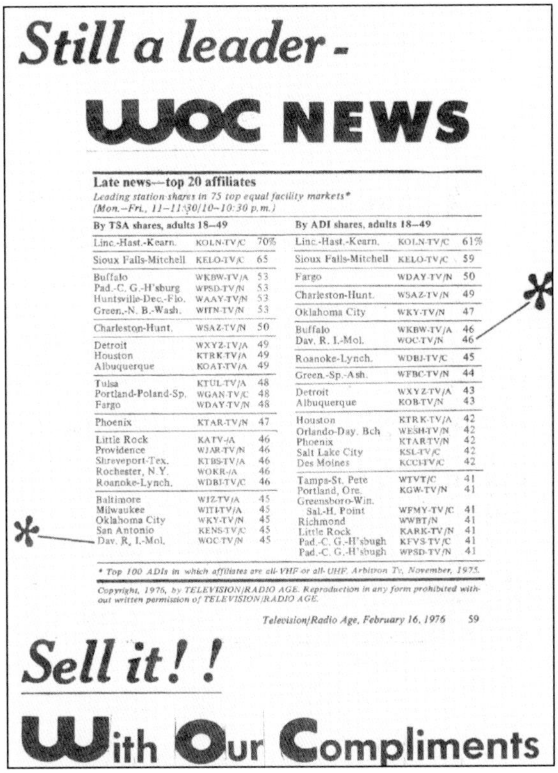

Still a leader -

WOC NEWS

Late news—top 20 affiliates

*Leading station shares in 75 top equal facility markets**
(Mon.–Fri., 11–11:30/10–10:30 p.m.)

By TSA shares, adults 18–49		
Linc.-Hast.-Kearn.	KOLN-TV/C	70%
Sioux Falls-Mitchell	KELO-TV/C	65
Buffalo	WKBW-TV/A	53
Pad.-C. G.-H'sburg	WPSD-TV/N	53
Huntsville-Dec.-Flo.	WAAY-TV/N	53
Green.-N. B.-Wash.	WITN-TV/N	53
Charleston-Hunt.	WSAZ-TV/N	50
Detroit	WXYZ-TV/A	49
Houston	KTRK-TV/A	49
Albuquerque	KOAT-TV/A	49
Tulsa	KTUL-TV/A	48
Portland-Poland-Sp.	WGAN-TV/C	48
Fargo	WDAY-TV/N	48
Phoenix	KTAR-TV/N	47
Little Rock	KATV-/A	46
Providence	WJAR-TV/N	46
Shreveport-Tex.	KTBS-TV/A	46
Rochester, N.Y.	WOKR-/A	46
Roanoke-Lynch.	WDBJ-TV/C	46
Baltimore	WJZ-TV/A	45
Milwaukee	WITI-TV/A	45
Oklahoma City	WKY-TV/N	45
San Antonio	KENS-TV/C	45
* Dav. R. I.-Mol.	WOC-TV/N	45

By ADI shares, adults 18–49		
Linc.-Hast.-Kearn.	KOLN-TV/C	61%
Sioux Falls-Mitchell	KELO-TV/C	59
Fargo	WDAY-TV/N	50
Charleston-Hunt.	WSAZ-TV/N	49
Oklahoma City	WKY-TV/N	47
Buffalo	WKBW-TV/A	46
Dav. R. I.-Mol.	WOC-TV/N	46 *
Roanoke-Lynch.	WDBJ-TV/C	45
Green.-Sp.-Ash.	WFBC-TV/N	44
Detroit	WXYZ-TV/A	43
Albuquerque	KOB-TV/N	43
Houston	KTRK-TV/A	42
Orlando-Day. Bch	WESH-TV/N	42
Phoenix	KTAR-TV/N	42
Salt Lake City	KSL-TV/C	42
Des Moines	KCCI-TV/C	42
Tampa-St. Pete	WTVT/C	41
Portland, Ore.	KGW-TV/N	41
Greensboro-Win. Sal.-H. Point	WFMY-TV/C	41
Richmond	WWBT/N	41
Little Rock	KARK-TV/N	41
Pad.-C. G.-H'sbugh	KFVS-TV/C	41
Pad.-C. G.-H'sbugh	WPSD-TV/N	41

** Top 100 ADIs in which affiliates are all-VHF or all-UHF. Arbitron Tv, November, 1975.*

Television/Radio Age, February 16, 1976 59

Sell it! !

With Our Compliments

WOC-TV salesmen used this handout to convince clients to spend their advertising dollars on the channel 6 news. During a 1975 ratings period, 46 percent of all adults aged 18–49 in the station's primary viewing area were tuned to the *Ten O'clock Edition* newscast. That rating is impressive, considering that the other 54 percent of the viewing audience was split between the two other local stations. (Courtesy of Don Rhyne.)

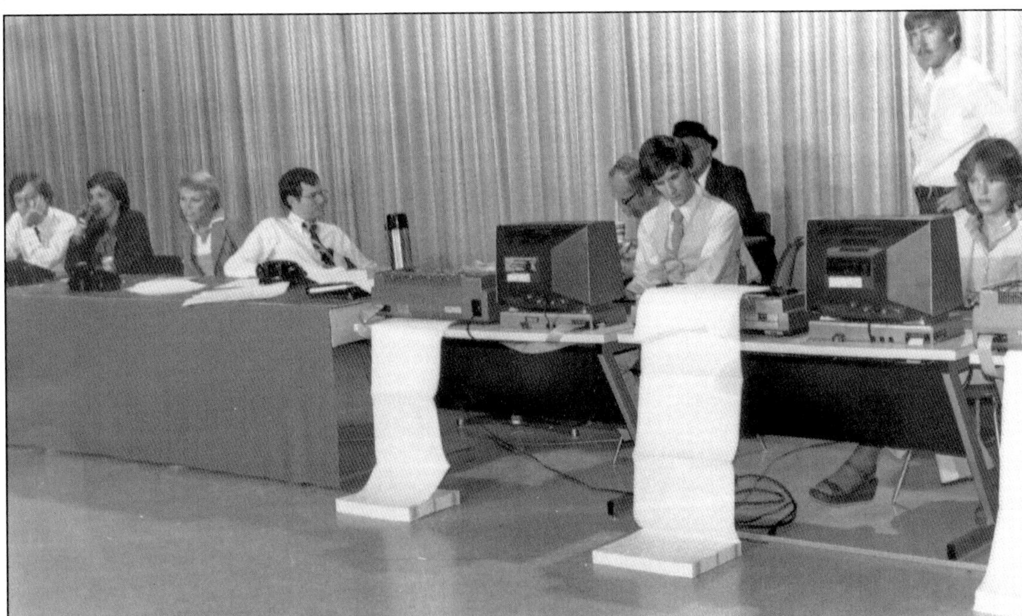

Gathering the news is not always exciting, especially during elections. This group of staff members appears bored while waiting for the local vote counts to begin arriving. Poll watchers in key precincts, courthouse clerks, telephones, and computers are all part of the information gathering process for election night coverage. John Collins (fourth from left) seems totally engrossed in the activity taking place behind the computer operator. (Courtesy of KWQC-TV.)

One of the more popular segments of *Especially for You* was the frequent visit of Helen Plagman (right), a leading area authority on plants and flowers. Many of Plagman's segments would feature flowers used at famous locations to celebrate key holidays. After the celebration, the arrangements would be shipped to WOC for use on television and then sent to hospitals and nursing homes. (Courtesy of Anita Sundin.)

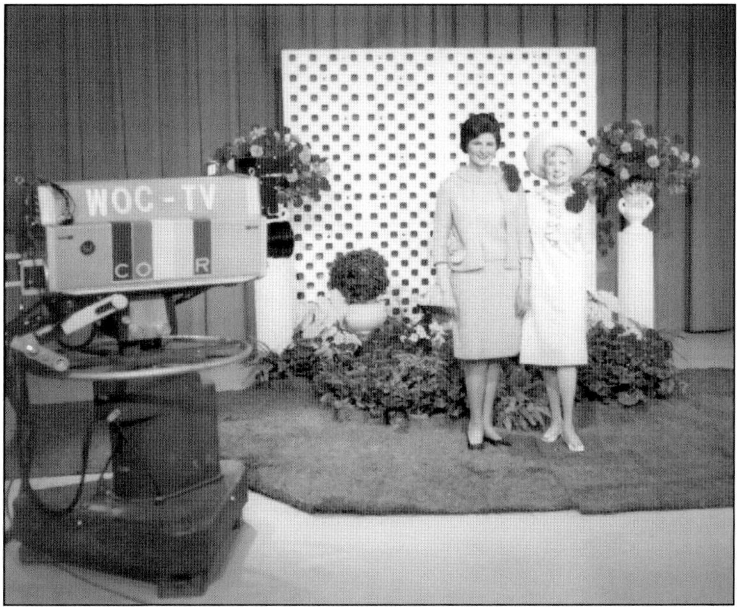

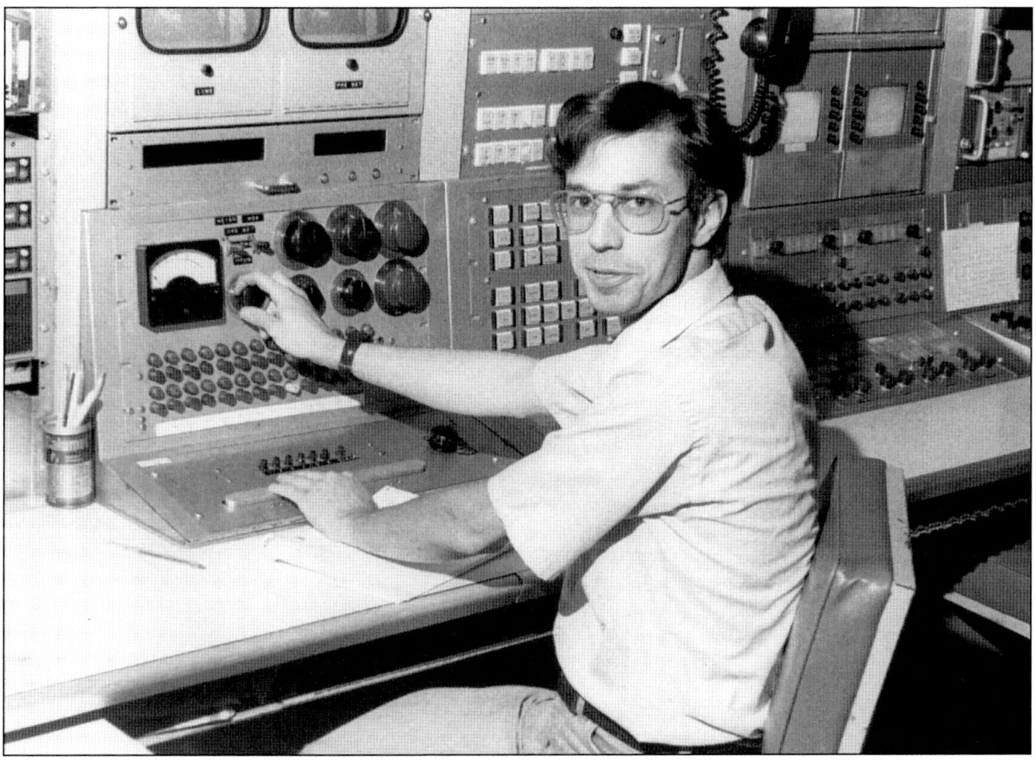

Channel 6 master control was reworked from the original design, pictured on page 60, into this configuration. Manning the controls is Jon Book, who started at the station in radio production and as part of the TV camera crew. Book learned his electronics well, as he became the chief engineer for WOC Radio in 1989. He now oversees five more stations owned by Clear Channel. (Courtesy of KWQC-TV.)

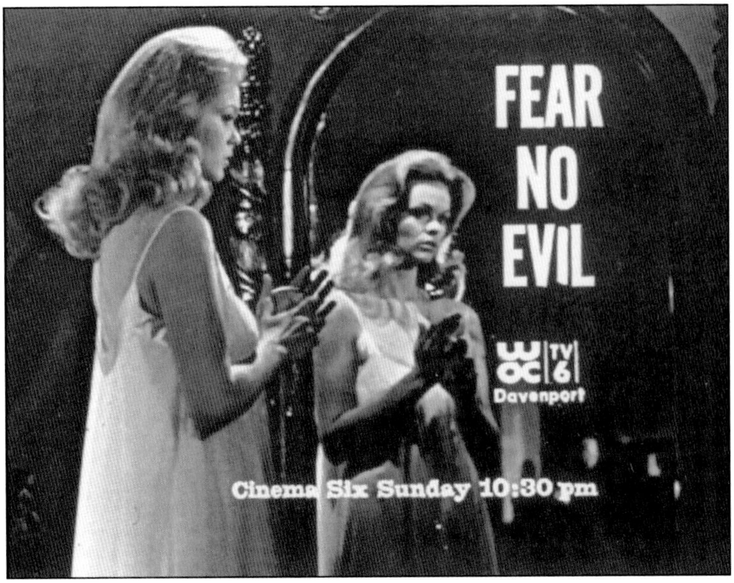

How does a station advertise and promote its Sunday night movie? With an action or perhaps provocative still photograph from that movie. Catching the viewer's eye is actress Linda Day George in a scene from the featured movie. Because the slide carried the station's call letters and location, it also doubled as legal station identification at the top or bottom of the hour. (Courtesy of Jon Book.)

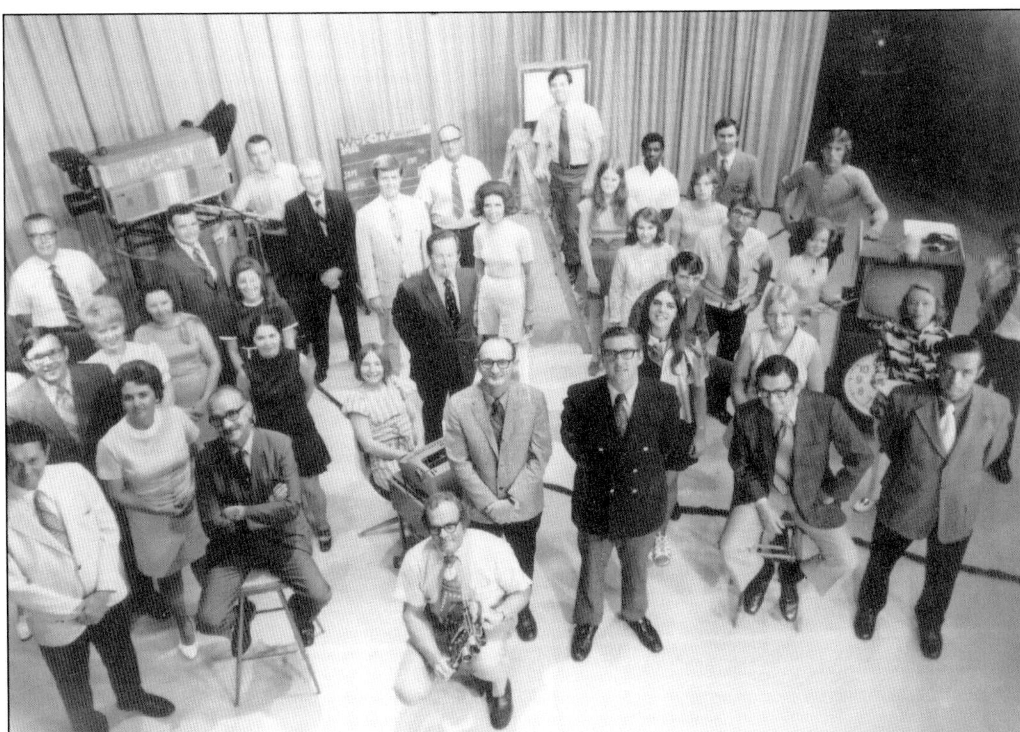

This photograph from the early 1970s was featured in print advertisements titled "Who's Who at WOC." The premise to the message was that there were many team members "behind the scenes" that helped put the WOC-TV's product "on the air," not just the people on-screen and behind the microphones. Pictured members included directors, engineers, traffic, continuity, accounting, and sales personnel, stage crew, and management. (Courtesy of Rick McGuire.)

Five

Cowboys, Cartoons, and Kids

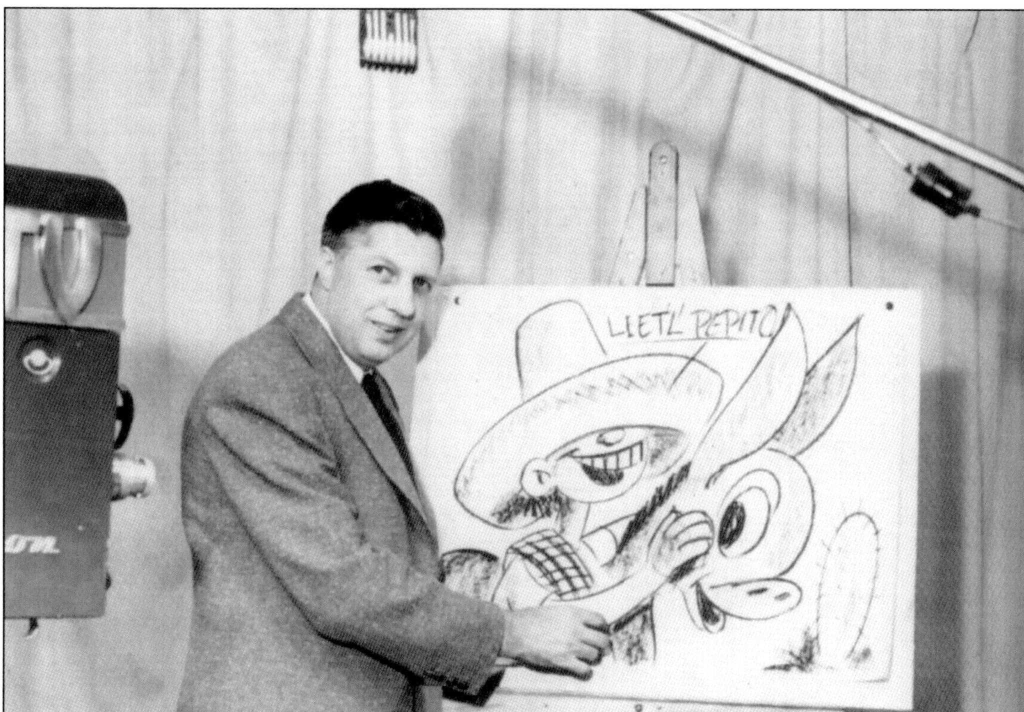

Commercial artist and theater owner Ken Wagner heard about the formation of WOC-TV and decided he wanted to be part of the new medium. He brought an idea for a children's show to management that combined storytelling with art and puppetry. Management liked the concept and *Comic Cutups* was born. The 15-minute show was on WOC-TV from the station's first day on the air. (Courtesy of KWQC-TV.)

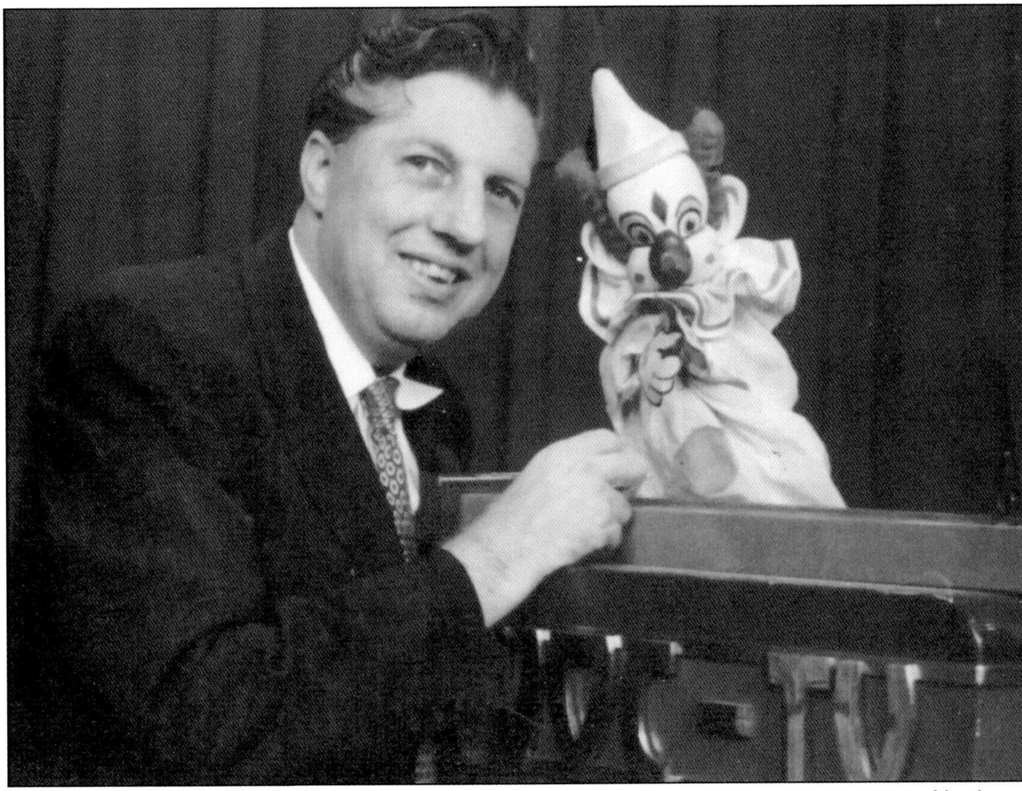

With his background as an artist and a theater owner, Ken Wagner became WOC-TV's film buyer and staff artist. In front of the camera, Wagner brought fact and fictional stories to life through his drawings. His sidekick, PeeWee the Clown, always managed to offer up some suggestions and provided a little comedy. Wagner's own children, Ken Jr. and later Linda, provided PeeWee's voice and action. (Courtesy of KWQC-TV.)

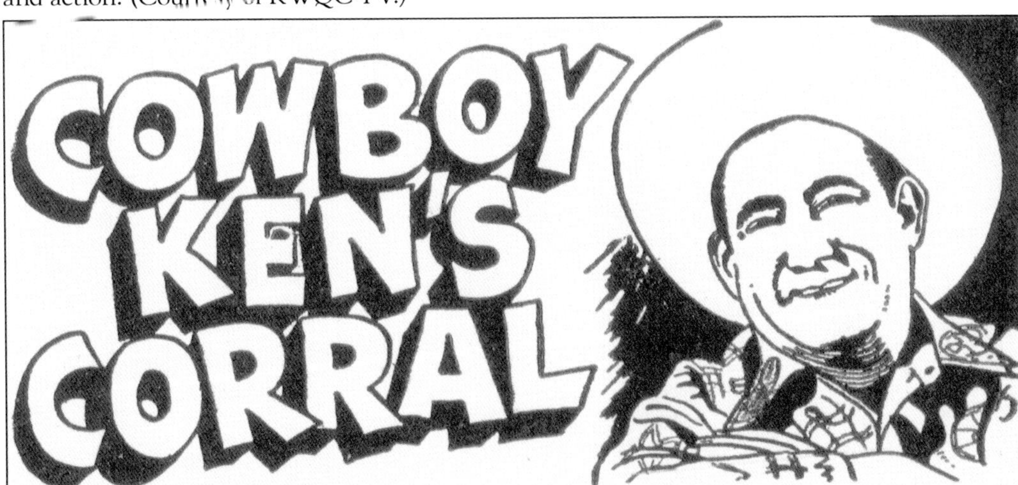

"Cowboy" Ken Houchins was the host of WOC-TV's second children's show. Though it was only 15 minutes in length, Houchins would feature a Western serial episode, offer safety and good citizenship tips, and sing a Western song or two for the children. This was Houchins's second stop in Davenport, as he had been heard years earlier as a singer on WOC Radio.

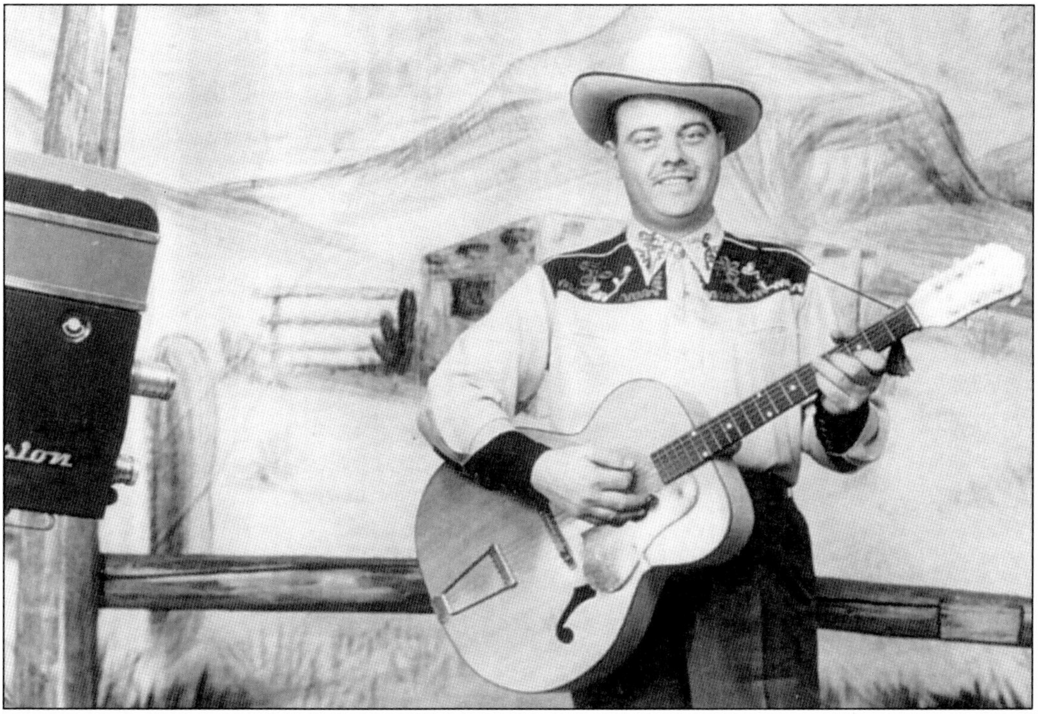

The Singin' Sheriff was a 15-minute program that replaced *Cowboy Ken's Corral* during the early 1950s. Forrest Edkin, known on the show as Eddie Forrest, played his guitar and sang songs that children would enjoy. The show did not run the Western episodes that *Cowboy Ken* did. Edkin later became a chiropractor in Muscatine, Iowa, and also recorded several Christian music albums. (Courtesy of KWQC-TV.)

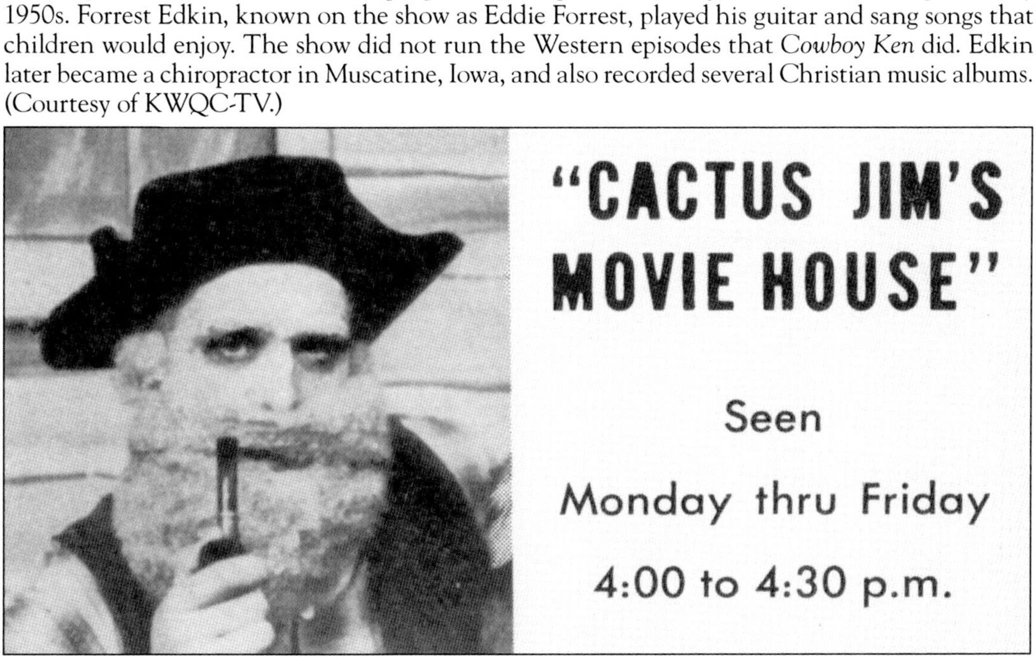

Announcer Bob Allard portrayed the friendly, old prospector Cactus Jim. His "movie house" presented old theatrical cliffhangers every afternoon. One of the more popular titles in this genre was *Tailspin Tommy*, which presented plenty of World War I–style biplanes flying and crashing. Kids could not wait for the next day's episode to find out how Tailspin would manage to escape from the pending crash of his airplane.

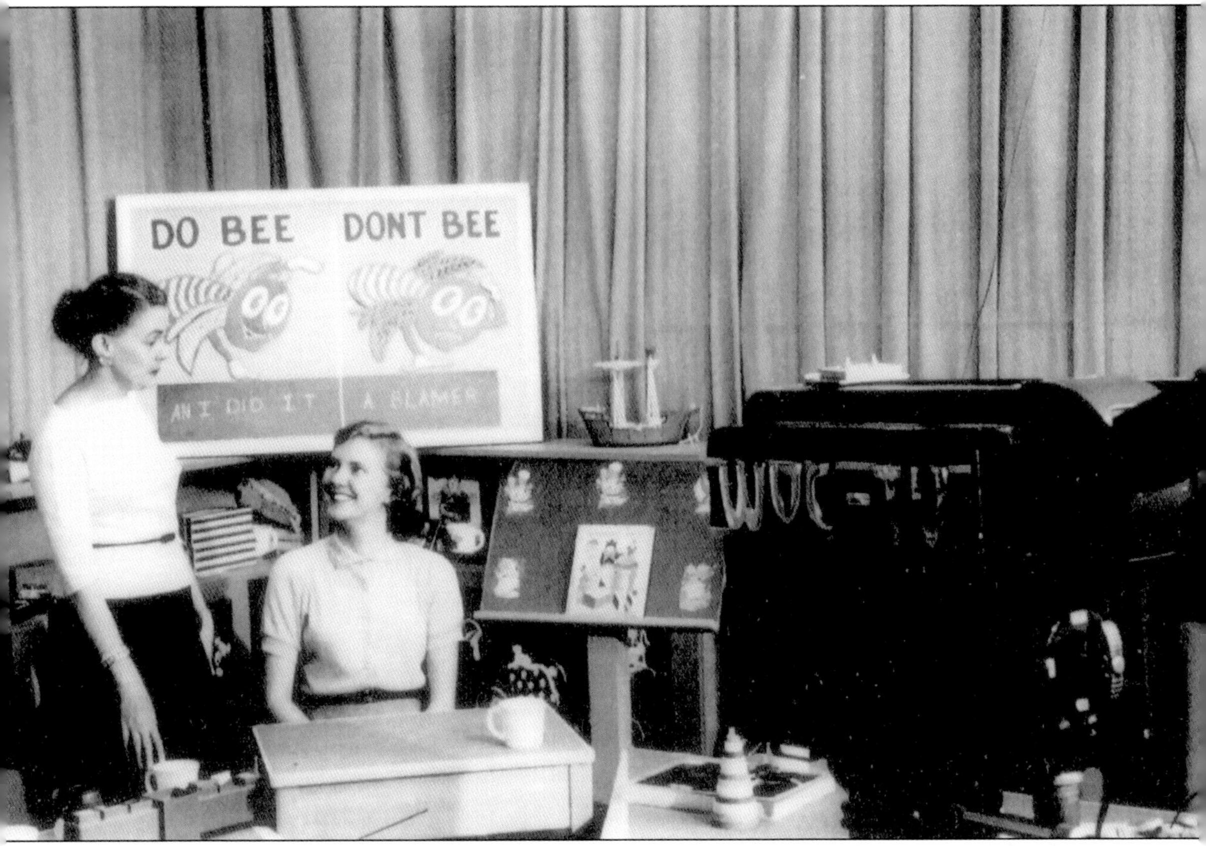

Romper Room was the brainchild of Burt Claster Productions in Baltimore, Maryland. It was nationally syndicated, and stations could either take a national airing of the show or produce their own version. However, Claster created the script for each day's show, and the local show had to exactly follow that script. WOC-TV was the first station in the Quad Cities to run the program. Each morning, the show's hostess would lead children in songs and games and give them lessons on manners or on being good. The closing to the show was probably most exciting for the children at home. The hostess would look through a "mirror," actually the frame of a handheld mirror, and pretend to be looking into children's homes. She would call out, "I see Bobby, Jane, and Billy. Are Carol, Marilyn, and Gary being good?" Each child whose name was spoken thought he or she was actually being singled out. This photograph from 1953 shows director Edith Glidden (left) with WOC-TV's first Romper Room hostess, Barbara Gorham. (Courtesy of Don McGonegle.)

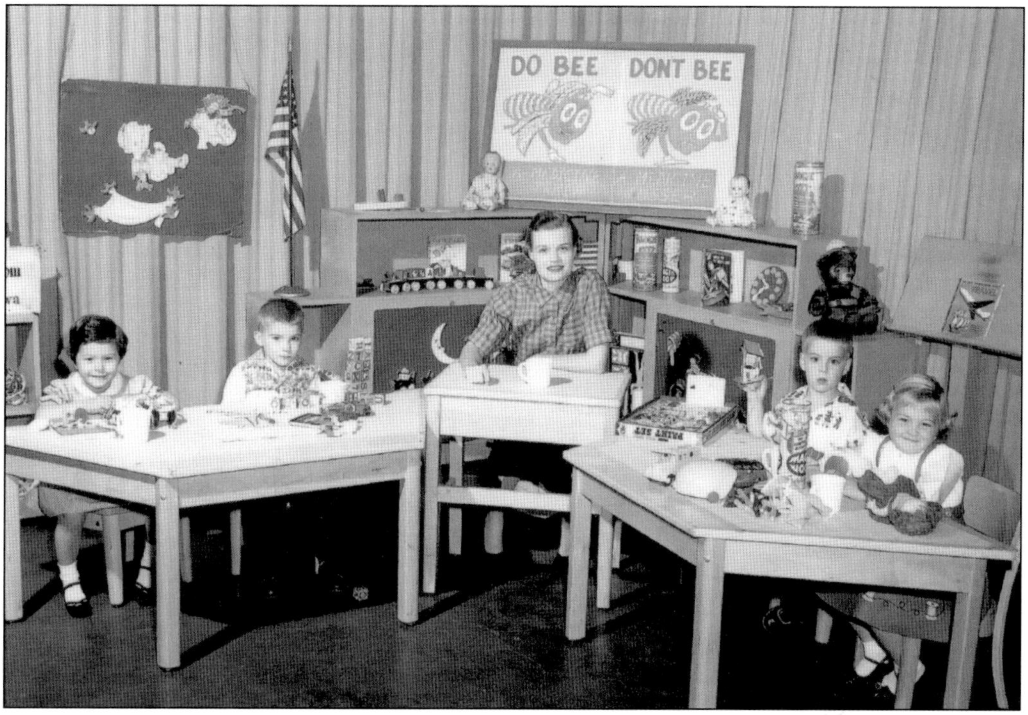

Former kindergarten teacher Gwen Korn became the second hostess of *Romper Room* in 1957. She proved to be extremely popular with her preschool viewers, if the bags of fan mail she would take home were any indication. "Miss Gwen" answered every piece and also chose the in-studio children from that mail. Although she had no television experience, as a teacher and a mother she made the perfect hostess. (Courtesy of Gwen Korn.)

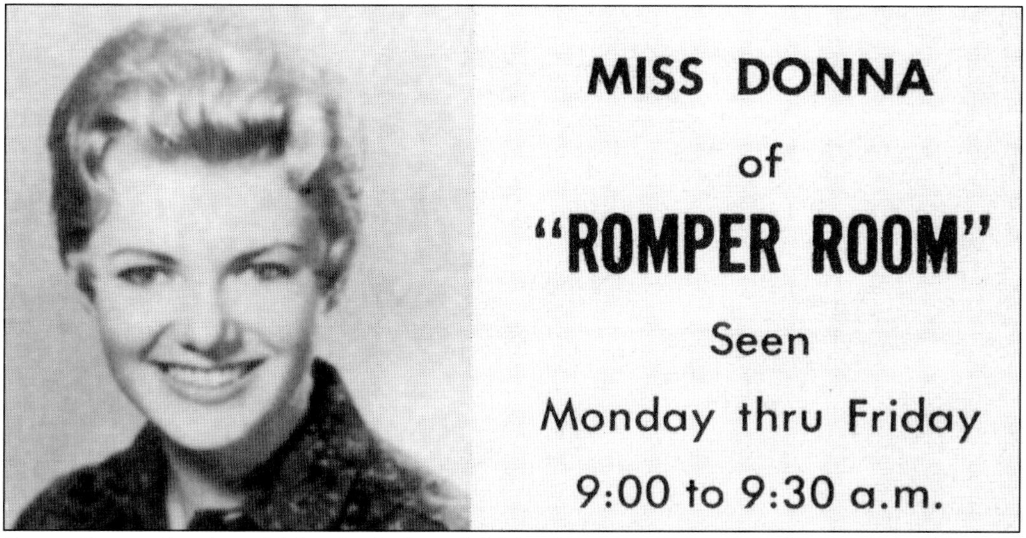

Donna Scott, a local model that had taken child development courses in college, was the third and last *Romper Room* hostess. The show was cancelled not because it had lost popularity, but because it lost its sponsor, a toy distributing company that carried the *Romper Room* brand. Through her modeling agency work, Scott would appear or be heard in many commercials throughout the region for Jewel-Osco and Eagle Foods, among others.

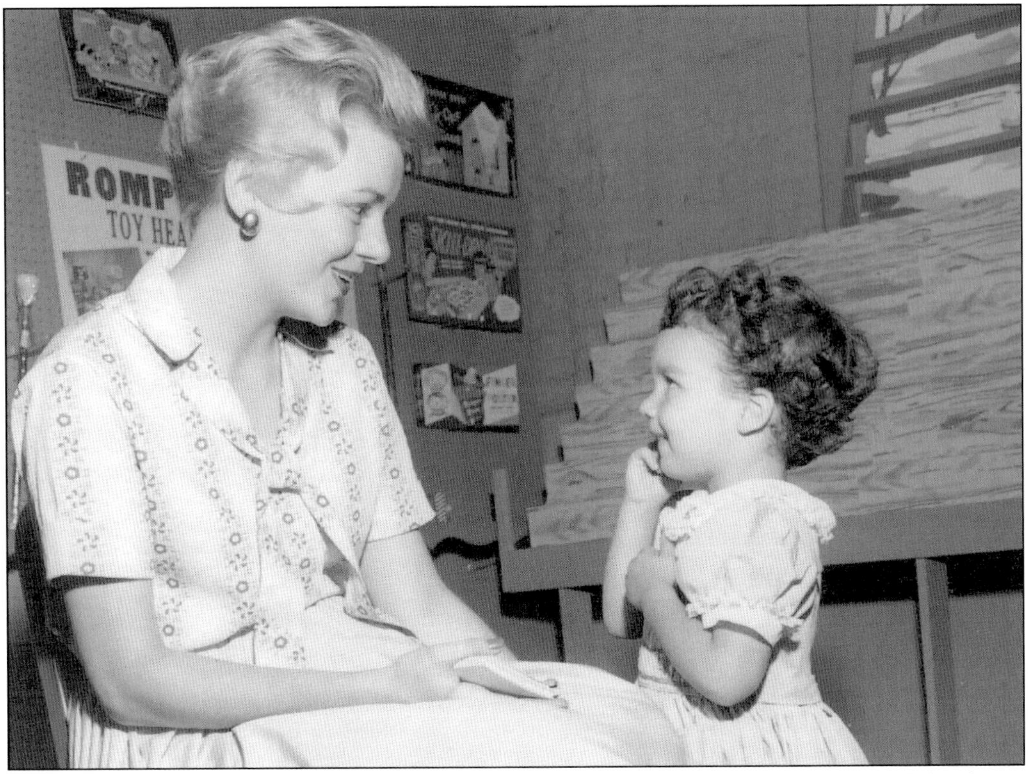

Romper Room's Miss Gwen and Miss Donna made personal appearances on behalf of the show's sponsor, Pioneer Distributing. That firm handled sales of the *Romper Room* branded educational books, toys, and games to department stores and hobby shops throughout the WOC-TV viewing area. This photograph captures Miss Donna, seated around the products, greeting one of her young fans at Ray's Hobby Shop in Galesburg, Illinois. (Courtesy of Ray Johansen.)

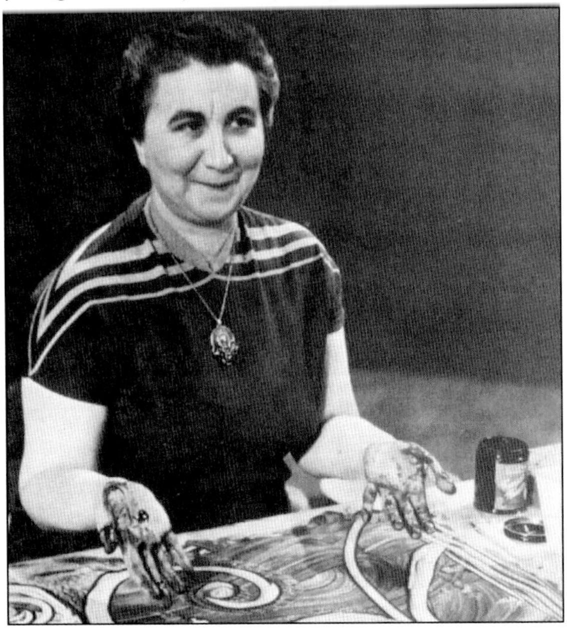

Ding Dong School was in the forefront of quality programming to preschool children and their parents. Hosted by "Miss Frances" Horwich, the show gave daily instruction on a variety of children's activities and usually ended with a brief talk about parenting. One of Miss Frances's most popular activities, as shown in this photograph, was finger painting. The NBC program was carried by WOC-TV from 1952 until 1956.

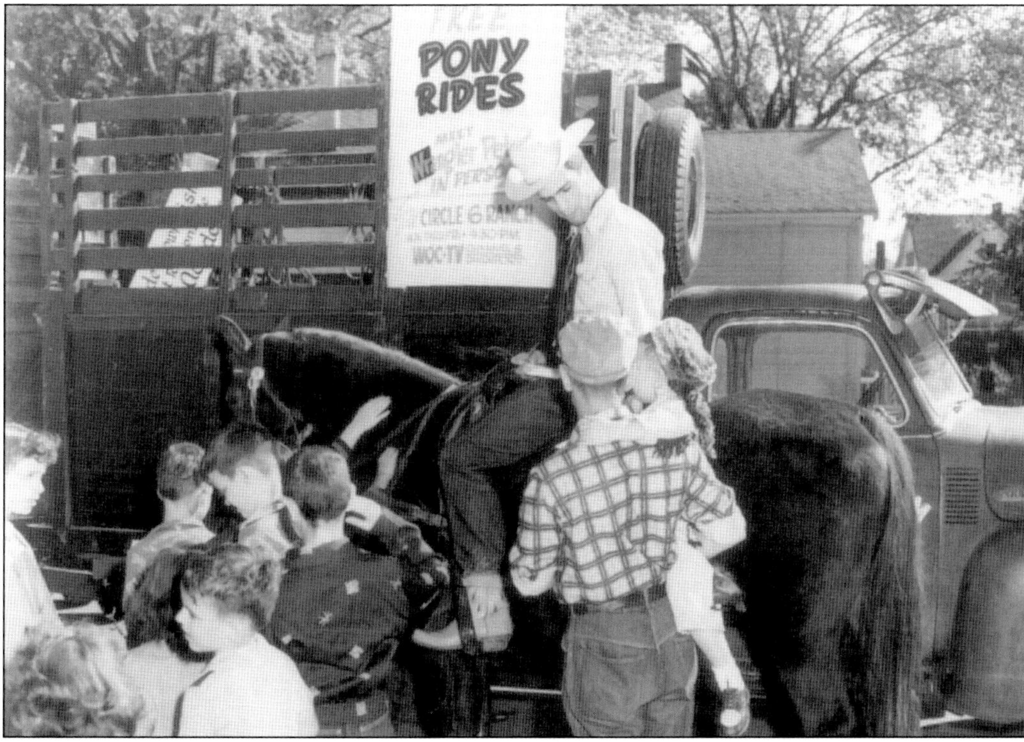

Walt Reno as "Cowboy Whitey" was the original host of the *Circle 5 Ranch*. Following his departure, there were several more hosts who stayed only briefly. One of those was "Wrangler Pete," played by Peter Vagenas, shown here in the mid-1950s providing area children with free pony rides. The show's name had been changed to *Circle 6 Ranch* by that time. (Courtesy of KWQC-TV.)

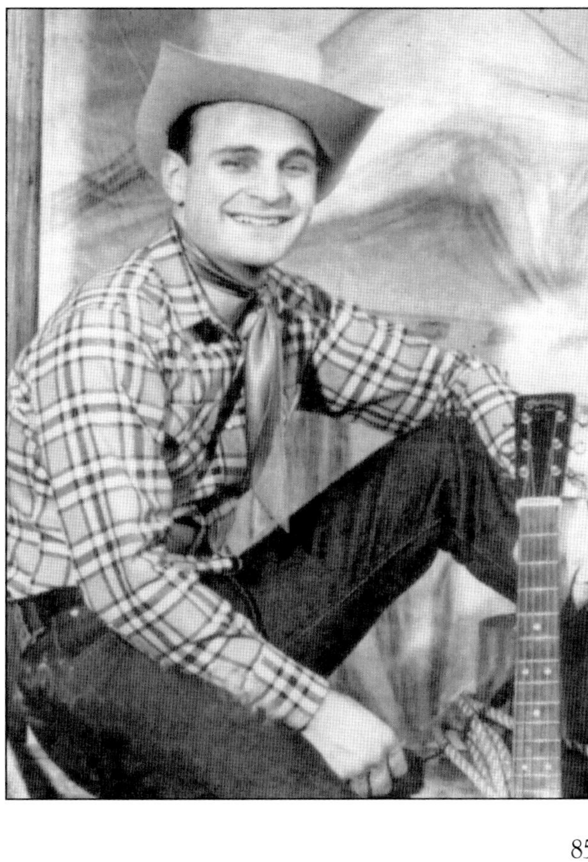

Wes Holly was the boss of the *Circle 6 Ranch*, following several other "cowboys." Holly entertained children at home and in the "bunkhouse" with the Western movies of Roy Rogers and Gene Autry. He would also sing a song or two and interview guests. After the show moved to Sunday mornings, the "ranch" became the *Cartoon Corral*. (With permission of Palmer College of Chiropractic, Special Collections and Archives.)

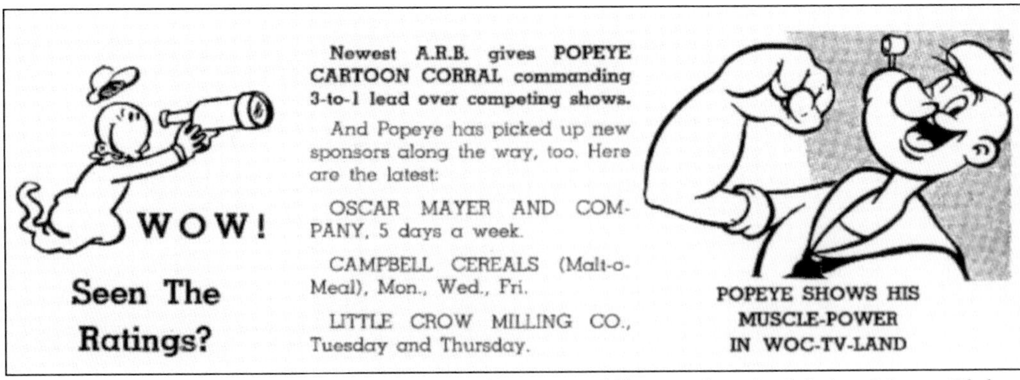

Even though the *Circle 6 Ranch* and Wes Holly were wildly popular, the *Mickey Mouse Club* on WHBF-TV was beating the *Ranch* in the ratings by nearly three to one. WOC-TV purchased a package of Warner Brothers cartoons, dropped the Western movies, and renamed the show the *Circle 6 Cartoon Corral*. The ratings suddenly reversed, as noted by this *c*. 1957 trade publication advertisement. (Courtesy of Gwen Korn.)

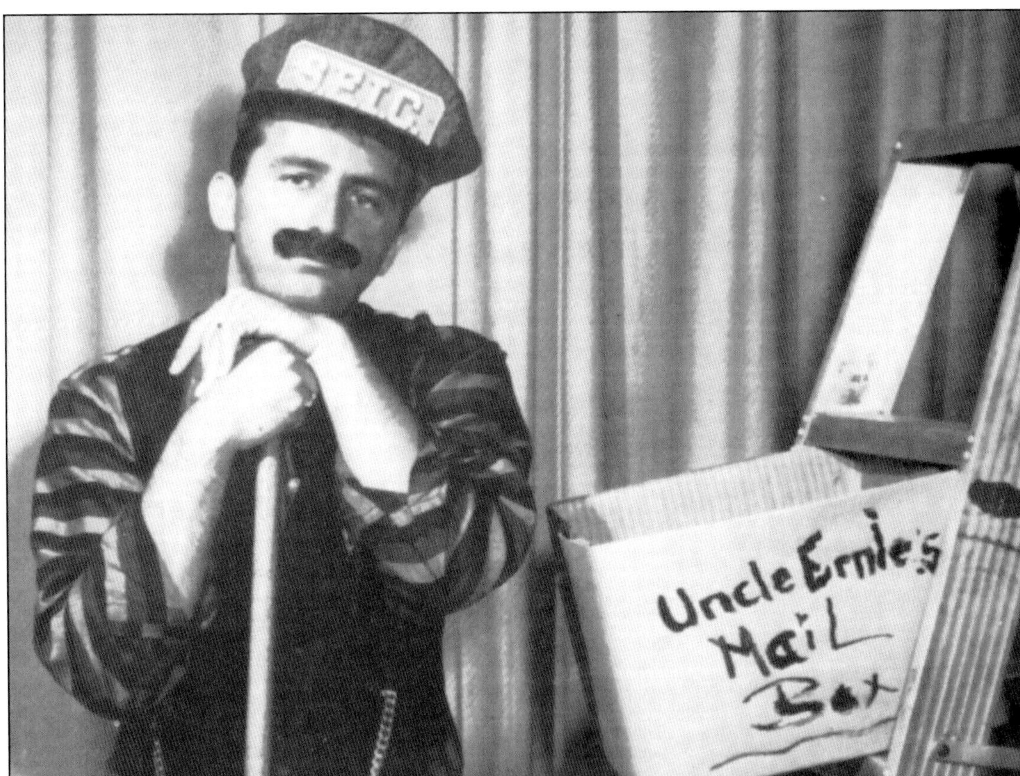

When Wes Holly left the Sunday morning *Cartoon Corral* program, station management wanted a cartoon show to continue in that time slot. The question would be, who would host the show, and what form would it take? Enter Ernie Mimms portraying the station's janitor. He introduced himself as "Uncle Ernie," and as long as the kids joined him, they would have some fun and watch cartoons together. (Courtesy of KWQC-TV.)

In addition to cartoons, *Uncle Ernie's Cartoon Carnival* offered segments of interest to its young viewers. This c. 1961 photograph shows director Don McGonegle (center) conferring with Uncle Ernie regarding how the upcoming scene with the Davenport motorcycle policeman should be carried out. The police department had just placed their new motorcycles in service, and the show was a good venue to display one. (Courtesy of Don McGonegle.)

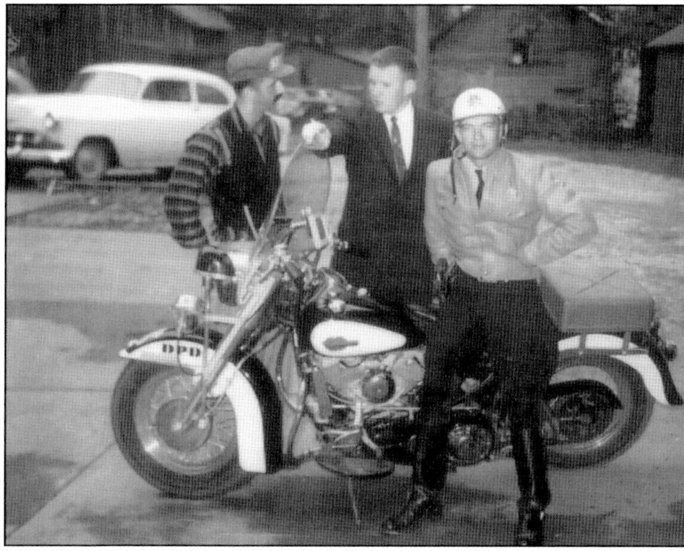

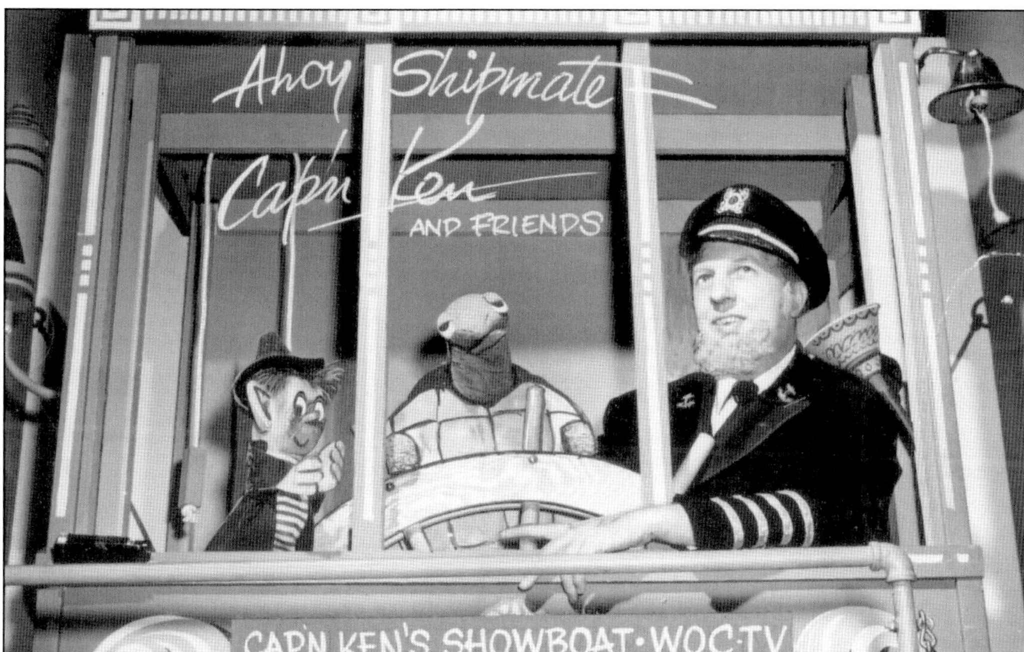

When channel 6 revamped the afternoon cartoon show, Ken Wagner became a host once again, this time as "Captain Ken." Puppets Tommy, the inquisitive cabin boy, and Calliope, the turtle with all the answers, aided the good captain with his vignettes between the cartoons. Wagner's daughter Linda served as the puppeteer. Like *Comic Cutups*, Wagner's show included his graphic art talents and contained educational elements to involve his young audience.

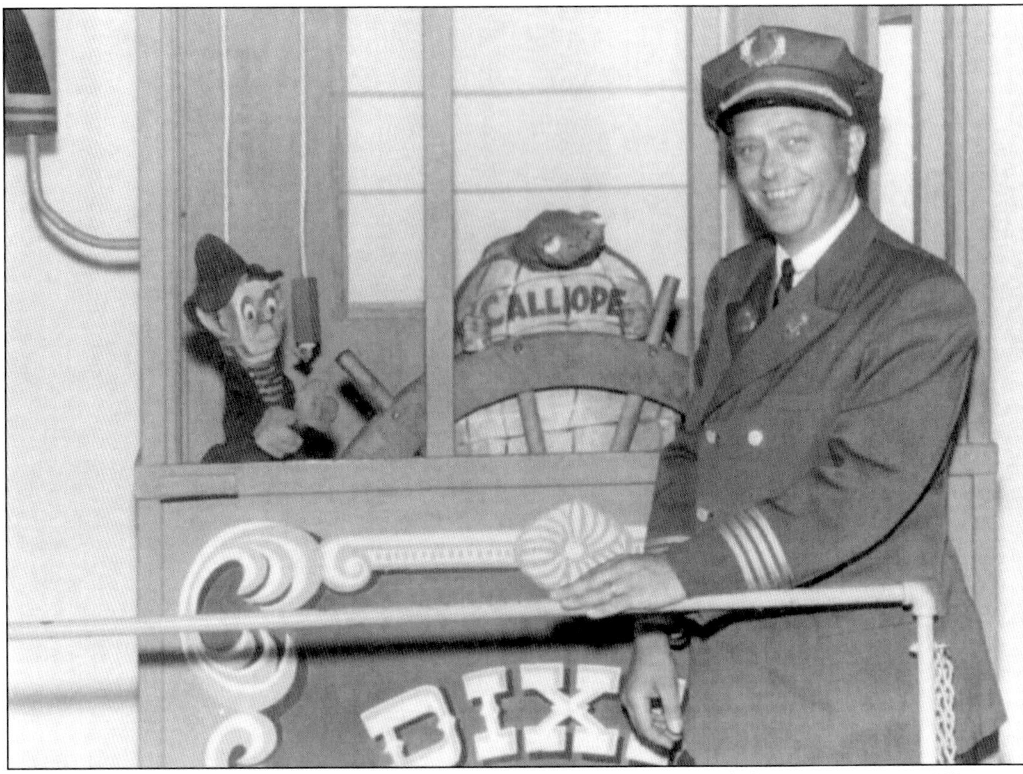

Ken Wagner left WOC-TV in 1959, and Vern Gielow became the second "captain" of the *Cartoon Showboat*. Gielow was the television production manager and easily stepped into the role. The popular elements of the program remained the same, including the byplay of puppets Tommy and Calliope. Gielow remained as head of the showboat until 1964, when he joined Palmer College of Chiropractic. (Courtesy of KWQC-TV.)

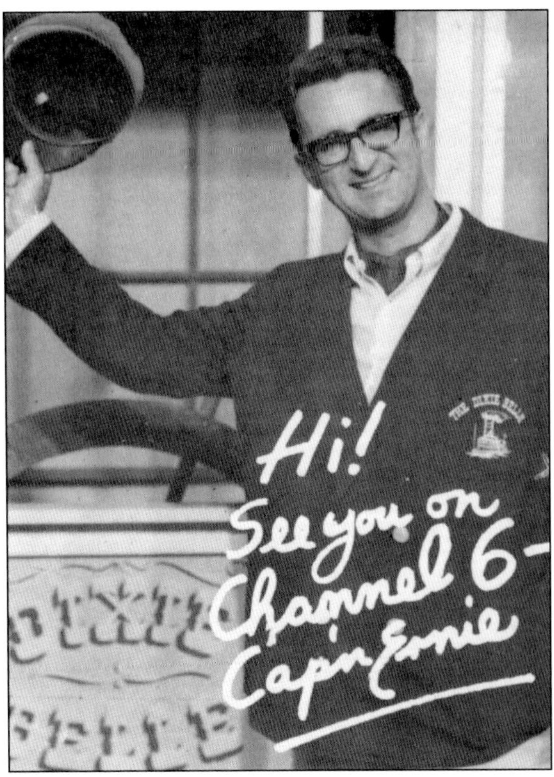

Ernie Mimms was the fourth and last "captain" of the *Cartoon Showboat*, and he was perhaps the most watched by children. Mimms believed that the show should be just about fun. Cartoons, the Three Stooges, treasure chest drawings, visits with the in-studio children, and special guests like Lorne Green of NBC's *Bonanza*, Jim Fowler from *Wild Kingdom*, and Kirby Grant of *Sky King* all made for an hour of good entertainment. (Courtesy of Jon Book.)

Six

Radio Changes

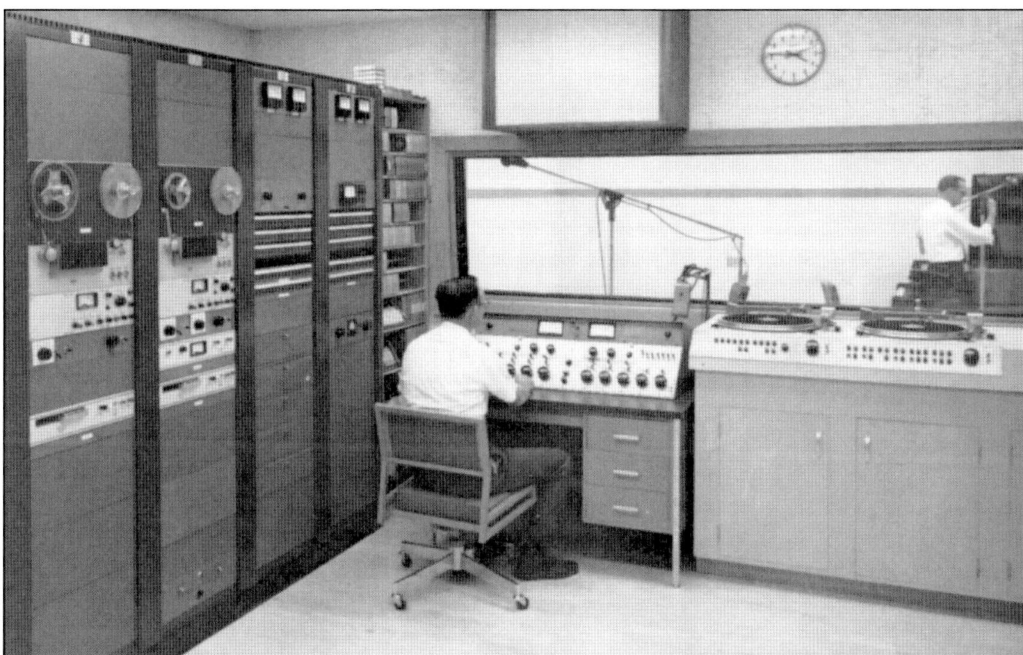

Up until 1972, WOC-FM duplicated the programs heard on WOC-AM. One program line from the studio fed both radio transmitters. Exceptions were high school football games or when the major-league baseball season overlapped with professional football games. AM radio carried one game, while FM radio carried the other. When separate programs were broadcast, the WOC production studio was placed in control of the FM feed. (Courtesy of *RCA Broadcast News*.)

KiiK

STEREO • ROCK • 104

Pressured by a FCC ruling in the early 1970s, stations had to end the practice of duplicating their AM signal on FM. WOC-FM became KIIK-FM in August 1972 and offered rock-and-roll hits in stereo around the clock. Live deejays were used during morning and afternoon drive times, but an automation unit was employed to play announcements, music, and commercials during the remaining hours.

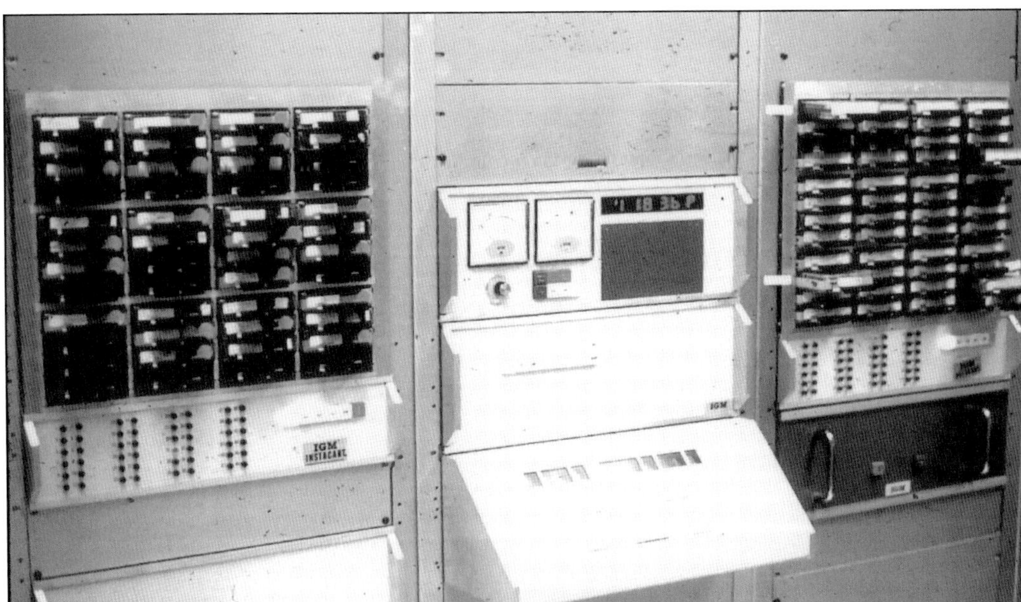

KIIK-FM first used this automation equipment to run its programming when live announcers were not scheduled. Cartridge tapes of music were inserted on one side of the computer (center), and commercials and announcements were on the other side. At times, the computer seemed to have a mind of its own, as a commercial or two might play at the same time as the song being aired. (Courtesy of Rick McGuire.)

The creation of KIIK-FM from the old WOC-FM signal created opportunities to interact with its new audience. Remote broadcasts from various events not only put the station out into the public, but also helped generate interest in the events the station visited. This KIIK announcer waits his turn to begin broadcasting from the Mississippi Valley Fair. Note the wireless equipment used to send his signal back to the station. (Courtesy of KWQC-TV.)

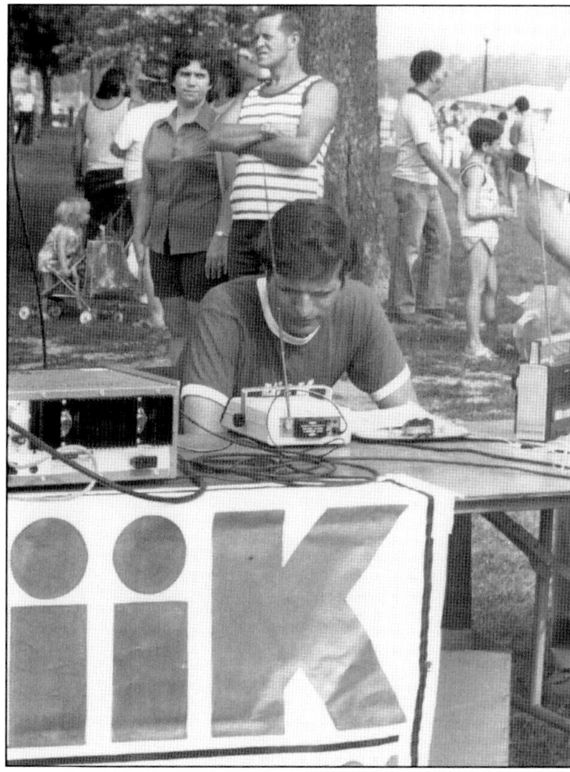

Pity the poor engineers who carried this to where a radio remote was to take place in the mid-1950s. Unlike the equipment shown in the photograph at the right of the page, this unit contains a small audio console, microphone, speaker, and turntables. Where are the turntables? They are contained in each of the black boxes on top of the console. Note the on-air warning light. (Courtesy of KWQC-TV.)

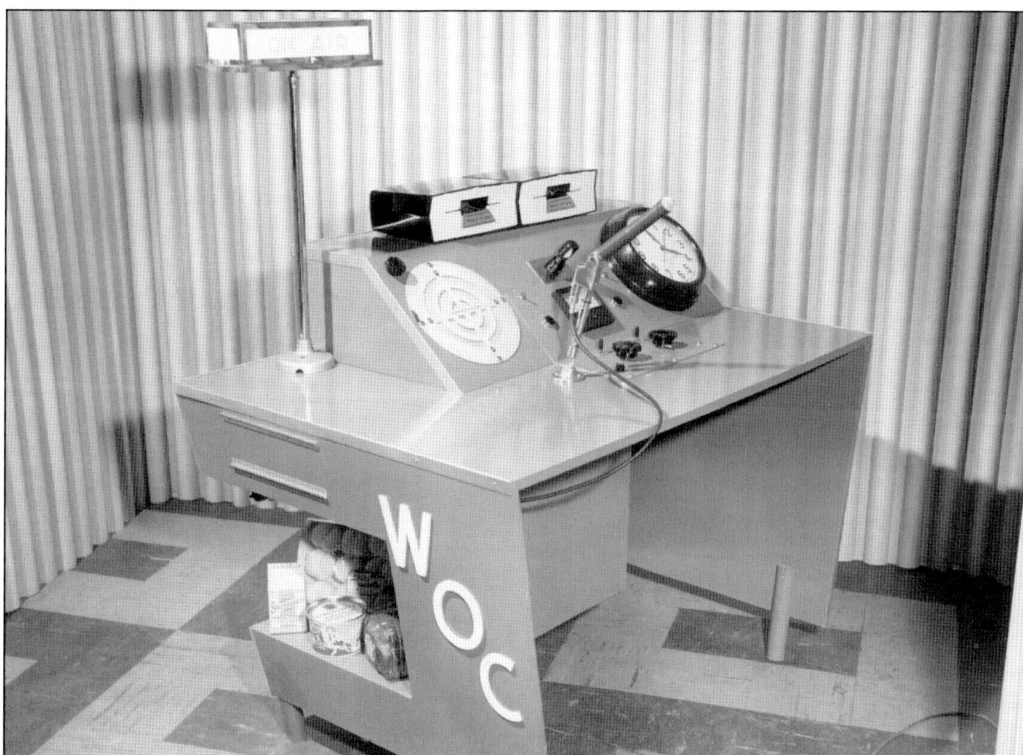

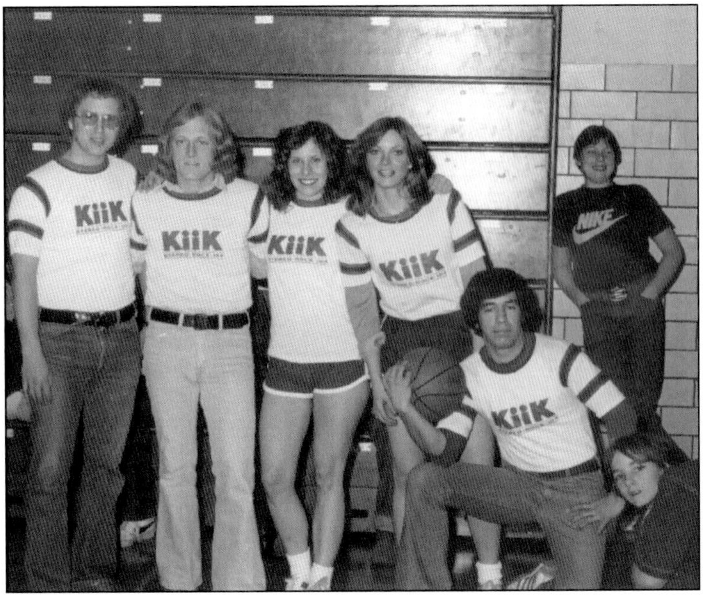

Several area radio stations used basketball teams for promoting the station, and KIIK-FM was certainly no different. Players included station on-air personalities and, sometimes, anyone else who could dribble and shoot a basketball. Station teams would play nonprofit groups and schools to help raise money for charitable causes. KIIK team members included, from left to right, Dave Stark, Paul Fredericks, Mary Shore, Beth Wood, and Kevin Vargas. (Courtesy of KWQC-TV.)

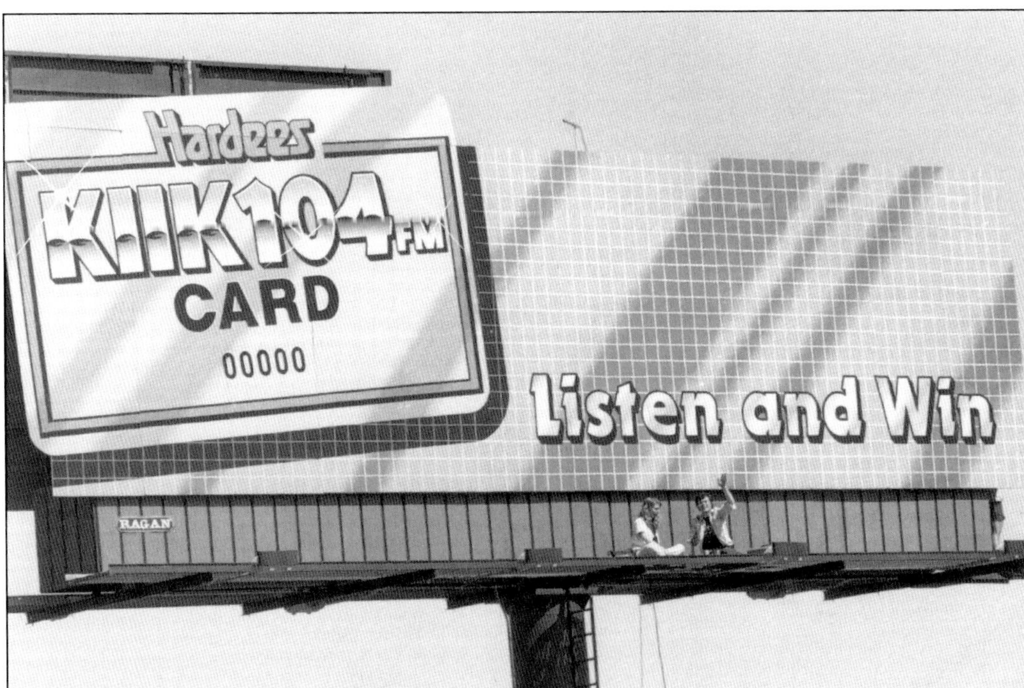

Money or prize giveaways are always good promotions for radio stations. It gets listeners to tune in and offers a chance to win something as a reward. Hardee's restaurants teamed with KIIK-FM in the early 1980s to offer the "KIIK card." Listeners received discounts on food and a chance to win big prizes. Deejay Sue Chekouras and general manager Jim O'Hara broadcast from this billboard to initiate the promotion. (Courtesy of KWQC-TV.)

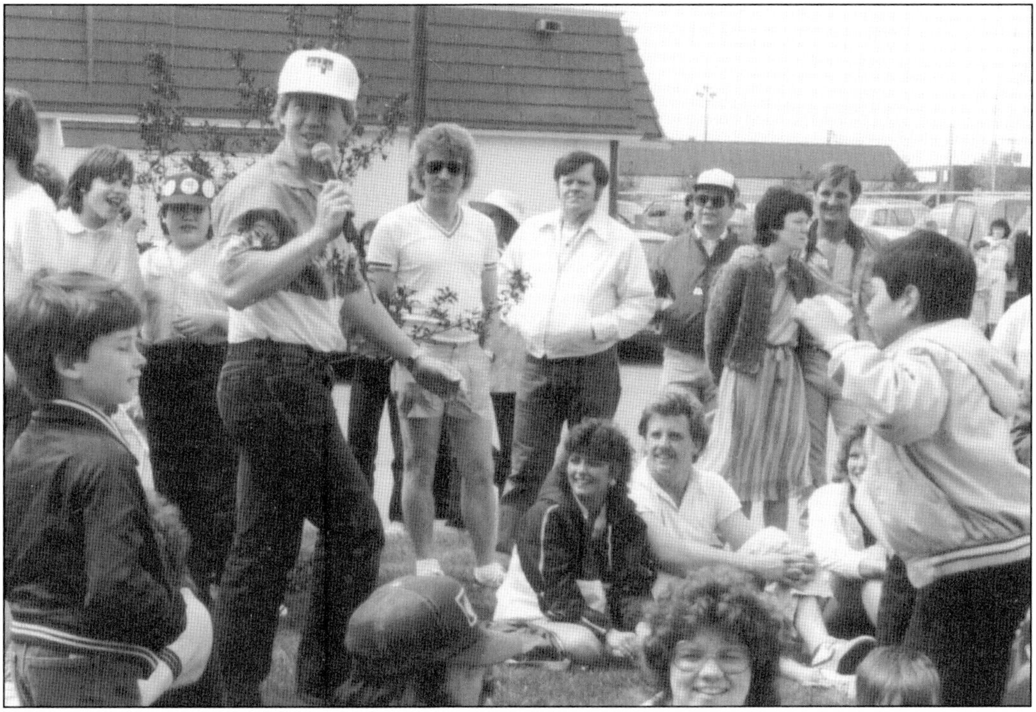

One of the most popular announcers to ever work in the Quad Cities was East Moline native William "Spike" O'Dell. He began his working career in the plant protection department of the Farmall tractor factory. With a radio always on in the guardhouse, O'Dell thought to himself, "I could do that." He enrolled in broadcasting school and worked part-time at several local stations. In 1977, while still working at Farmall, he was hired at KSTT as the morning-drive personality. "Spike at the Mike" took the area by storm. With his humor and infectious laugh, he was just "one of his listeners." In 1983, O'Dell joined KIIK-FM and brought his audience along with him. He ruled the morning ratings until 1987 when Chicago's WGN Radio lured him away from Davenport. He became WGN's top-rated morning announcer for many years.

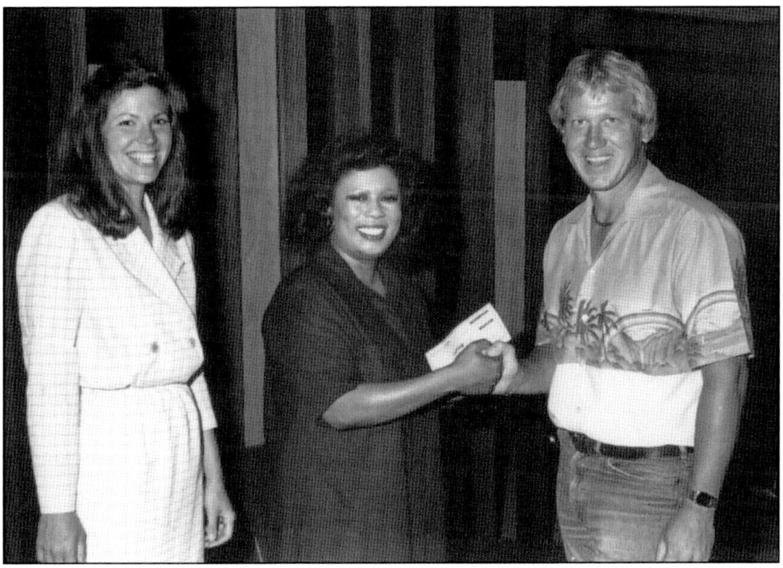

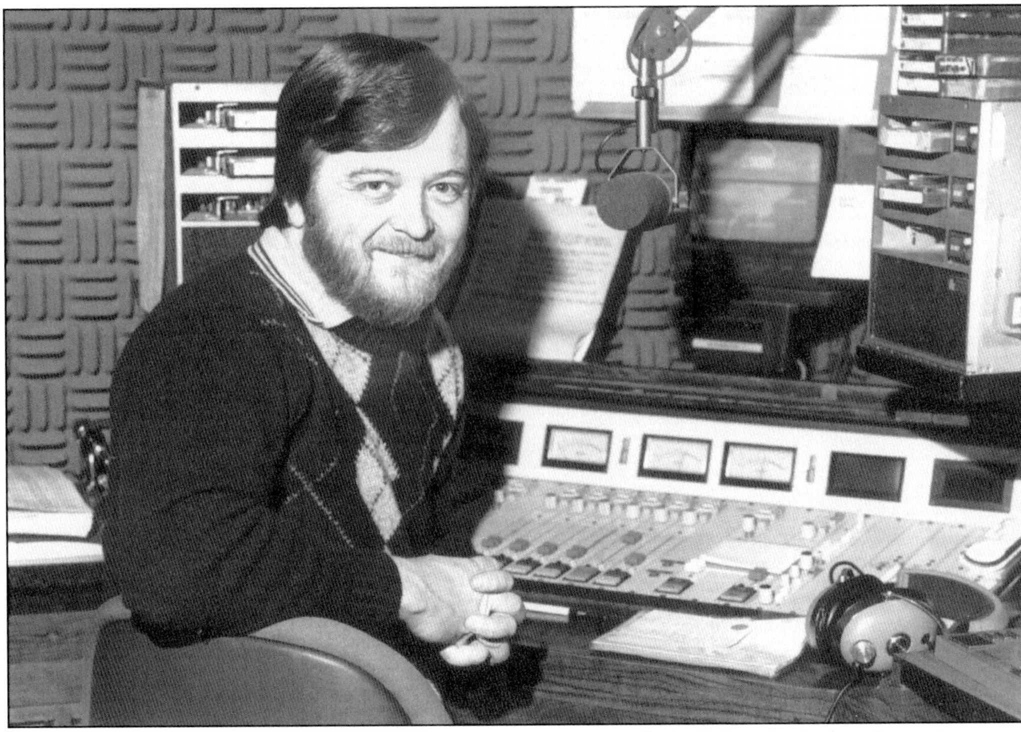

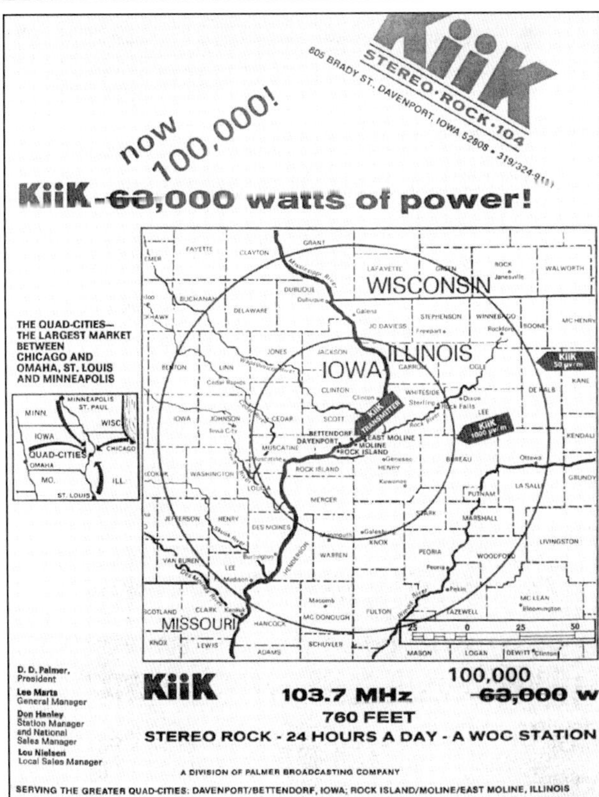

Bob Gelms had already made a name for himself at WLUP in Chicago. He and his family moved to the Quad City area when they purchased a Victorian mansion to restore. After opening a bed and breakfast, Gelms joined KIIK-FM in the mid-1980s as a weekend announcer. He moved to full-time afternoons when he purchased another home to restore and reconstruction bills came in higher than the quotations. (Courtesy of KWQC-TV.)

This contour map shows the KIIK-FM signal range. The inner circle is the primary signal, and the outer circle shows the signals fringe reception area. In the early 1970s, KIIK-FM's radiated power increased to 100,000 watts. Its primary signal now reached nearly to that outer circle. Listeners were calling the station from well into Wisconsin to request their favorite songs.

WOC NewsTalk 1420 am

By the late 1970s, stereo FM stations had grown in number and drew listeners away from AM stations that still played music. This was happening all across the country, and WOC was no exception. While KIIK-FM gained in popularity, WOC's "pure gold" format was beginning to sound worn out. Following many other AM stations, WOC dropped music altogether and changed to a news and talk format. (Courtesy of WOC.)

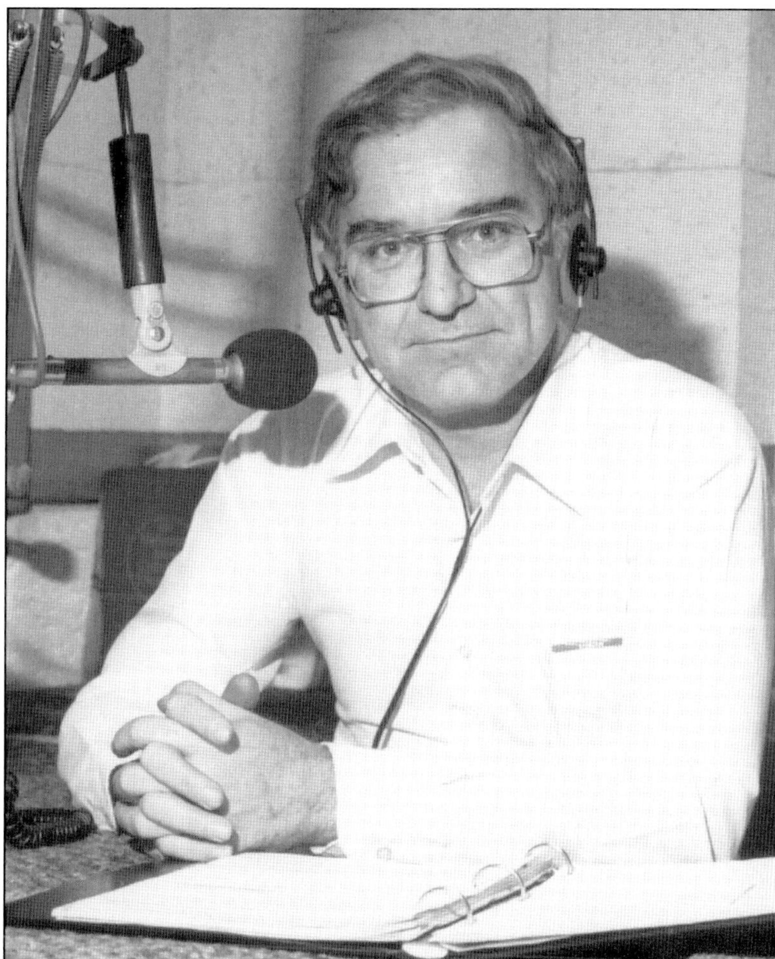

Jim Fisher always had something on his mind and it was usually thought provoking. He started with WOC in the early 1970s playing "pure gold" music. When the station's format changed to news and talk, Fisher invited his listeners to join the discussions. Never afraid to tackle the issues, Fisher had an opinion on them all. And he usually managed to press someone's "hot button" in the process. (Courtesy of WOC.)

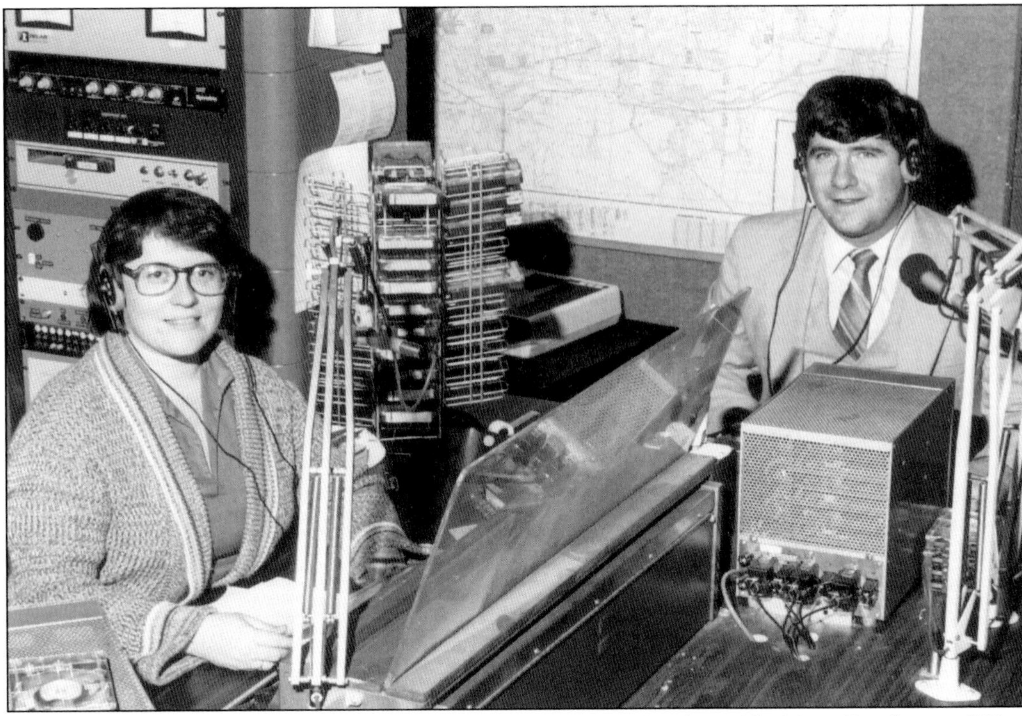

News, weather, and sports filled the WOC *Morning Report*. Anchored by Nora Sanders and Tony Little, the program aired each weekday from 5:30 to 9:00 a.m. At 9:00 a.m., Sanders remained on the air with her two-hour daily talk show. That program addressed many liberal views and provided good balance to WOC's other popular talk-show host, Jim Fisher, who took a more conservative look at issues. (Courtesy of WOC.)

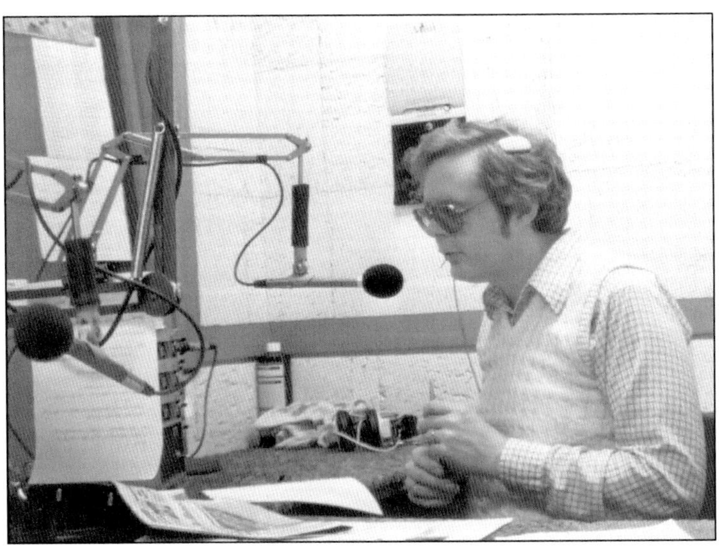

Talk-show hosts gather topical information from a variety of sources. Newswire services, weekly news magazines, and national and local newspapers provide the subject matter that will elicit comments from both the host and the callers. In this photograph from the late 1970s, show host Bob Sidney consults one such newspaper article to help initiate the on-air conversation with his audience. (Courtesy of KWQC-TV.)

From WOC's first days, agricultural news was an important part of the station's programming. A large part of WOC's audience was, and still is, engaged in the farming industry. Full-time farm director Daryl Albaugh provided grain and livestock prices and complete market analysis. Albaugh also produced daily reports and discussions concerning a wide variety of farm issues, conservation, and agriculture-related legislation. (Courtesy of KWQC-TV.)

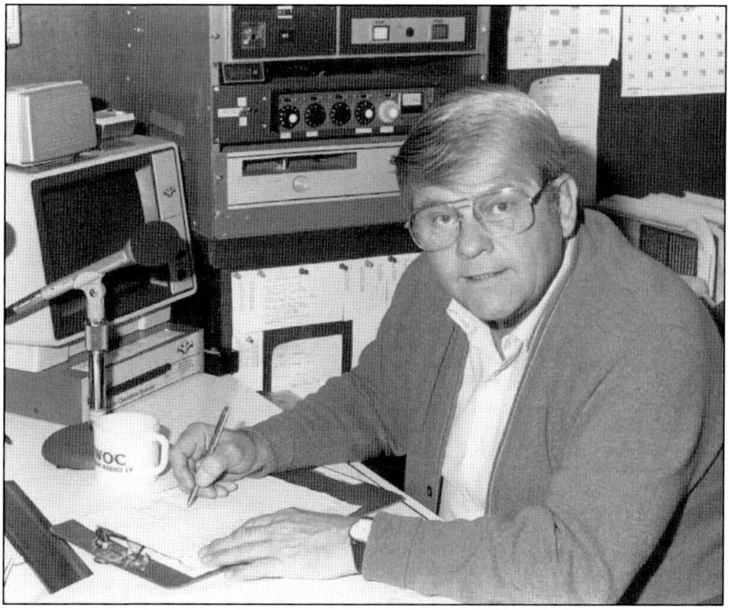

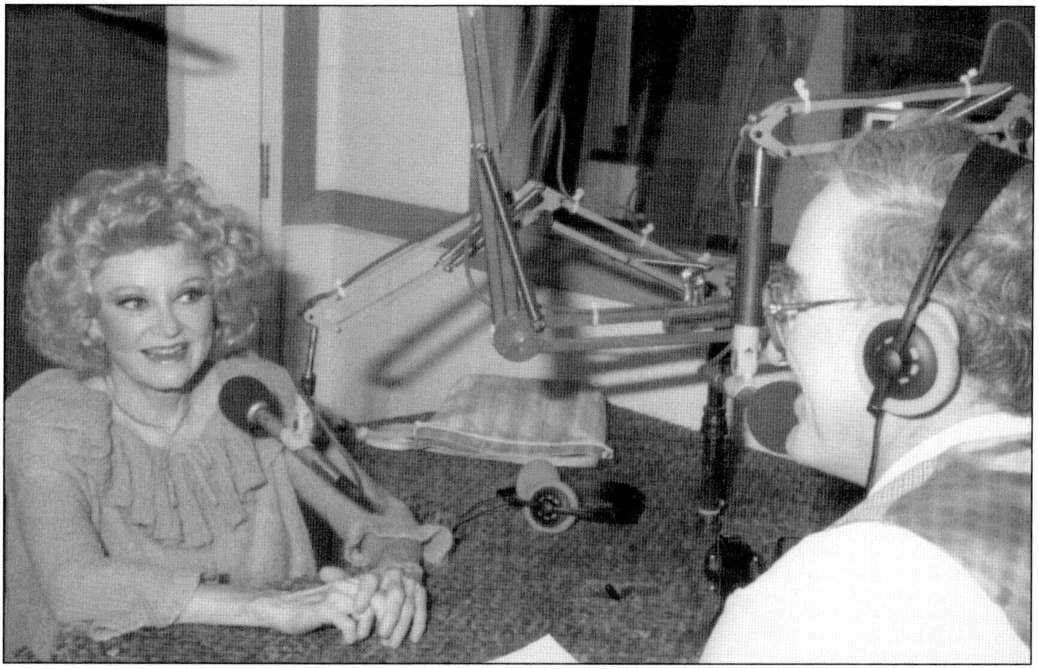

Sitting in a studio for several hours a day does tend to have its benefits. Hosts do occasionally get to meet famous people in the world of politics and entertainment. While in Davenport for a personal appearance, comedienne Phyllis Diller dropped in on Jim Fisher's afternoon WOC talk show. As Diller was noted for her zany wit, no doubt Fisher and his audience were well entertained. (Courtesy of KWQC-TV.)

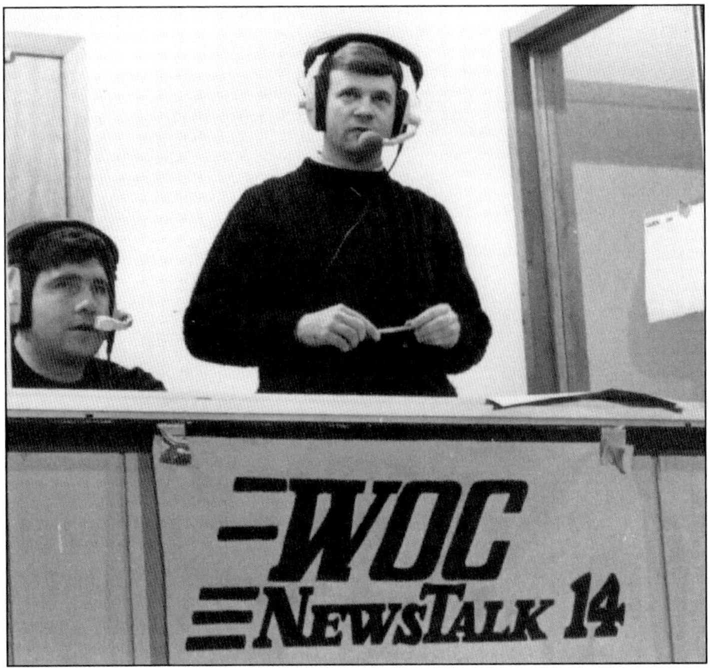

WOC became Newstalk 1420 in the late 1970s, but that did not stop the station from offering a slate of high school and college football and basketball games. While collegiate games were aired from networks like Learfield Sports, high school games were originated by WOC. Tony Little (left) provided the game's color commentary and statistics, while Lee Bright called the play-by-play action. Bright was also a talk-show host. (Courtesy of KWQC-TV.)

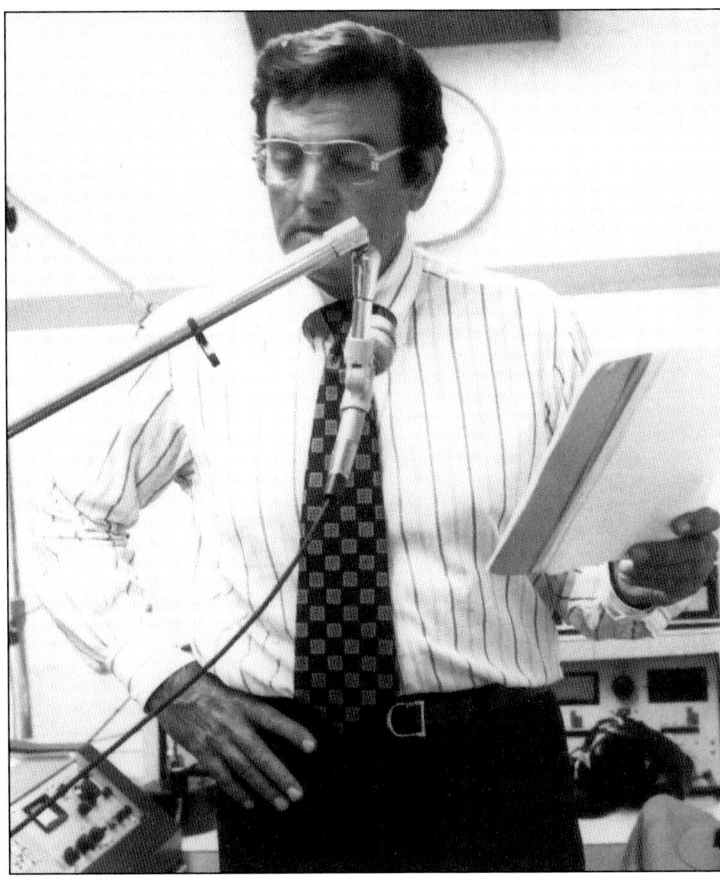

The star of CBS television's popular series *Mannix* was not an announcer at either WOC or KIIK-FM. But actor Mike Connors did agree to record some promotional announcements for the stations, as this photograph from the early 1970s reveals. Actors and entertainers are usually glad to provide announcements and comical drop-ins, as it provides them with continued name recognition by the public. (Courtesy of KWQC-TV.)

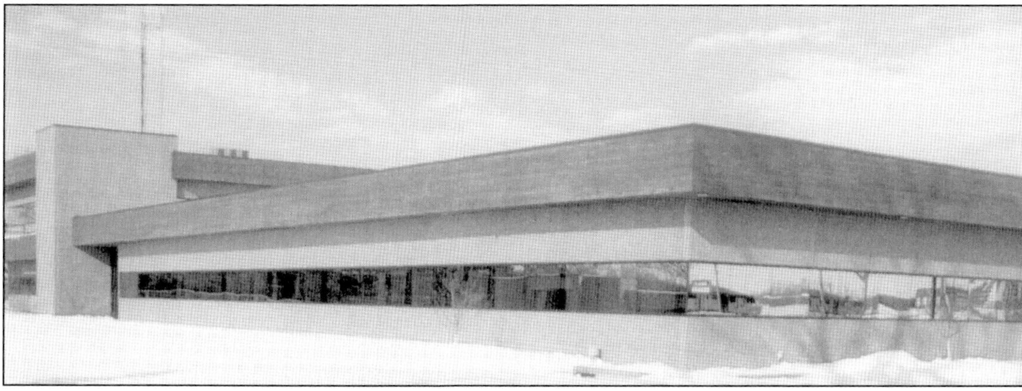

The functional new offices and studios of Signal Hill Communications are seen in this 1988 photograph. Located on the Davenport border with Bettendorf, the building overlooks Duck Creek Golf Course. It housed production and air studios, offices, and an area for future video production. Today the building is home to six radio stations and the offices of the Quad Cities Radio Group, owned by Clear Channel Communications. (Courtesy of WOC.)

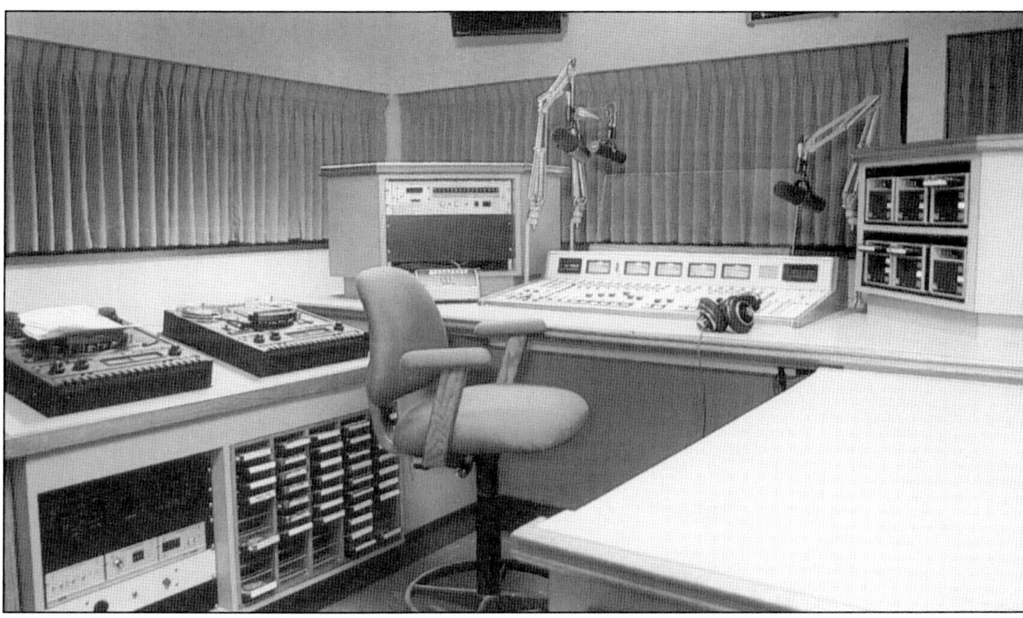

The first thing one notices about the new KIIK-FM air studio is that there are no turntables. Records had become a thing of the past as far as radio stations were concerned. All music was recorded onto cartridge tapes for better audio quality. The reel-to-reel machines on the left, used to play public service programs, would soon become obsolete as well. (Courtesy of KUUL-FM.)

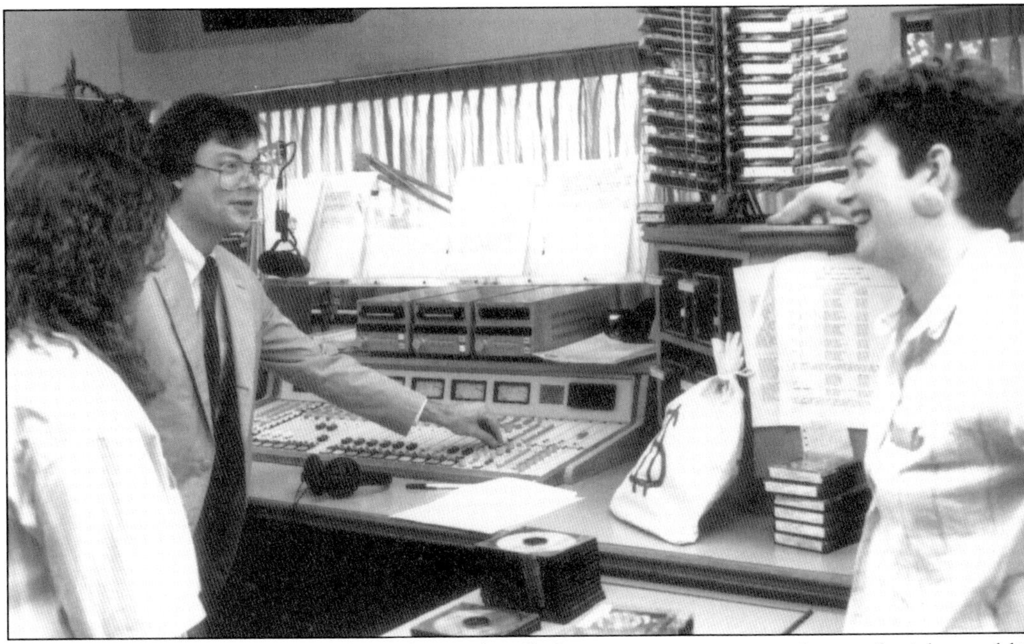

The completion of the new studios of Signal Hill Communications was observed with a public open house. Hundreds of avid listeners to both WOC and KIIK-FM toured the building to see exactly how the sound they enjoyed got into their radios. KIIK-FM's Jim O'Hara demonstrates the audio board to two of his studio guests. (Courtesy of KUUL-FM.)

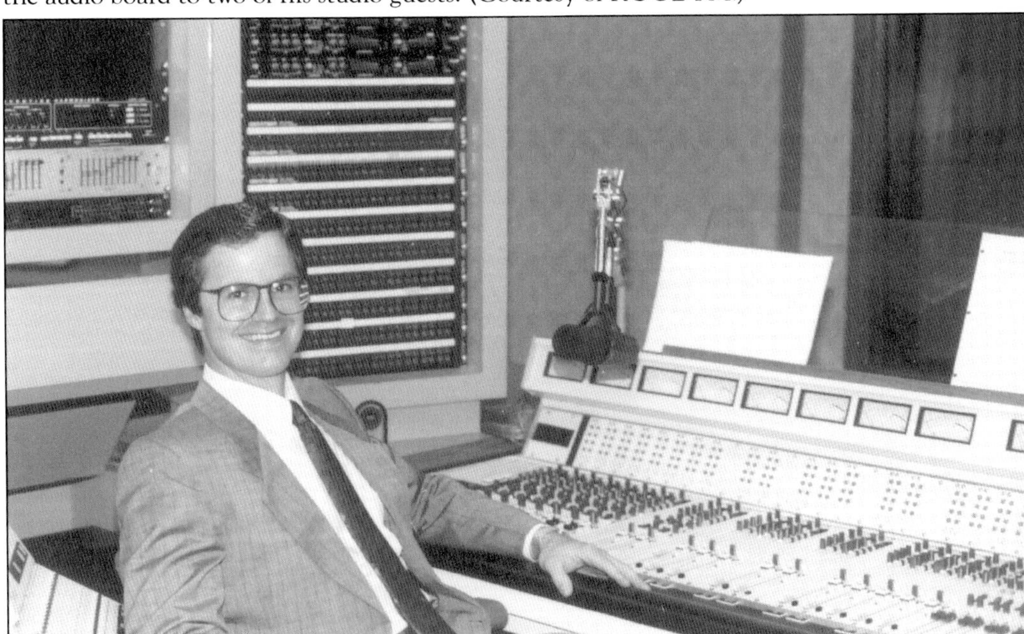

Jerry Pelletier joined KIIK-FM as the evening deejay, but became so popular with listeners that he was moved to afternoon-drive time. He is photographed here in the KIIK production studio. All commercials and promotional announcements were created in this studio. A wide variety of electronic equipment contained here could be used to create the special audio effects heard on many of the station's productions. (Courtesy of KUUL-FM.)

Two old "captains" reminisce about their days as pilots of the *Dixie Bell*. Vern Gielow (left) and Ernie Mimms treated listeners of WOC Radio to their memories of the cartoons, the children, and the special guests of the *Cartoon Showboat* during a WOC broadcast from its new studios. For nearly 20 years, the *Cartoon Showboat* entertained tens of thousands of area children in-studio and at home. (Courtesy of Jon Book.)

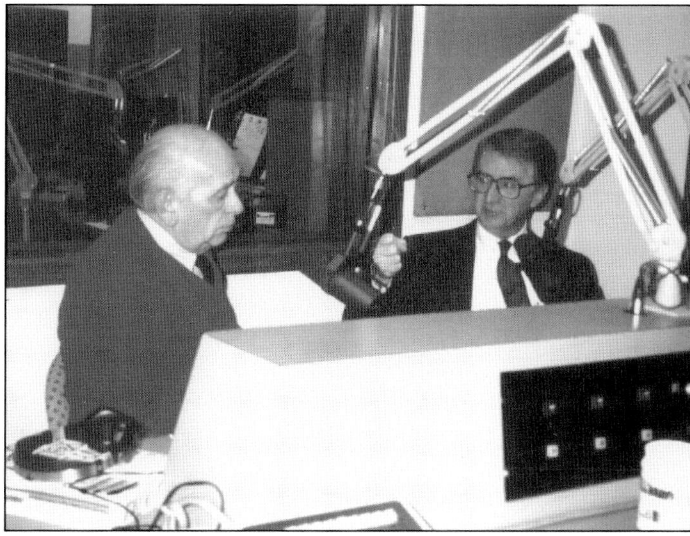

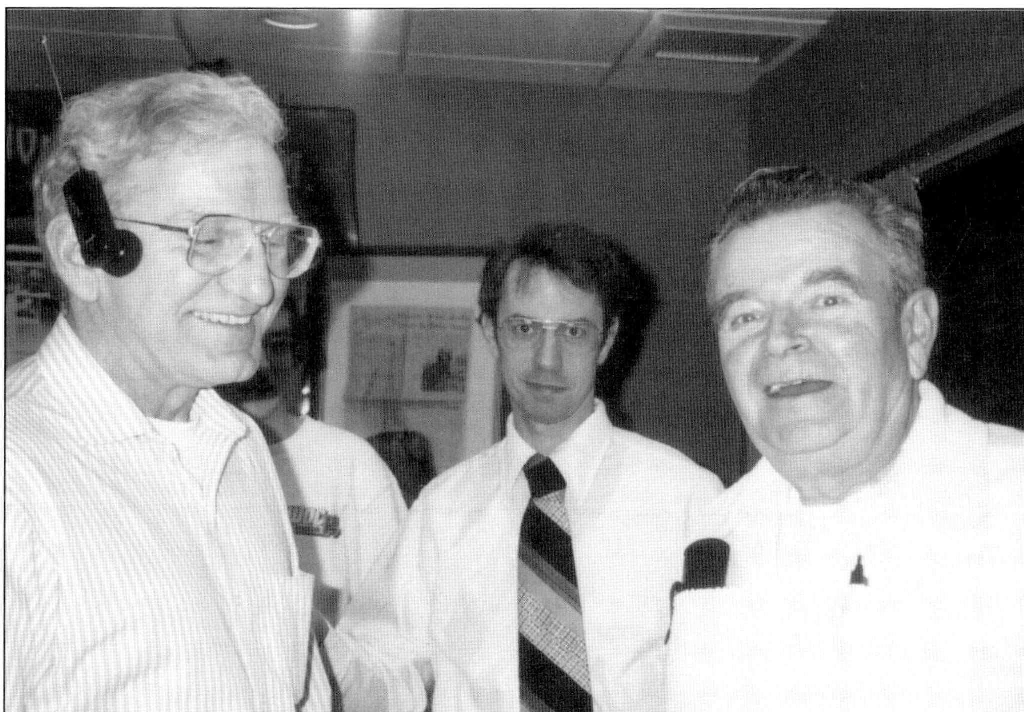

WOC Radio aired special programming celebrating its 65th anniversary. Former radio employees were invited to the new Signal Hill Communications building for an open house. Afternoon talk-show host Jim Fisher (left) interviews longtime engineer and consultant Gene McHenry (right) regarding all the changes in technology, while current chief engineer Jon Book (center) looks on. (Courtesy of Anita Sundin.)

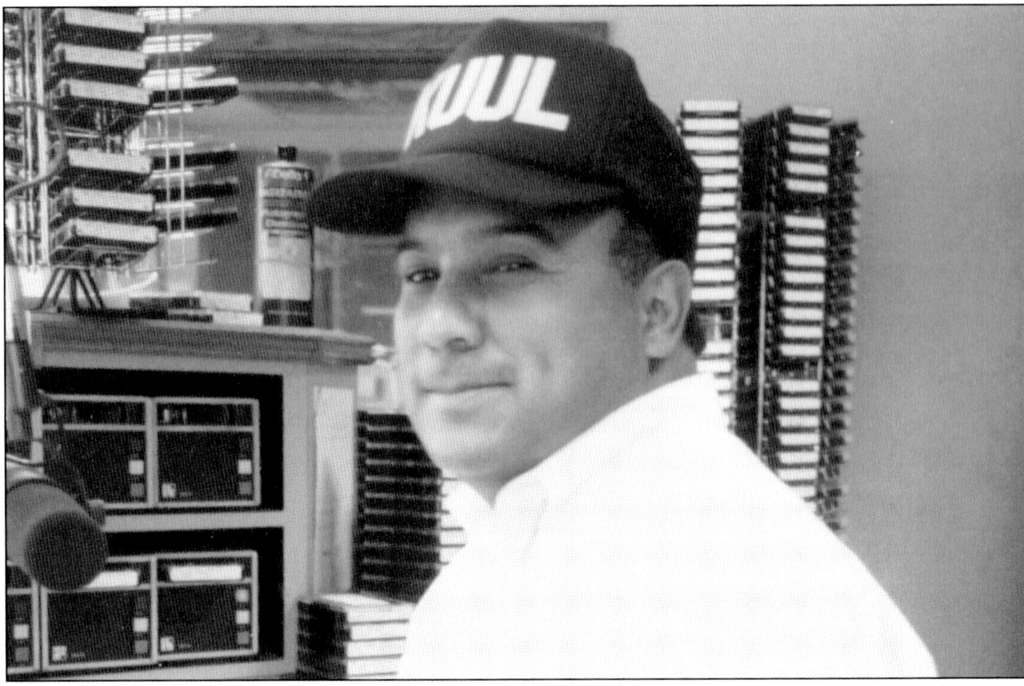

After KIIK-FM's change in format to "oldies," its call letters were changed to KUUL-FM. Afternoon-drive time announcer Joey Denero became a listener favorite. As a teen, Denero frequented Davenport's Draught House and Col Ballroom to hear the rock-and-roll bands of the 1960s. Audiences could relate well with him, as they remembered the same period of time covered by the station's new format. (Courtesy of KUUL-FM.)

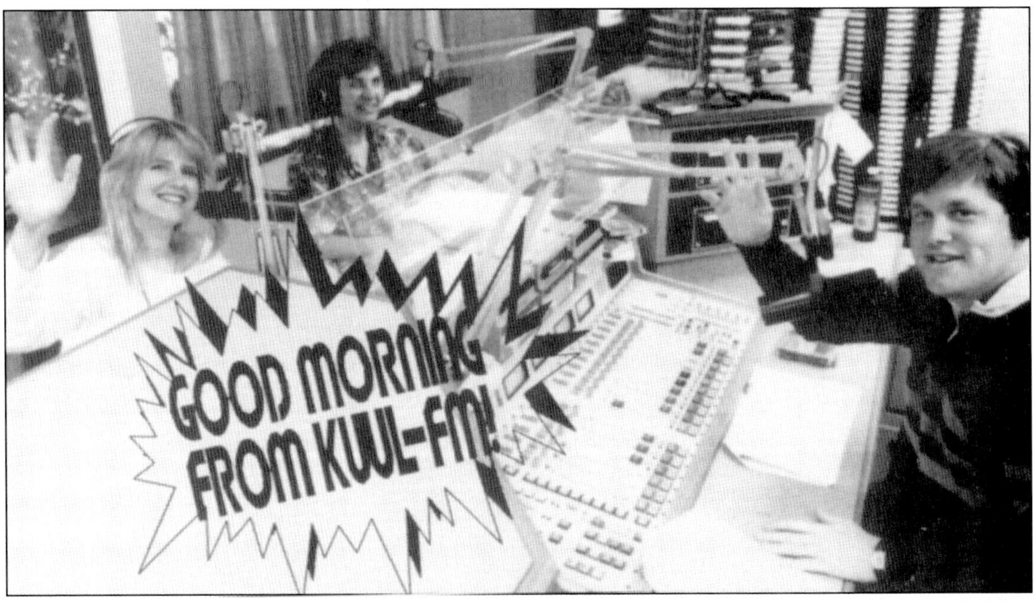

This promotional photograph captures KUUL-FM's talented morning team. Debbie McFadden (left), Susan McBride, and Matt Schwind woke listeners each morning to get their day started off on a bright and informed note. McBride reported the news, while McFadden and Schwind played hit music and added their own brand of humorous reports. (Courtesy of KUUL-FM.)

Seven

Reagan Returns

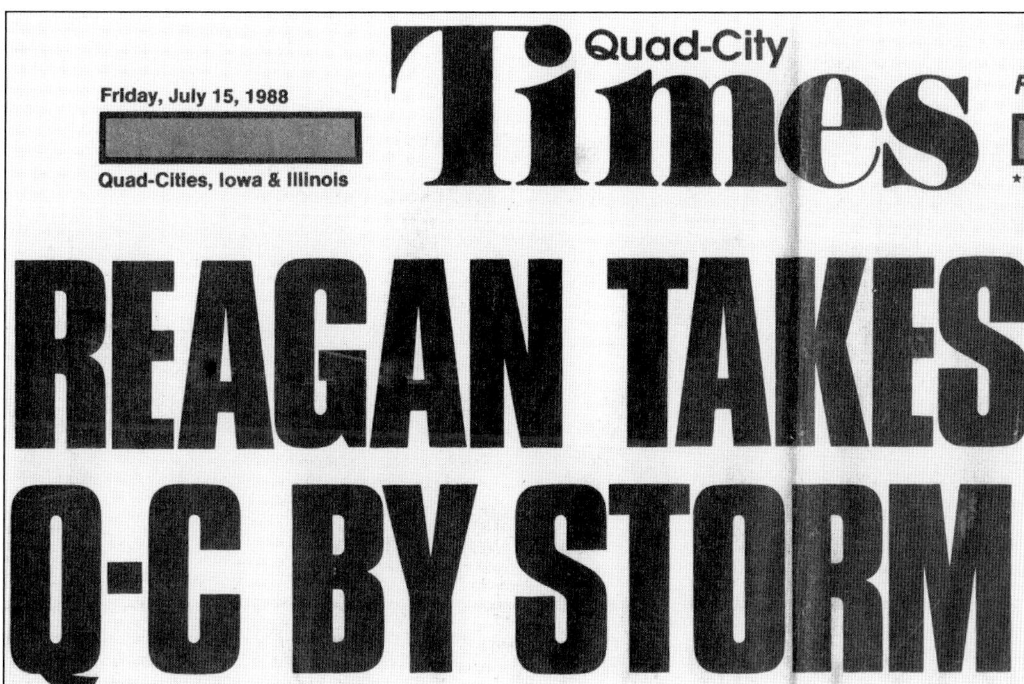

Friday, July 15, 1988

Quad-Cities, Iowa & Illinois

Quad-City Times

REAGAN TAKES Q-C BY STORM

This headline from the *Quad-City Times* says it all. Thousands turned out to catch a glimpse of Ronald Reagan, the former announcer, actor, corporate spokesman, governor, and now sitting president. His return to Davenport was to honor and be honored by WOC, the station that gave him his start in broadcasting and perhaps led to his nickname as "the Great Communicator."

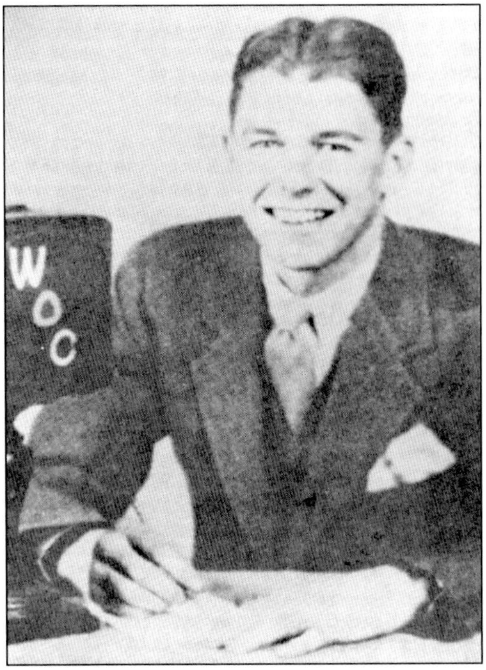

In this c. 1934 photograph, also seen earlier in the book, the handsome figure of Ronald "Dutch" Reagan is captured at the WOC microphone. From radio announcer to movies and television, and from governor to U.S. president, he is easily regarded as WOC Radio's most famous alumnus. It was a true honor to have President Reagan return to where it all started. (With permission of Palmer College of Chiropractic, Special Collections and Archives.)

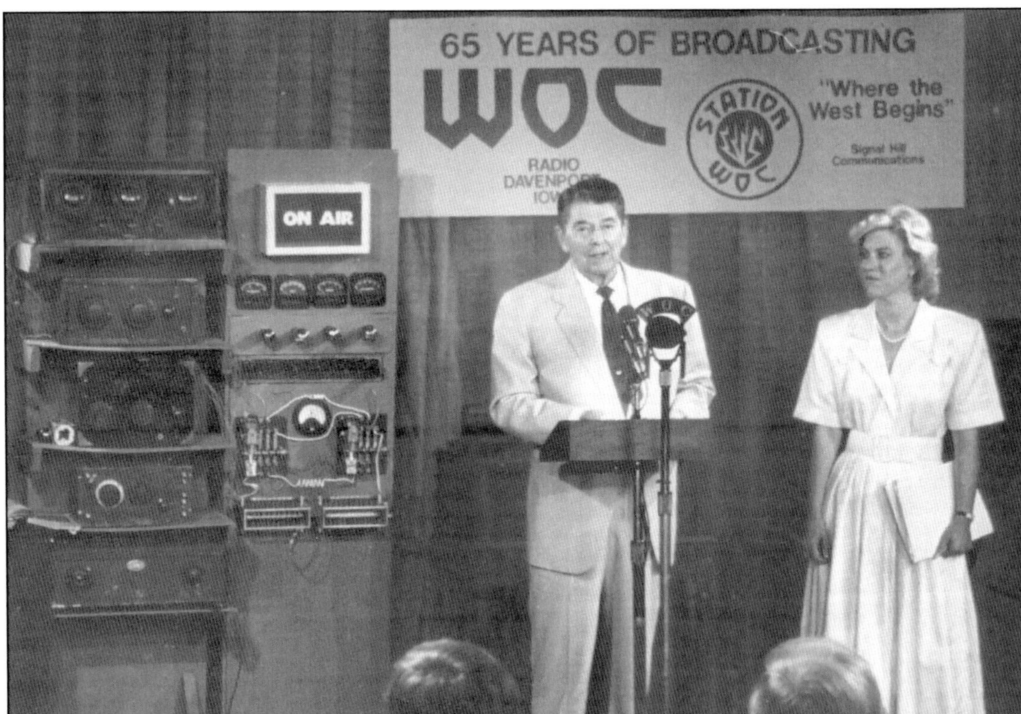

Behind a WOC microphone amid some 1930s-era station equipment, Pres. Ronald Reagan greets attendees at the dedication of Signal Hill Communications' new studios. Vickie Palmer, owner of Signal Hill, introduced him by saying these thrilling words, "It is indeed my great honor to welcome back to WOC our most famous alumnus; allow me to introduce the president of the United States." (Copyright Moline Dispatch Publishing Company, used with permission.)

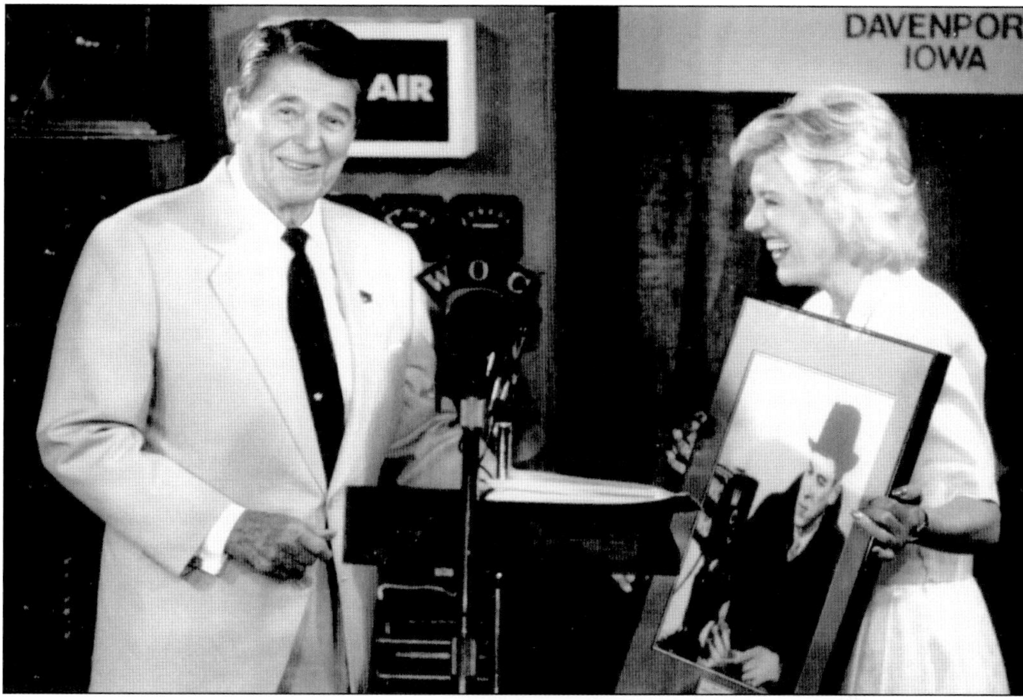

Vickie Palmer shares a laugh with President Reagan. The photographic portrait Palmer holds displays "Dutch" Reagan the sportscaster c. 1932. Reagan received $5 and bus fare to Iowa City to call the action of the Iowa-Minnesota college football game. He later was transferred to sister station WHO in Des Moines, where he spent several years as that station's sports director. (Copyright Moline Dispatch Publishing Company, used with permission.)

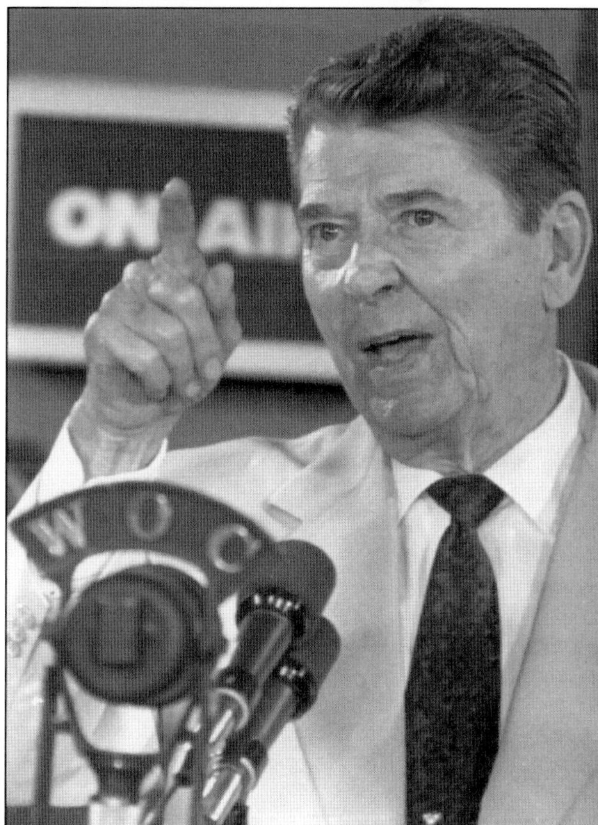

President Reagan emphasizes a point while addressing the attendees at the Signal Hill dedication. Reagan recounted how he auditioned for his job as a sports announcer, and how he nearly got fired for not mentioning the name of the funeral home that provided a half-hour of live, free organ music to the station. He also spoke on serious issues that faced the country. (Copyright Moline Dispatch Publishing Company, used with permission.)

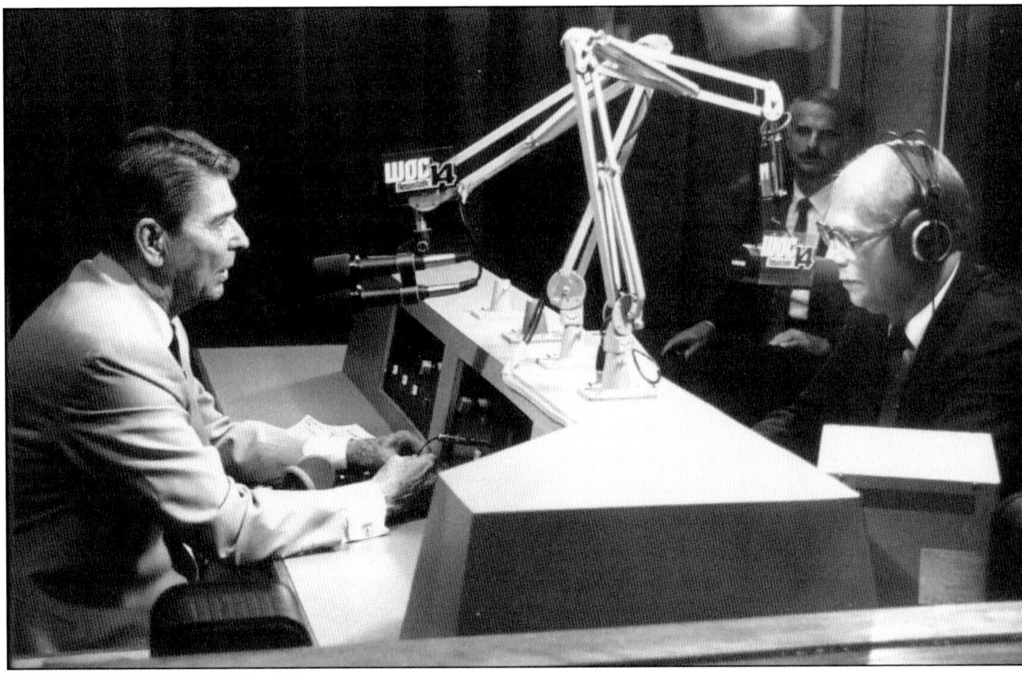

News director Mark Minnick (right) interviewed President Reagan and discussed his career at WOC. Reagan related the time he was re-creating a baseball game from the wire-service ticker when that machine quit working. Until the ticker tape restarted, Reagan filled time by having the batter hit foul ball after foul ball. Note the U.S. Secret Service agent in the background of this photograph. (Copyright Moline Dispatch Publishing Company, used with permission.)

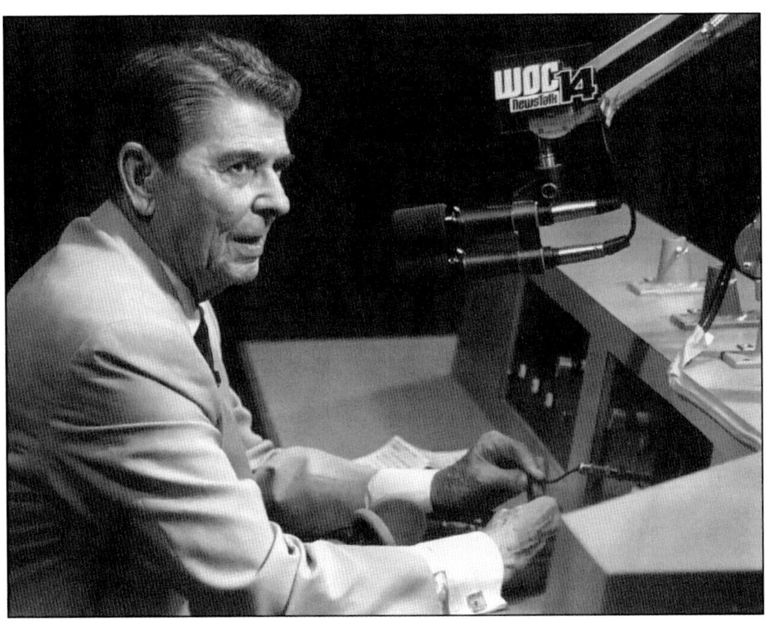

President Reagan appears caught in thought at the microphone, as he reminisces about how his broadcasting career was launched in Davenport. Reagan recalled, in great detail, who he worked with, where he lived, and his on-air bloopers. He even remembered the girls he dated. (Copyright Moline Dispatch Publishing Company, used with permission.)

Eight

SIGNAL HILL TODAY

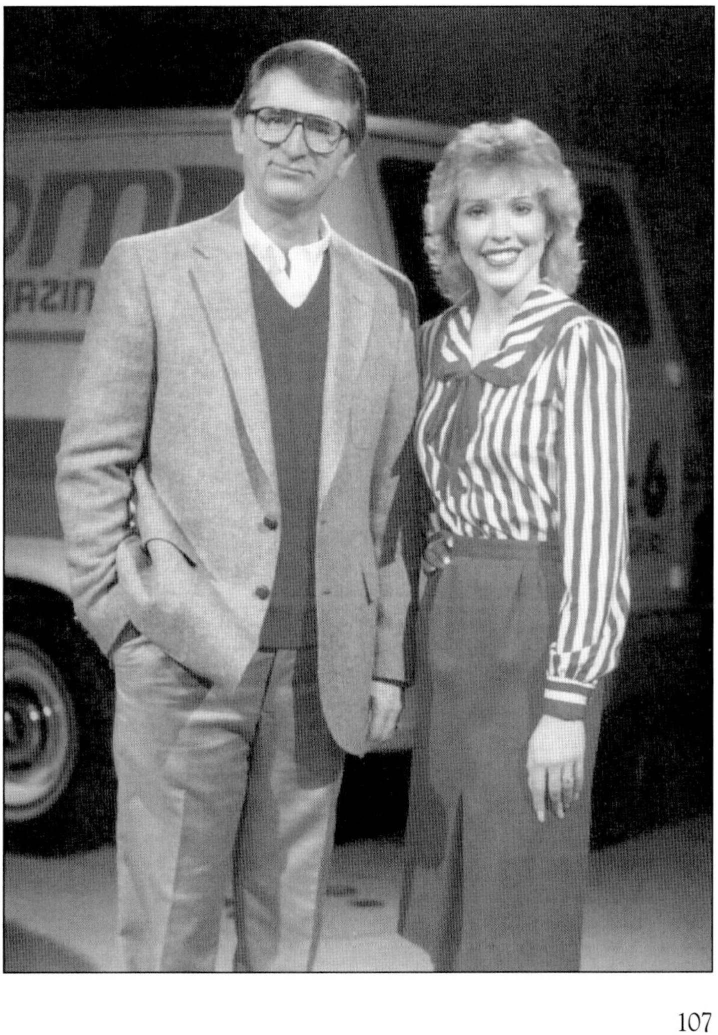

PM Magazine was a nationally syndicated program from Westinghouse Broadcasting that provided local stations with news and human-interest stories of a lighter nature. Based on the national story, local hosts would then present a segment that would appeal to their audience. Usually the local segment provided follow-up information with some light humor included. The show's hosts in the mid-1980s were Ernie Mimms (left) and Paula Sands. (Courtesy of KWQC-TV.)

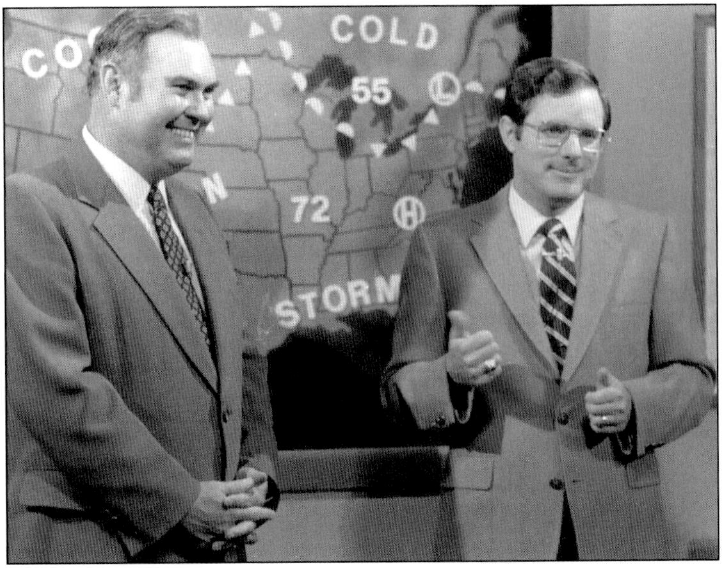

Whenever an NBC personality was in town, the local affiliate usually received a visit. In this case, it was the network's *Today Show* resident weatherman Willard Scott (left) hamming it up with channel 6 weatherman John Collins. In this case, Scott came to the station to help note a station promotional event and perhaps give Collins some pointers on forecasting the weather. (Courtesy of KWQC-TV.)

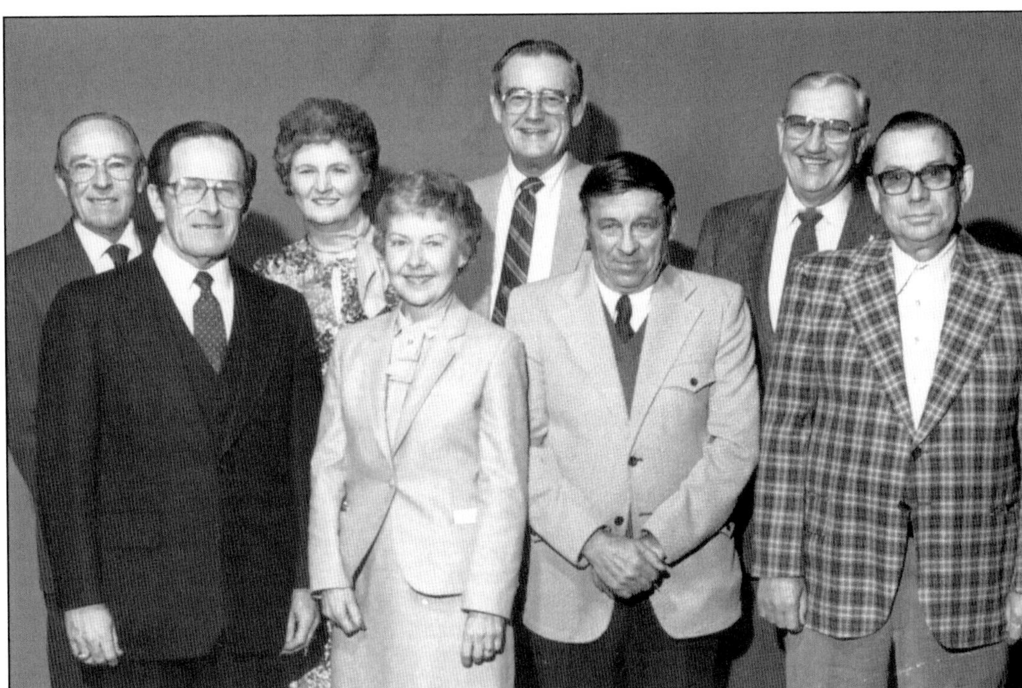

This is the last group of employees to retire from the WOC stations while still under the ownership of the Palmer family. Pictured here are, from left to right, sales executive Ran Jensen, sales executive John Goodall, continuity director Anita Sundin, sales secretary Ann Harrison, television sales manager Harold Heath, engineer Max Roth, radio sales manager Lou Nielsen, and engineer Bud Elliott. In total, the group represented 232 years of service. (Courtesy of Anita Sundin.)

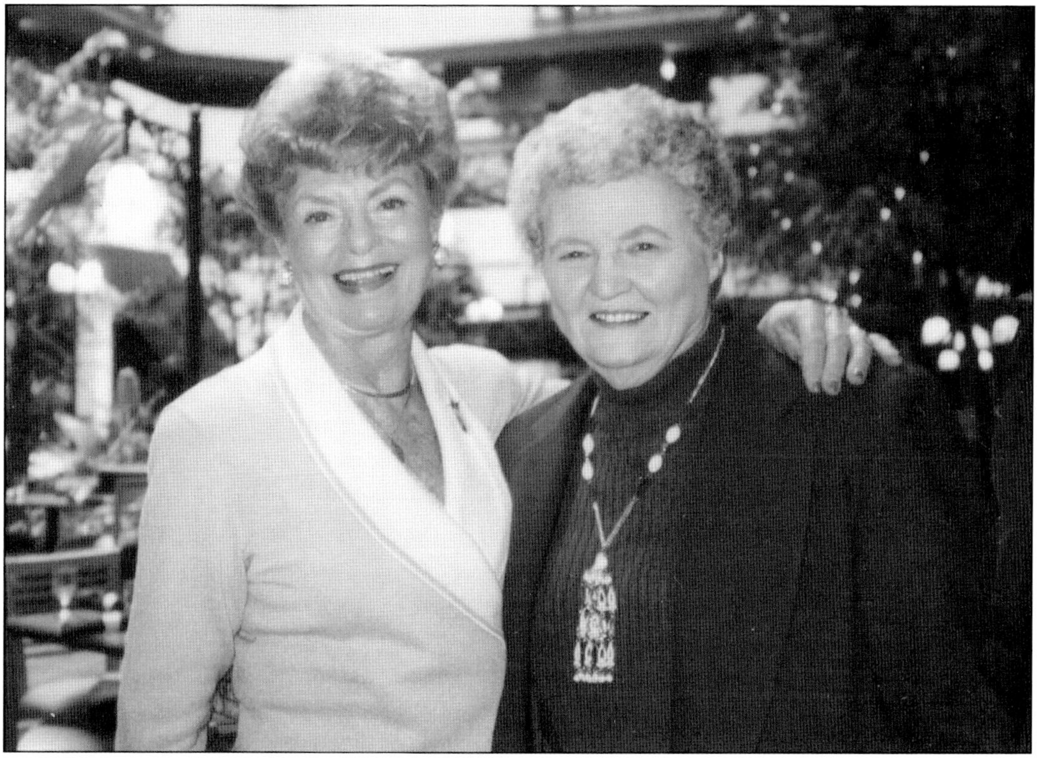

Together again after 30 years are *Especially for You* hostess Pat Sundine (left) and substitute hostess Anita Sundin. Both ladies had various radio shows on WOC and were seen or heard in many commercials over the years. The two are most remembered for their 16 years of informing viewers with interviews of local and national news makers and segments on cooking, fashion, and gardening. (Courtesy of Anita Sundin.)

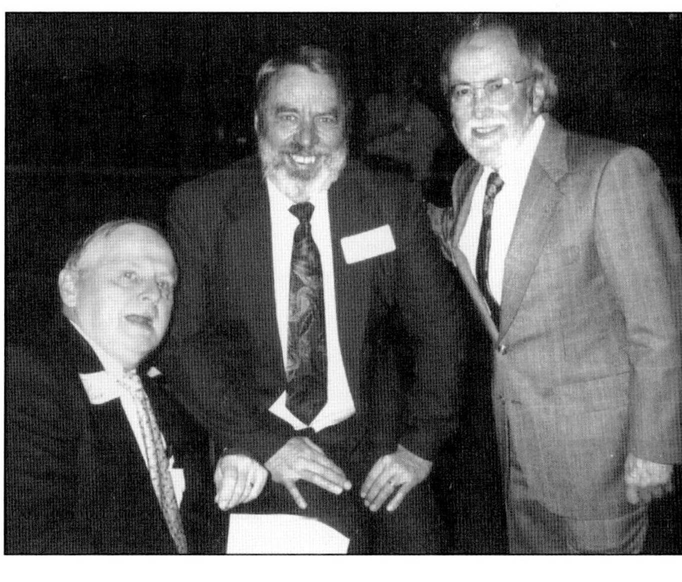

Over 30 years of sports broadcasting is represented in this photograph. Ed Zack (left), Wally Boller, and Hal Hart met up at WOC-TV's 50th anniversary celebration. Hart was the first on-air sports reporter, followed by Zack in 1961. Boller took over the sports anchor chair in 1967. All three had also been heard calling the action at football and basketball games on WOC Radio. (Courtesy of Anita Sundin.)

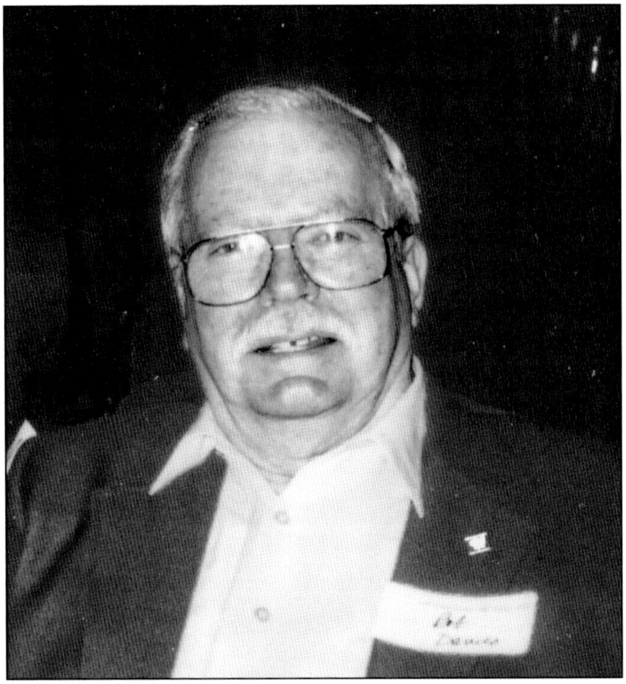

Announcer, weatherman, and children's program host were a few of Bob Danico's jobs at channel 6. However, he spent most of his career with the station as one of its directors. Newscasts, commercials, public affairs programs, and specials benefited from his creative touch. A musician, he worked with the audio engineer to bring out the best sound possible in the band, orchestra, and choral programs he directed. (Courtesy of Anita Sundin.)

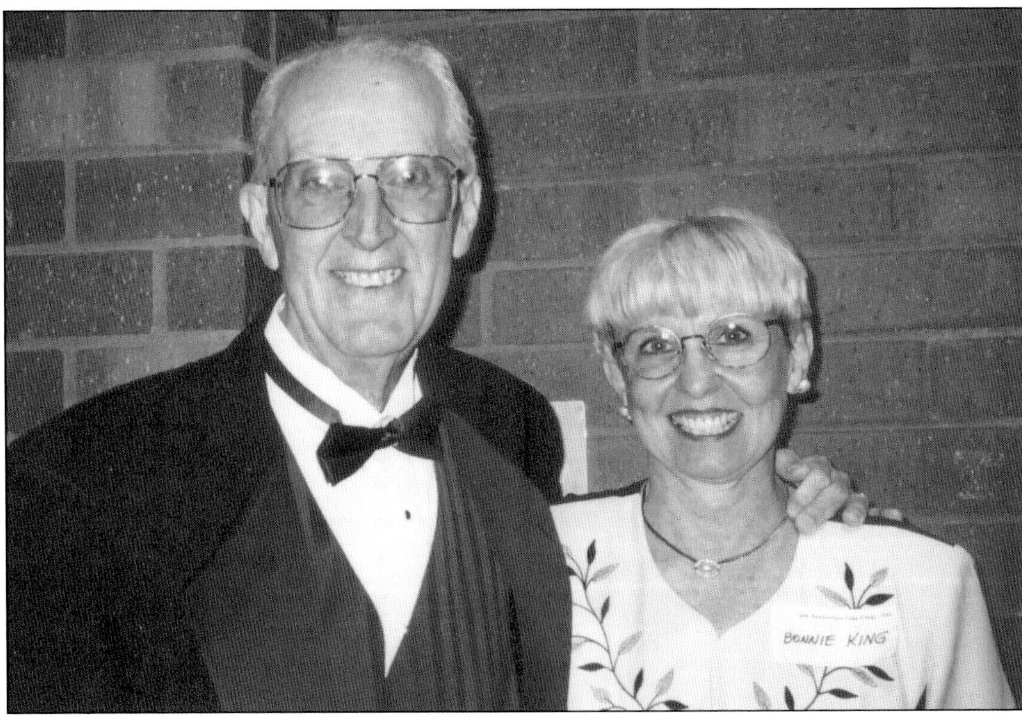

A viewer favorite was Charles King, shown with his wife, Bonnie, in a photograph from the 50th anniversary of channel 6. King was the popular anchor of *Quad Cities Today*, a two-hour morning program that featured news, weather, and interviews. Although now retired, his popularity was such that a travel firm hired his wife and him to host tours that now fill up quickly with former fans. (Courtesy of Anita Sundin.)

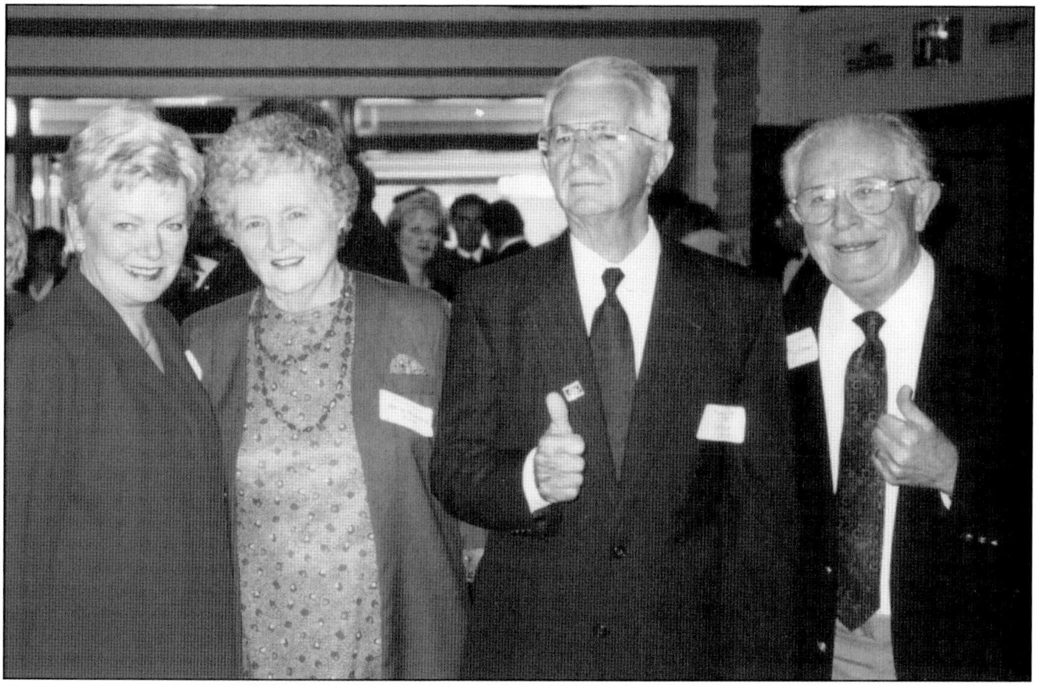

Former *Romper Room* hostess Donna Scott (left), *Especially for You* substitute hostess Anita Sundin, "Captain" Ernie Mimms, and director Ed Jones renew friendships at WOC-TV's 50th anniversary. Many employees of the stations, including the early stars of local television, returned to Davenport for the event. The gala celebration was held at the RiverCenter and was broadcast live on channel 6. (Courtesy of Anita Sundin.)

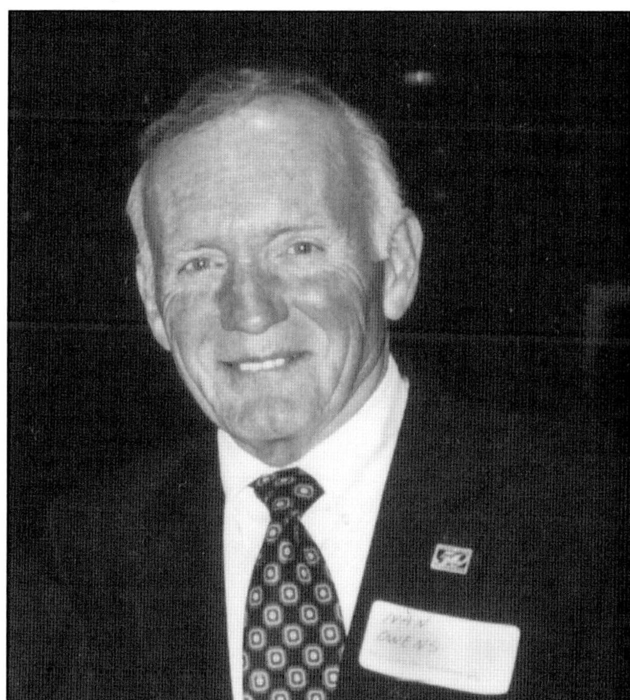

Ivan Owens spent 46 years at channel 6 and was stage manager for most of that time. In that position, he was responsible for providing many of the props used in commercial production and for designing and building the various sets. Channel 6's news sets always stood out as the best looking and most functional of any of the local stations. (Courtesy of Anita Sundin.)

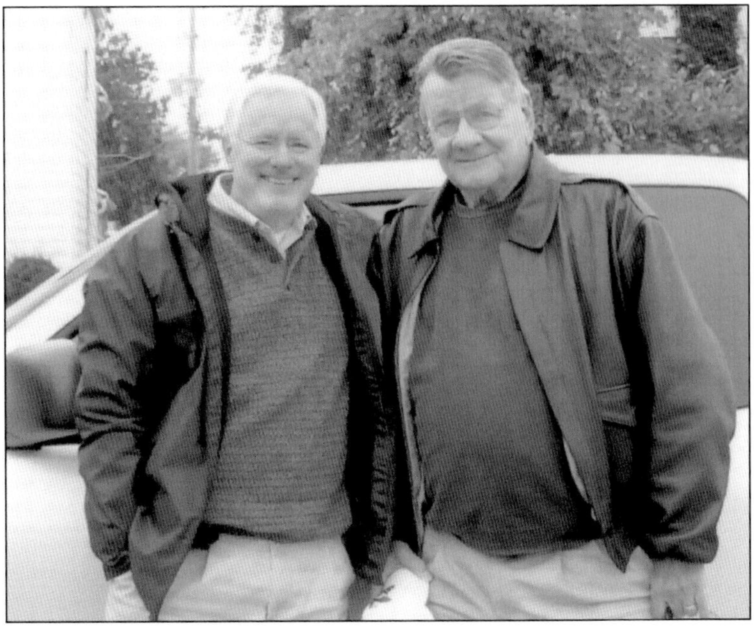

Former weatherman John Collins (left), back in town for a college reunion, meets up with former news anchor Don Rhyne. Rhyne is retired, but Collins is still in broadcasting. He left channel 6 in the mid-1980s to forecast weather for KIRO-TV in Seattle, Washington. For the past 20 years, Collins has been a weatherman at WBAL radio and television in Baltimore, Maryland. He also hosts a weekly gardening program.

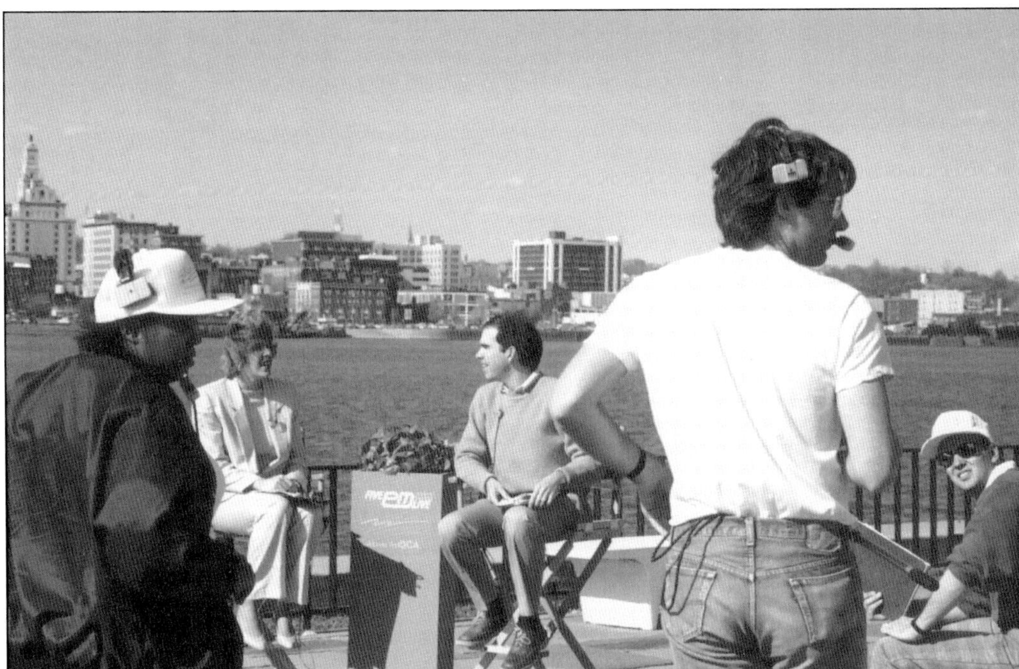

PM Magazine had run its course, but channel 6 created a new program titled *Five PM Live*. The show would feature human-interest stories from the local viewing area and highlight upcoming special events. It was not uncommon for the show to be carried out entirely on location, as seen here. Hosting the show from Modern Woodmen Insurance in Rock Island are Paula Sands (left) and John David. (Courtesy of KWQC-TV.)

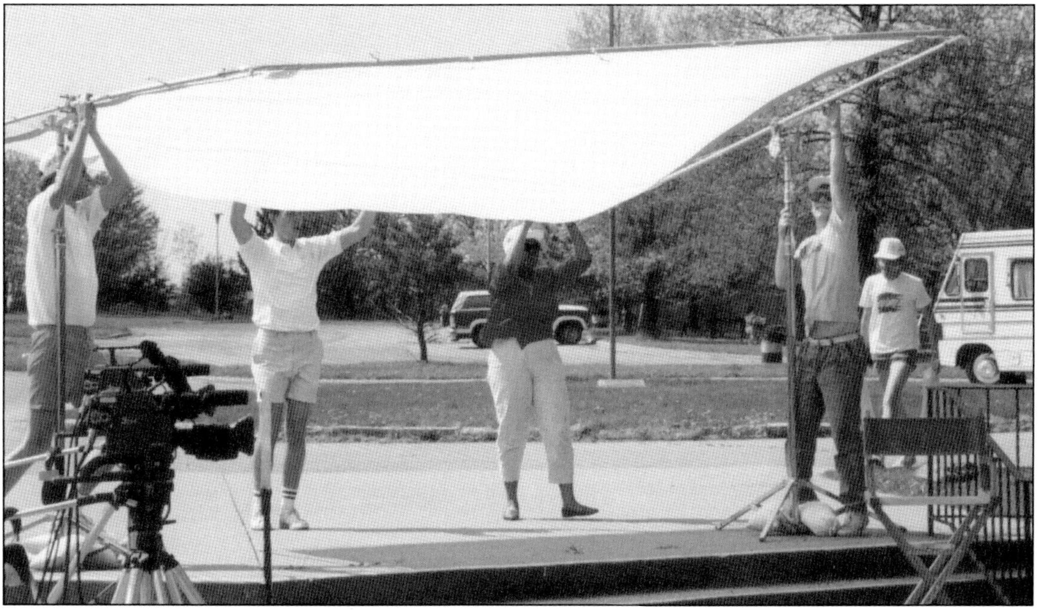

Productions away from the studio always mean plenty of work for the crew. While the studio has an ample amount of the correct lighting for the scene or talent, outdoor shoots pose a different problem. While there might be bright sunlight, it is not "focused" and can give a flat look to the scene. To compensate and to eliminate shadows, the crew sets up reflectors as seen here. (Courtesy of KWQC-TV.)

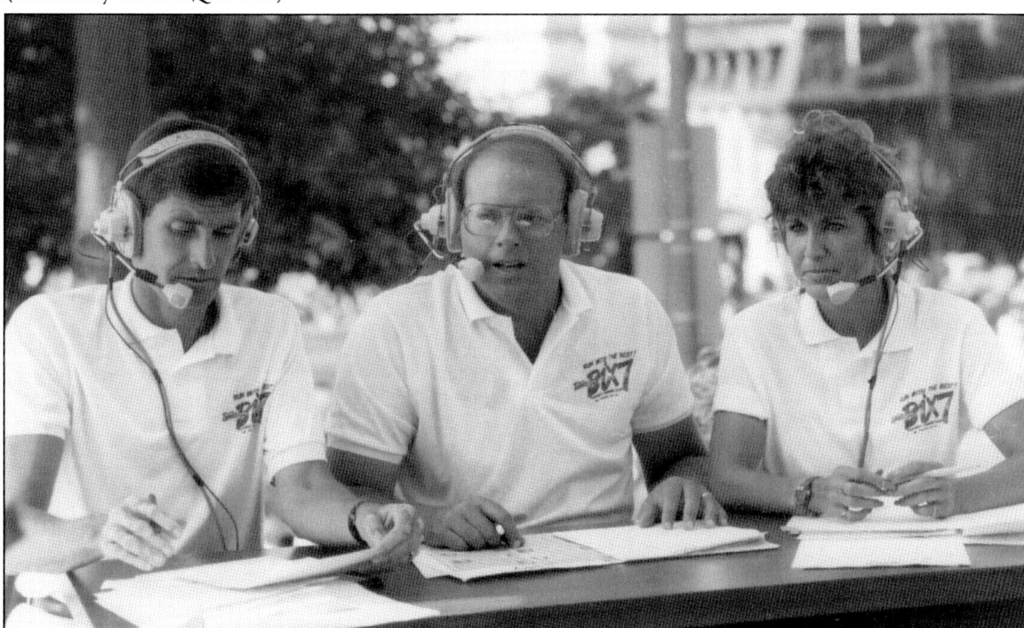

In 1983, channel 6 began live coverage of the Bix 7 Road Race. Using cameras in a helicopter, on a motorcycle, and at various fixed points along the course, the station covered runners over the entire course. Former Olympians Jim Ryun (left) and Gayle Barron (right) join sports director Thom Cornelis for race coverage and commentary. Their vantage point is just outside the station on Brady Street hill. (Courtesy of KWQC-TV.)

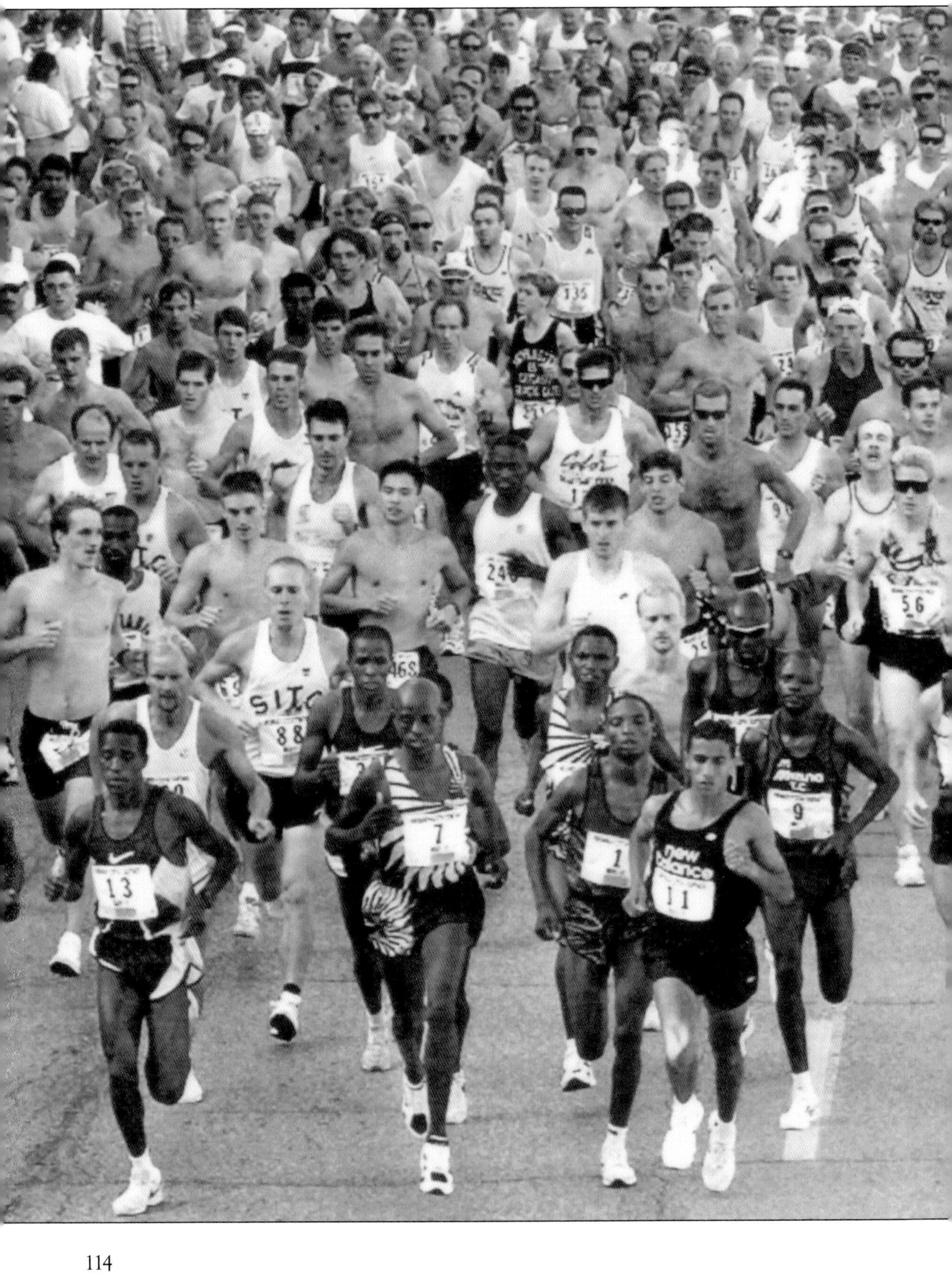
13
7
1
new balance
11
9
88
56

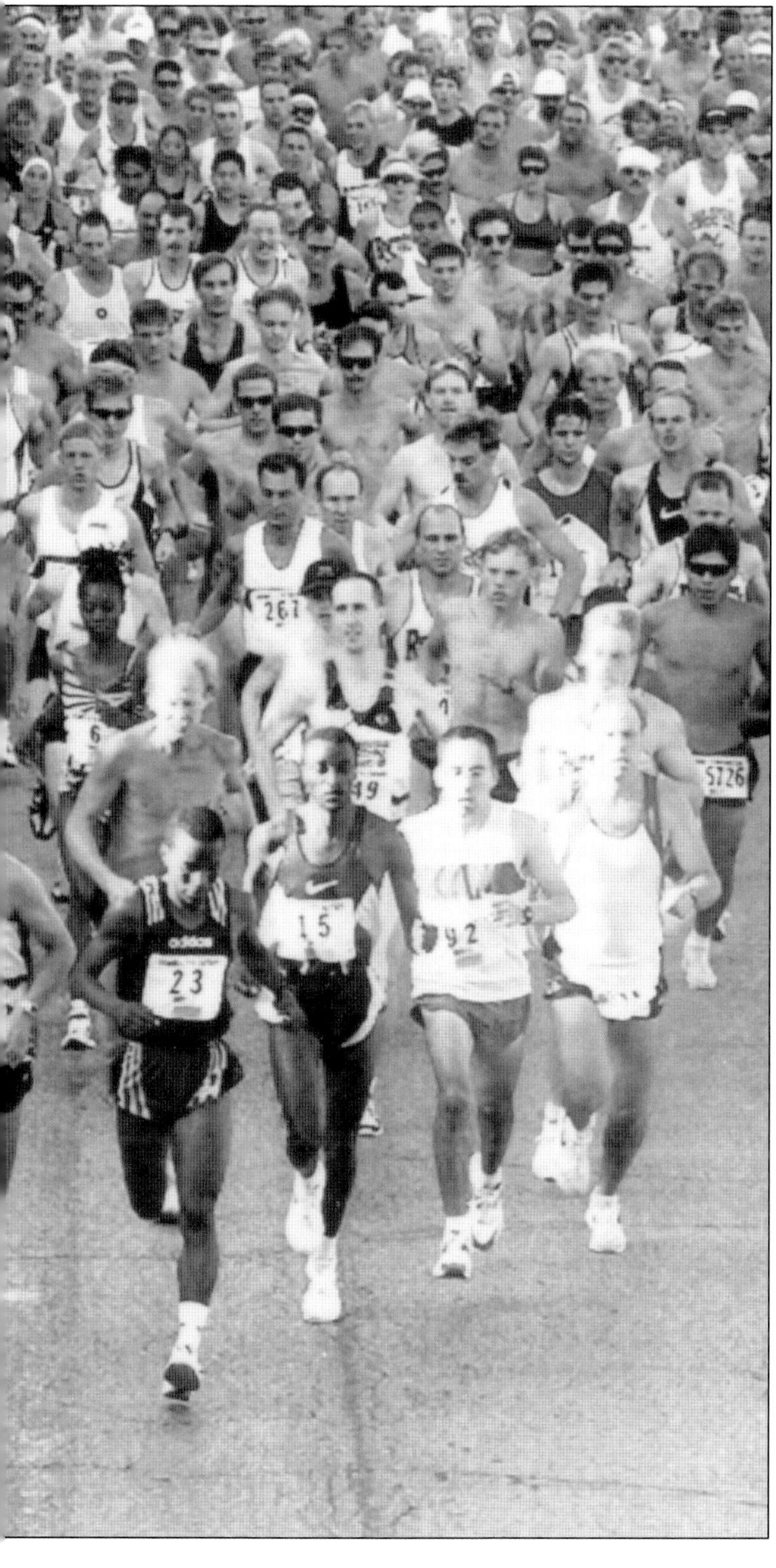

The Bix Beiderbecke Memorial Jazz Fest is a three-day festival of traditional jazz music. It was founded in 1972 to honor the accomplishments of Davenport's Bix Beiderbecke, a cornetist, pianist, and composer. Every year, it draws thousands to Davenport to listen to great jazz bands. In 1975, the first Bix 7 Road Race was held in conjunction with the festival. The course is 7 miles long and contains many hills. That first year, there were fewer than 100 runners. Since that first competition, the race has steadily grown into the largest non-marathon race in the Midwest. Typically 15,000–20,000 runners and walkers participate each year, including runners of international renown. This photograph shows the field as it begins the trek up the Brady Street hill, just two blocks from the starting line. Channel 6 has broadcast the race live since the mid-1980s. The station also transmits coverage on satellite for cable channels and the Armed Forces Television Network. (Courtesy of KWQC-TV.)

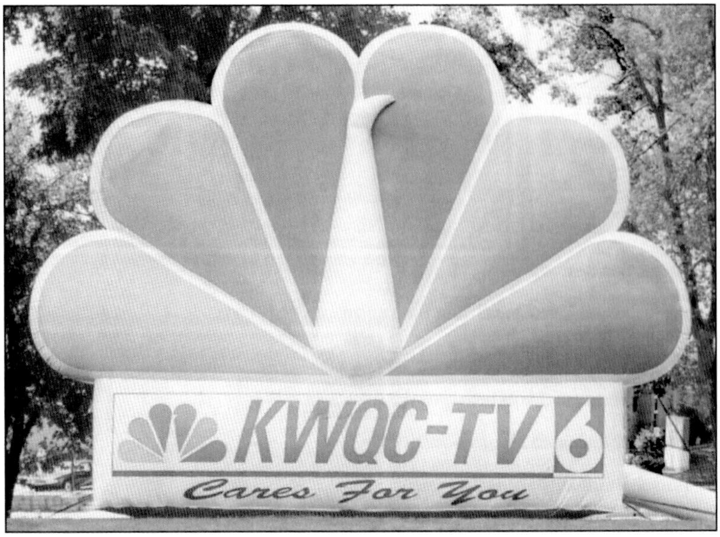

In the 1990s, channel 6 began branding itself as the station that "cares for you." It took sponsorship roles with many nonprofit events held across the Quad Cities and created some of its own events like the Women's Lifestyles Fair. The station also provided numerous on-air announcements for nonprofit groups at no charge. This balloon sign was used as a reminder of the station's sponsoring role. (Courtesy of KWQC-TV.)

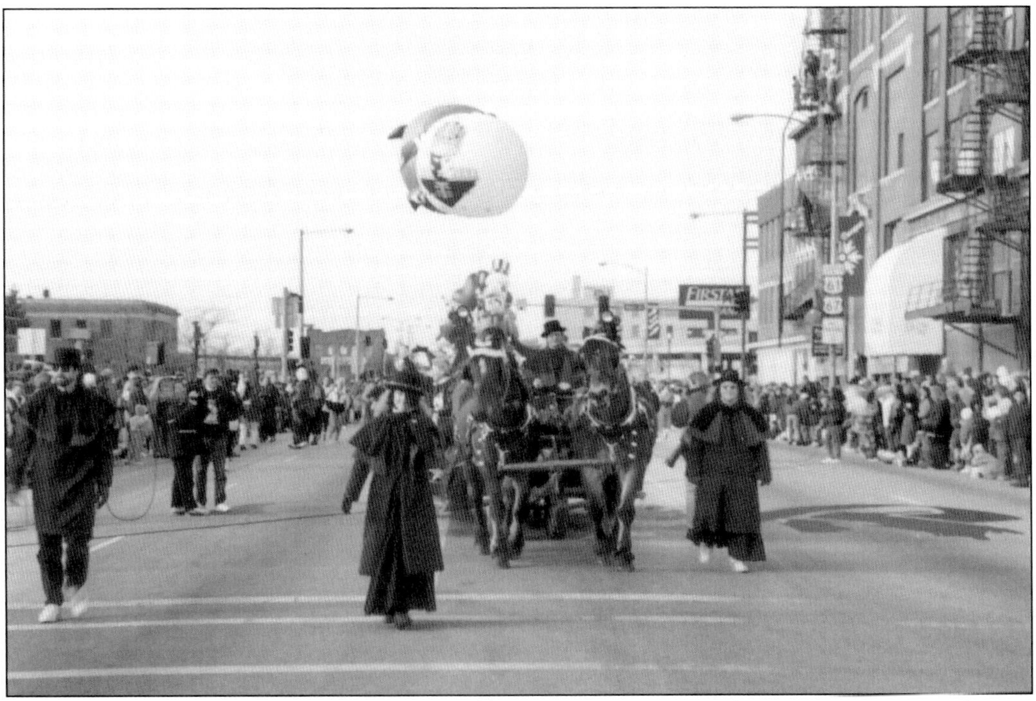

Just before Thanksgiving, the Quad City Arts Festival of Trees is staged at Davenport's RiverCenter. A variety of holiday-related events are held, along with the display of hundreds of decorated Christmas trees. One event is the holiday balloon parade through the downtown. Businesses sponsor the giant caricature balloons and many of the parade's floats. Channel 6 has televised the parade live since the late 1990s. (Courtesy of KWQC-TV.)

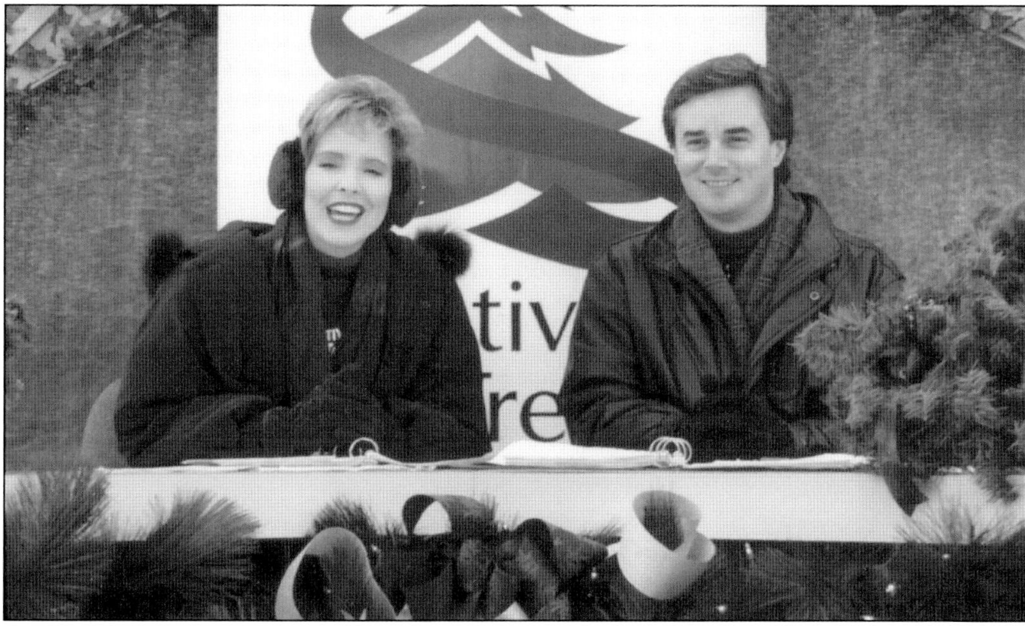

Paula Sands and John Mooney anchored televised coverage of the Festival of Trees holiday parade in the 1990s. Additional reporters covered the parade's preparations, including the filling of the huge helium-filled balloons and the parade's step-off. Participant interviews were also included. For people who could not attend, or did not like the weather conditions on parade day, television coverage still allowed them the opportunity of seeing this great event. (Courtesy of KWQC-TV.)

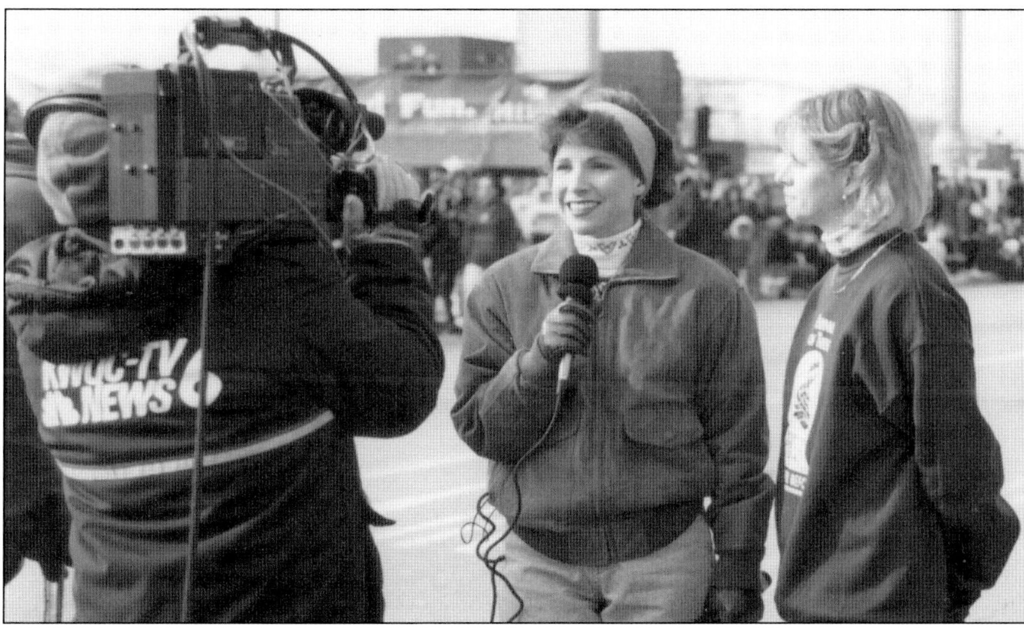

Over 3,500 volunteers, 650 tree designers, and 3,200 entertainers contribute to the many events that make up the Festival of Trees. The weeklong fest is the major fund-raiser for the Quad City Arts Council and is responsible for funding its many cultural programs. Channel 6 reporter and news anchor Marcia Lense (center) is seen interviewing one of the many parade volunteers. (Courtesy of KWQC-TV.)

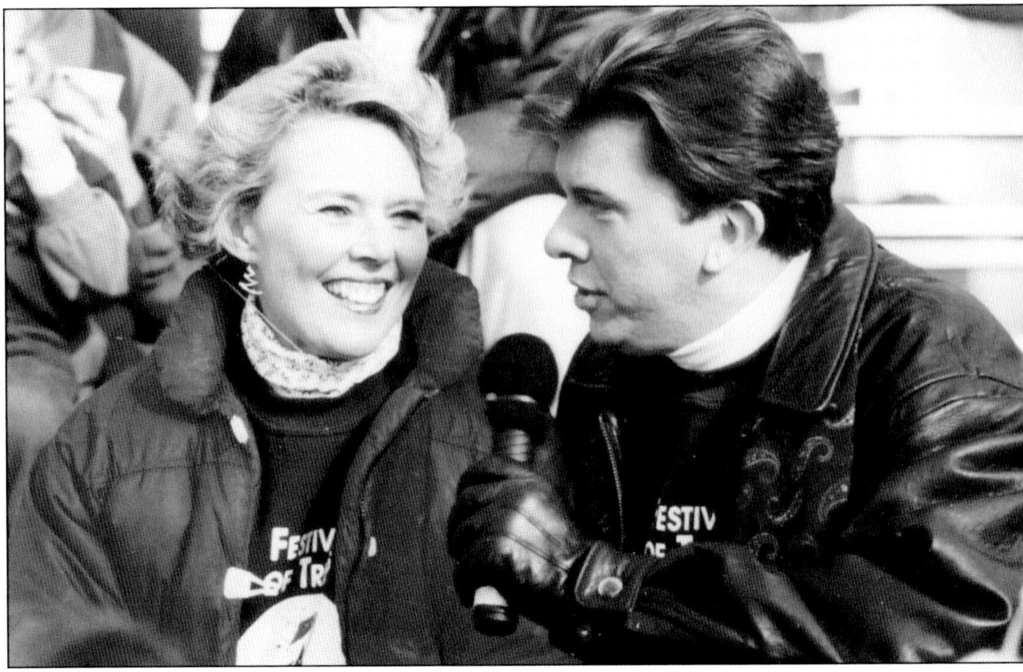

Mike Mickle interviews Festival of Trees director Karen Getz during a mid-1990s parade broadcast. Getz was a community volunteer who directed the entire festival from 1991 to 1994, was a member of the steering committee, and chaired the sponsorship committee. She was also the liaison between the festival and the Quad City Symphony's Holiday Pops Concert. Unfortunately Karen Getz passed away in 2007. (Courtesy of KWQC-TV.)

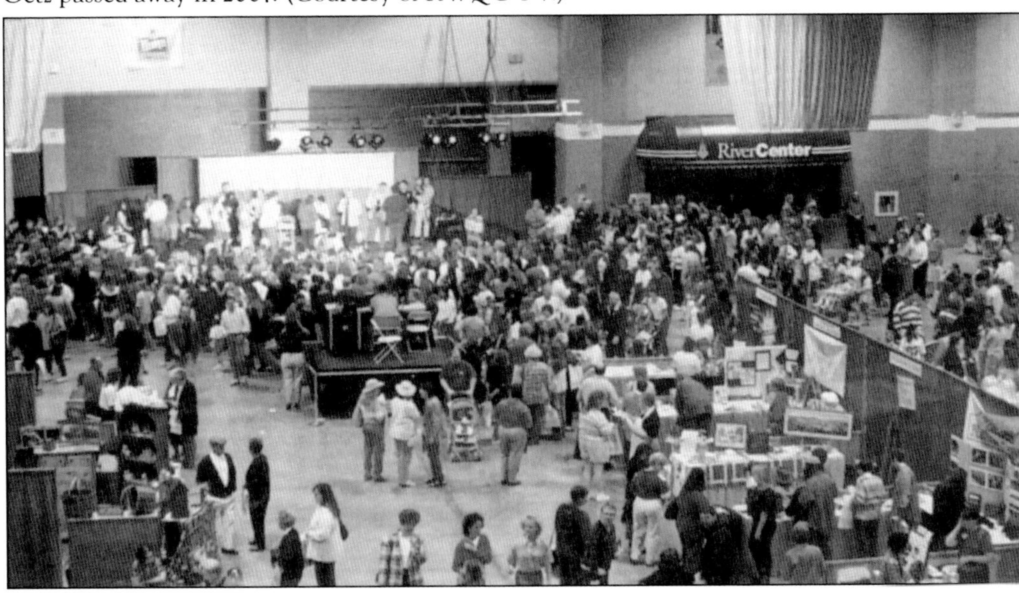

As part of the station's "KWQC-TV6 Cares for You" branding, it sponsored a variety of community events and produced one rather large one. The Women's Lifestyles Fair was an annual spring event that presented seminars, displays, and fashion shows. There were also special appearances by noted celebrities like Martha Stewart, network news anchor Faith Daniels, and actress Diahann Carroll. (Courtesy of KWQC-TV.)

A highlight at channel 6's annual Women's Lifestyles Fair was the guest speaker. Celebrity guests included journalists, chefs, food experts, exercise and health gurus, and television personalities. Before he slimmed down, NBC's *Today Show* weatherman and host Al Roker came to Davenport to address the fair attendees. (Courtesy of KWQC-TV.)

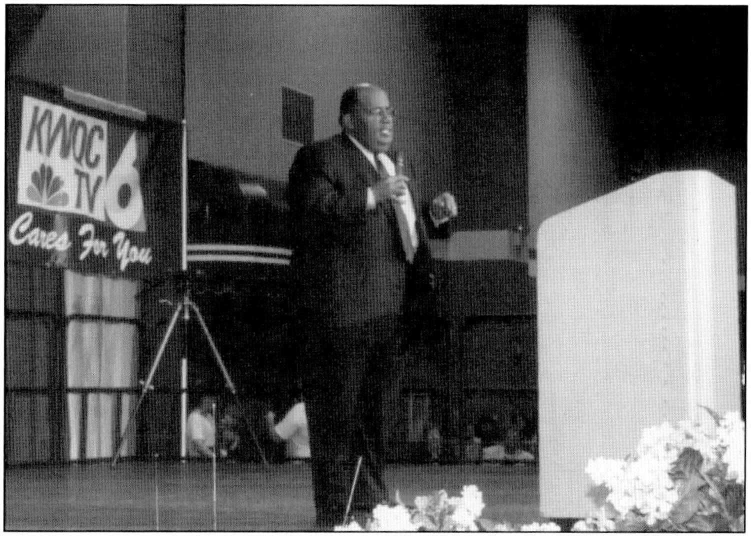

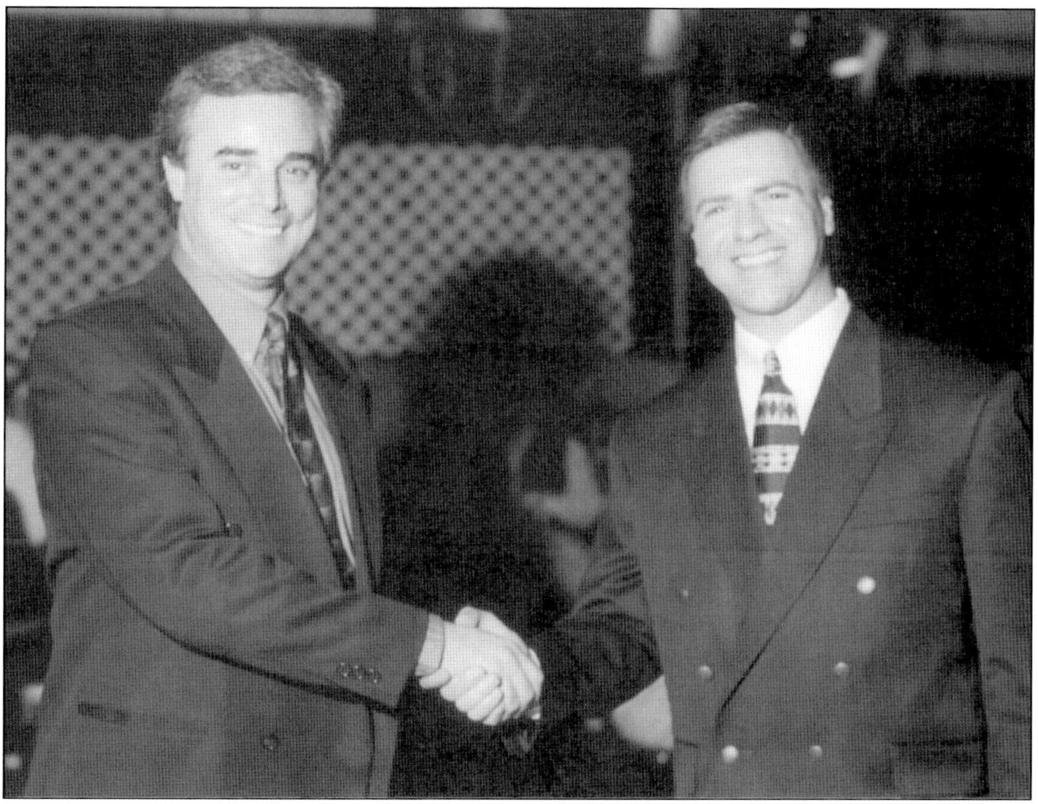

John Mooney (left) was a popular news anchor at channel 6 for six years. In 1998, he left for the anchor position at KAKE-TV in Wichita, Kansas. He is seen here welcoming his replacement at KWQC-TV, Gary Metivier. Metivier is certainly no stranger to news, having covered major earthquakes in California and the Oklahoma City bombing. He is one of the current anchors of channel 6's weekday newscasts. (Courtesy of KWQC-TV.)

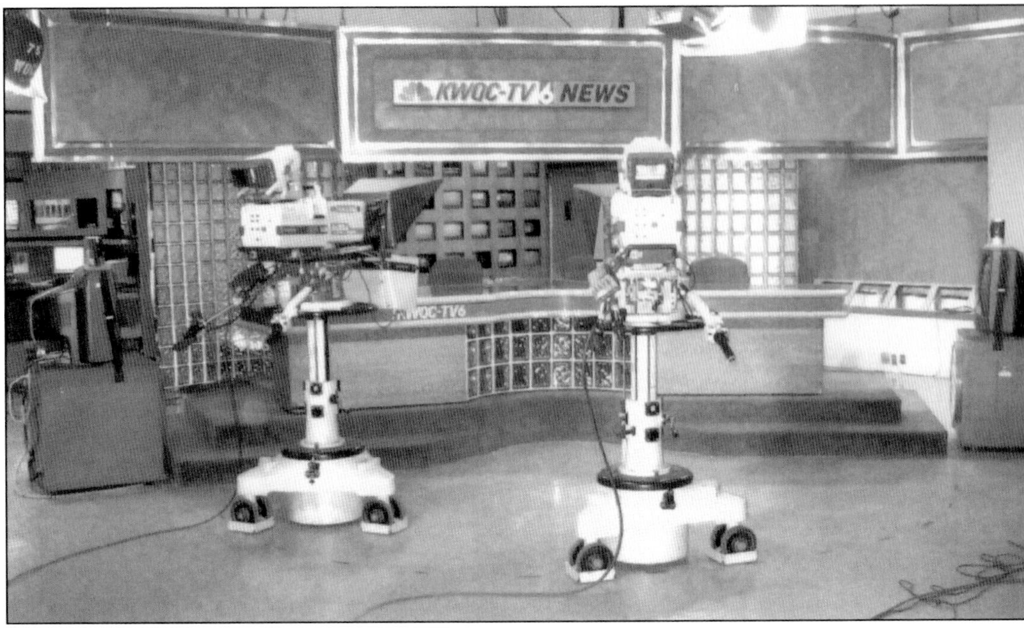

This is the channel 6 permanent news set as it appears today. New technology has made the cameras and cables much smaller and lighter than their earlier counterparts. A teleprompter can be clearly seen attached to the front of the camera on the left. It works by reflecting the rolling script, which only the on-air person can see, onto a piece of reflective ground glass in front of the camera lens.

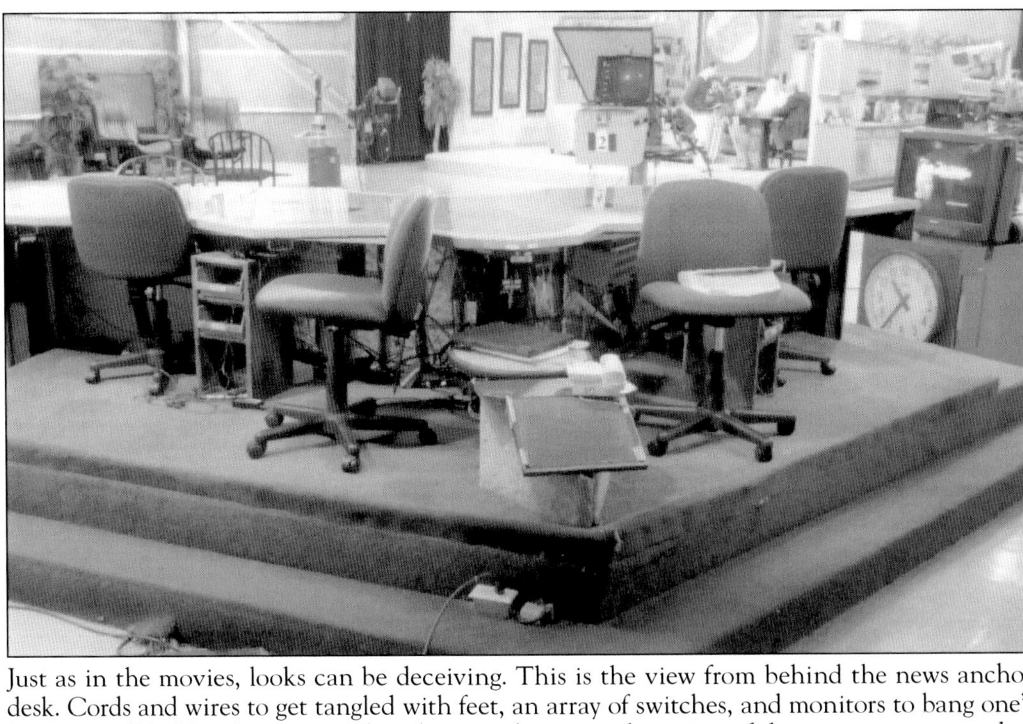

Just as in the movies, looks can be deceiving. This is the view from behind the news anchor desk. Cords and wires to get tangled with feet, an array of switches, and monitors to bang one's knees are all hidden from view. This photograph gives a clear view of the prompter mounted to the front of the camera.

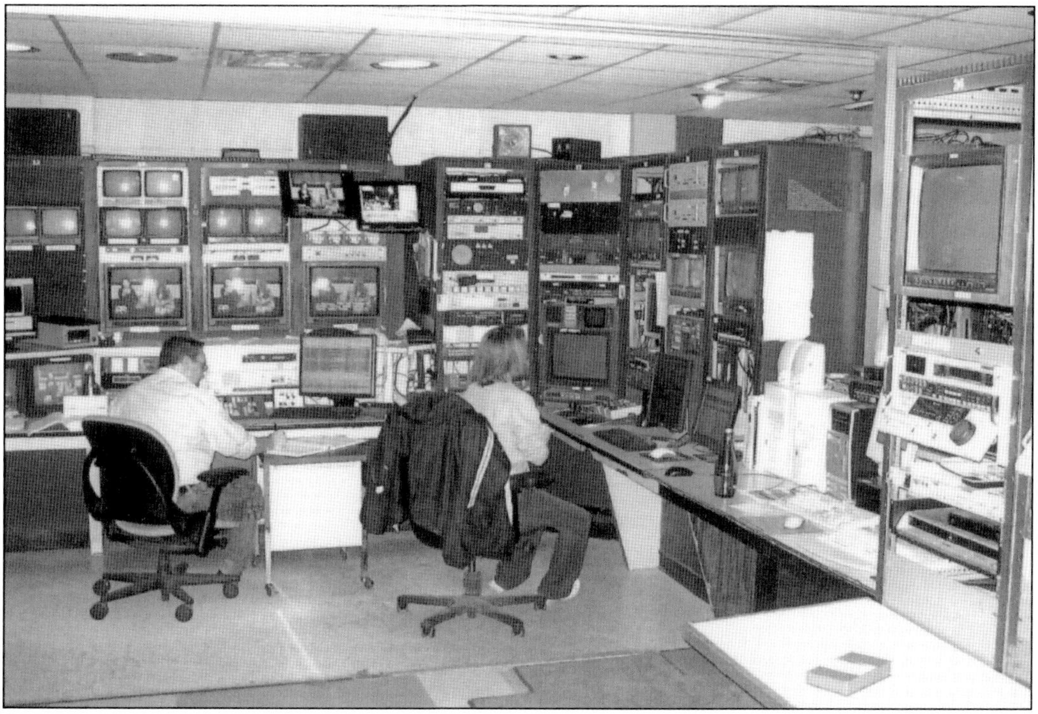

Sean Gorman (left) and Mary Haney are monitoring KWQC-TV's current master control area. Much of today's audio and video sources are now on computer hard-drive units and controlled by other computers. There are no more film or slide projectors or audio cartridge machines. On the right, under the monitor, is one of the few remaining videotape playback machines that are used primarily for local news stories.

This photograph of channel 6's current production control room shows the advances in television technology since the studios were built in 1963. Today the director chooses from many more incoming video sources, creates more on-screen graphics, and uses a much larger and more complex video switcher for putting the pictures seen at home on the air. Not shown is the audio board, which is behind the director's position.

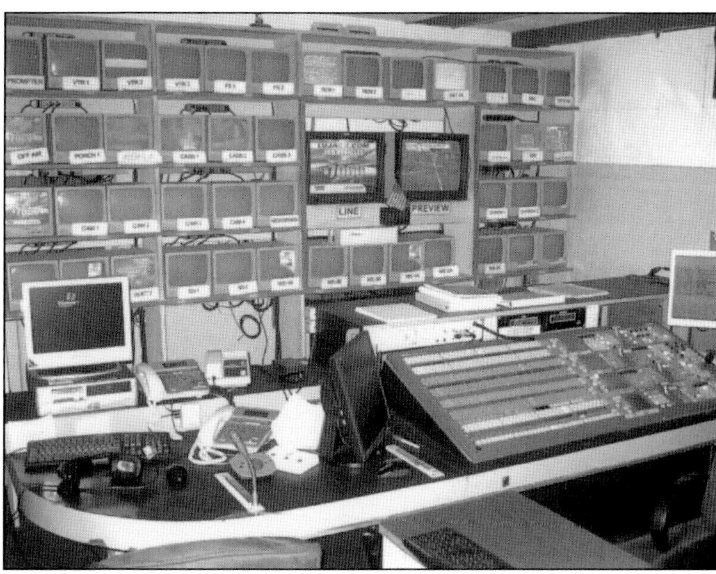

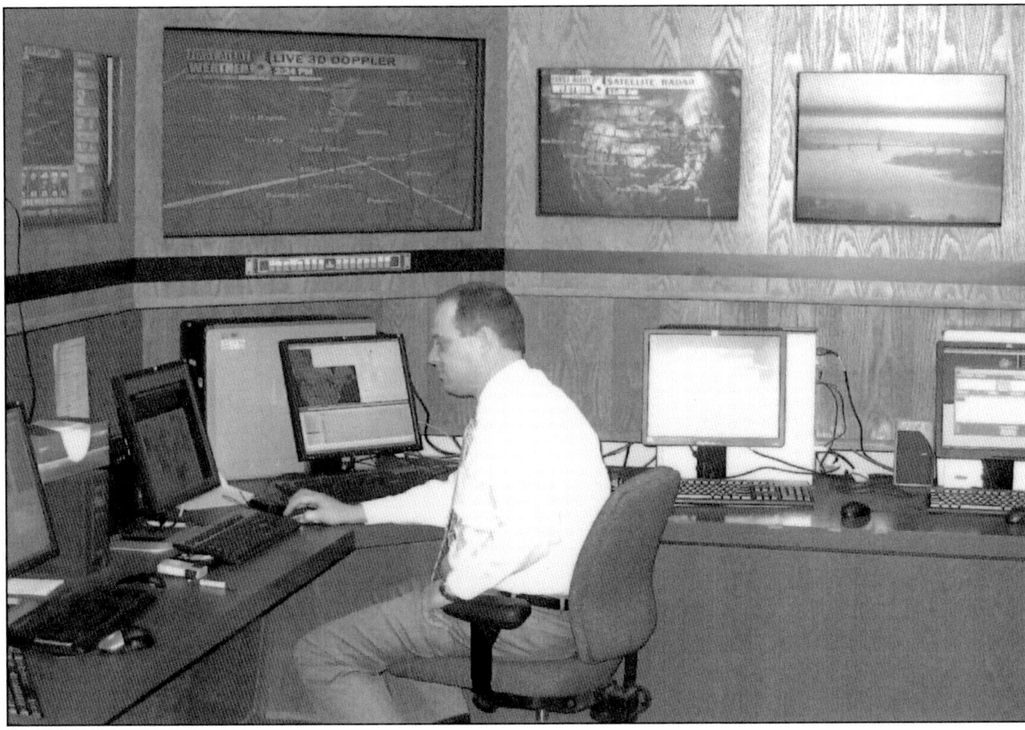

Channel 6 meteorologist Ryan Burchett is seen preparing for his evening weather report and forecast. The computers are used to download Doppler weather radar and satellite precipitation information from the U.S. Weather Bureau. A computer not shown generates the graphics that viewers see during the airing of the weather segments. Reporting the weather has come a long way from grease pencil lines and characters on a map.

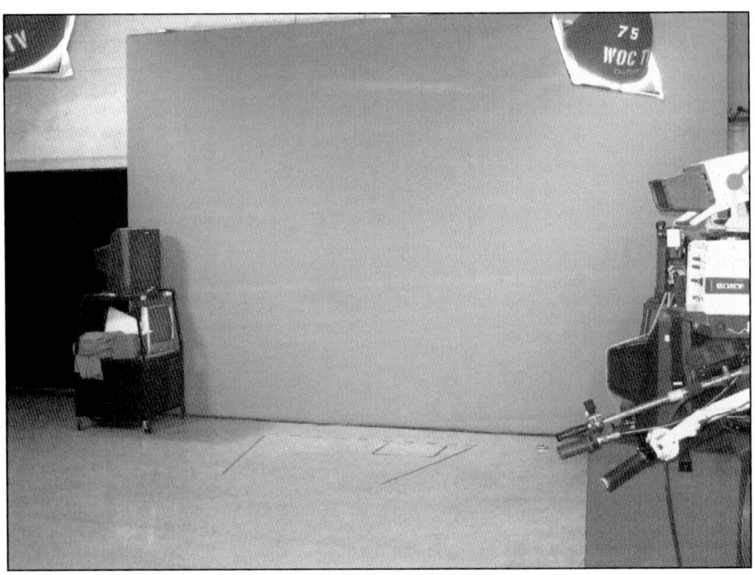

This is the location in the studio where the process of placing weather maps and live action scenes behind a reporter is accomplished. The process is called chroma key, and the reporter stands in front of a blank, green wall. The visual is then electronically inserted "into" the color green. Monitors on either side of the set allow the weatherman to see where he is pointing.

Broadcast technology has changed greatly since both WOC and WOC-TV began transmitting signals. Much of the electronic gear used to produce a signal to the transmitter has been reduced in size by transistors. Satellites replace telephone lines and audio and videotape machines are replaced by computer hard drives. Channel 6's chief engineer Doug Bierman adjusts a piece of high-definition broadcast equipment that is just one more technological progression.

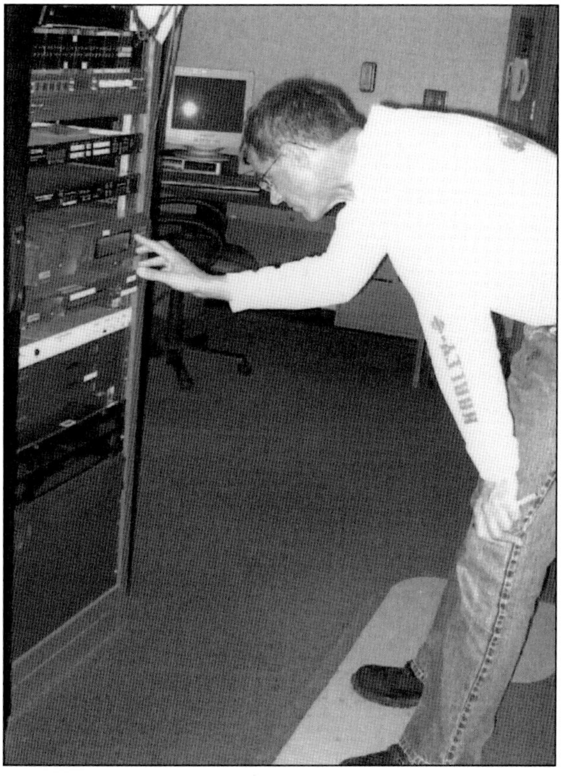

News department members in the early 2000s include, from left to right, (first row) Gary Metivier, anchor; Fran Riley, reporter; Terry Swails, weather; Sharon DeRycke, anchor; Charles King, anchor; and Thom Cornelis, sports; (second row) Paula Sands, anchor; Erik Maitland, weather; Mike Mickle, anchor; Jason DeRusha, reporter; Marcia Lense, anchor; Dan Pearson, sports; and Theresa Bryant, weather. Channel 6 news has been first in the ratings since the late 1960s. (Courtesy of KWQC-TV.)

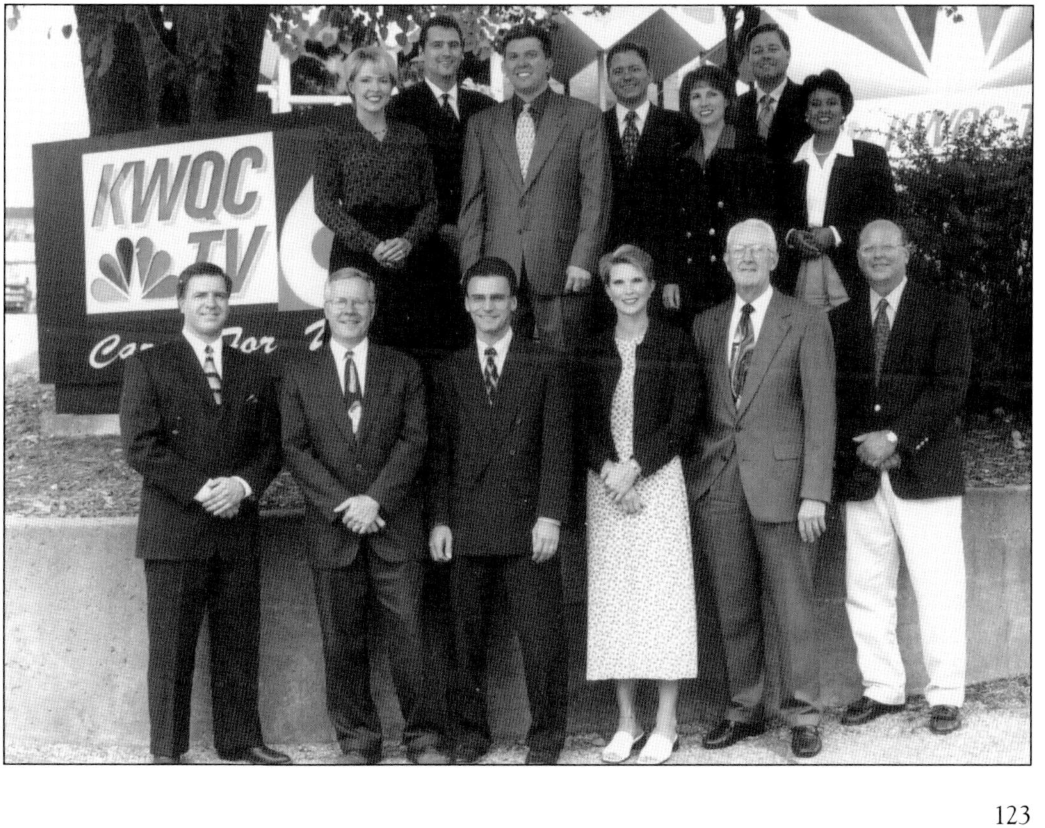

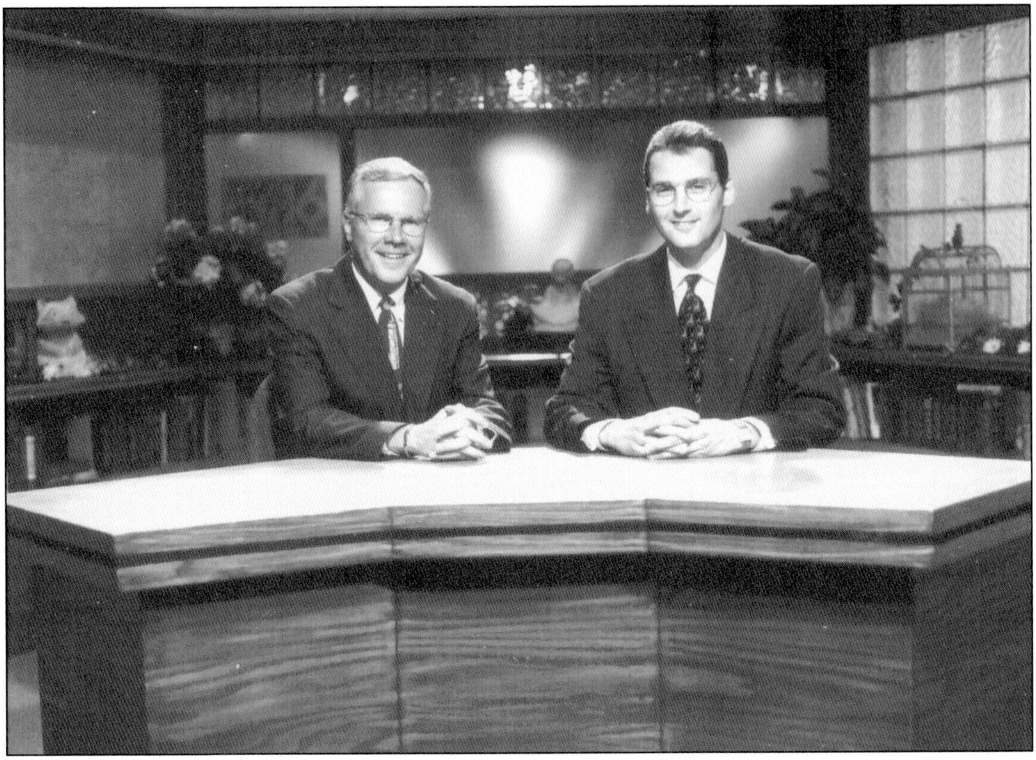

In the early 1990s, channel 6 used several different sets for their news programs depending upon what time of day the program was aired. This photograph captures reporter Fran Riley (left) and weatherman Erik Maitland at the *Quad Cities Today* early-morning news set. This set, as well as many others over the years, was designed and crafted by stage manager Ivan Owens. (Courtesy of KWQC-TV.)

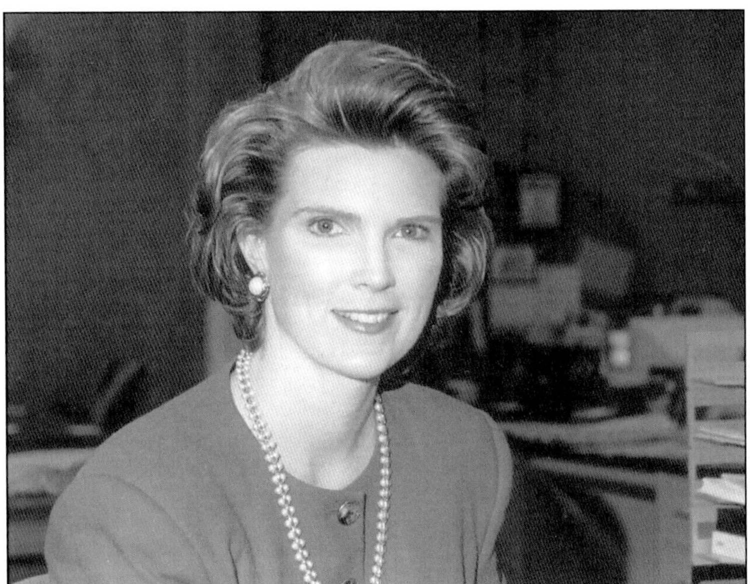

This promotional photograph captures Sharon DeRycke in the "big hair" days. DeRycke has been with channel 6 since 1989 and coanchors the KWQC news at 10:00 p.m. with Gary Metivier. She also files news stories for the 5:00 and 6:00 p.m. newscasts. When Paula Sands is on vacation, DeRycke becomes the substitute hostess for *Paula Sands Live*. (Courtesy of KWQC-TV.)

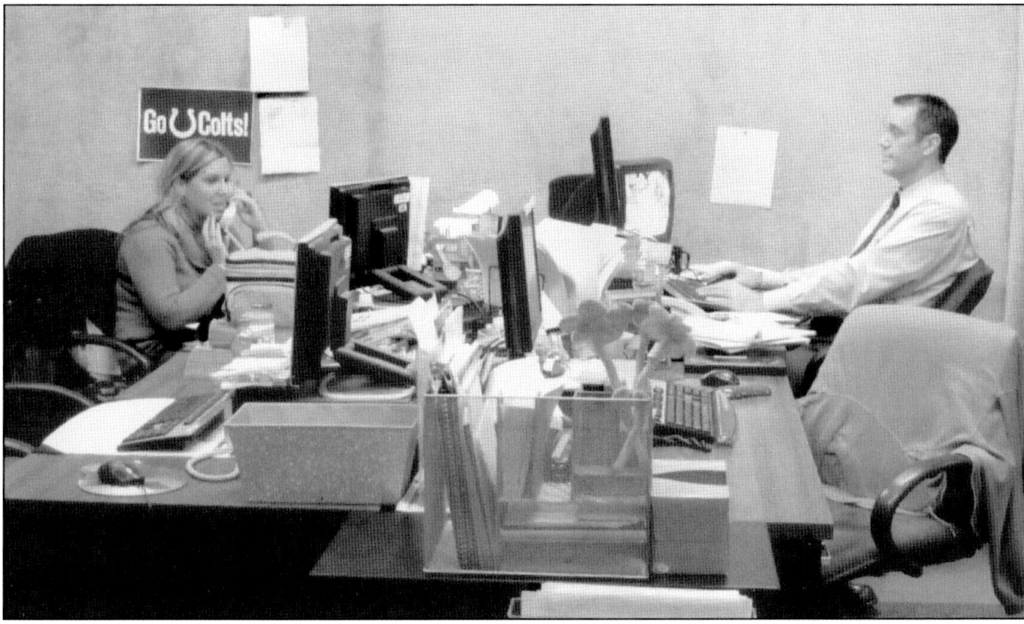

These two people rise early in the morning to bring viewers the news at 5:00 a.m. on *Quad Cities Today*. Meredith Haley (left) is usually out on the streets covering the news events that occurred in the early-morning hours. David Nelson coanchors the broadcast from the studio, and after the show's airing he hits the streets to cover developing news stories throughout the day.

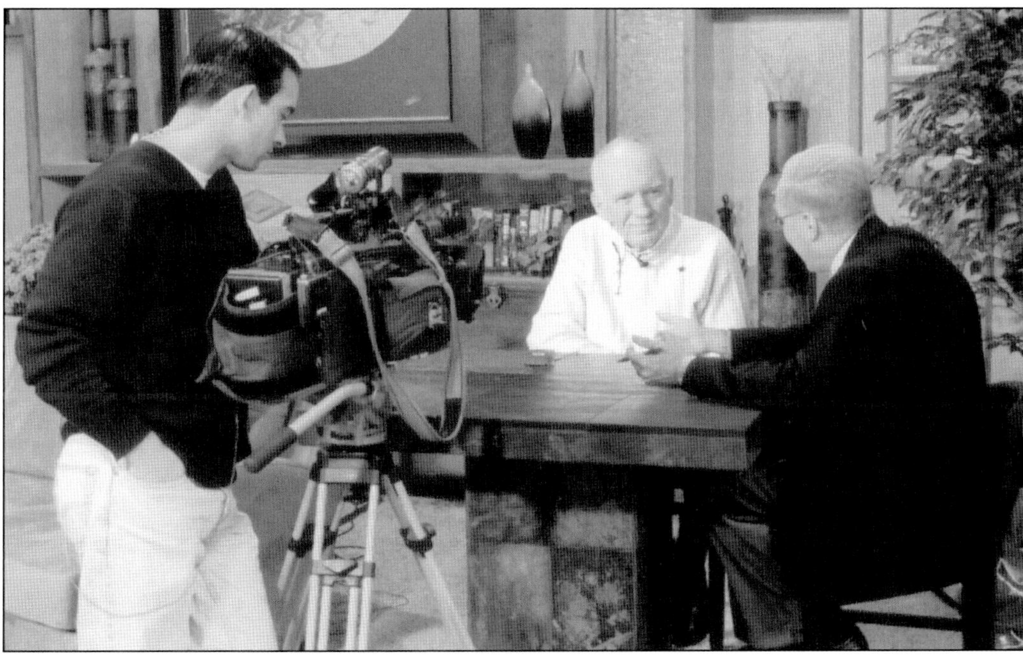

Kory Kuffler (left) records a discussion between Ivan Owens (center) and Fran Riley for Riley's four-part series on the 60th anniversary of channel 6. They are taping on one of the sets of *Paula Sands Live*, the last group of sets designed and built by Owens before retiring. *Paula Sands Live*, on the air since 1993, is the modern-day version of channel 6's earlier long-running program, *Especially for You*.

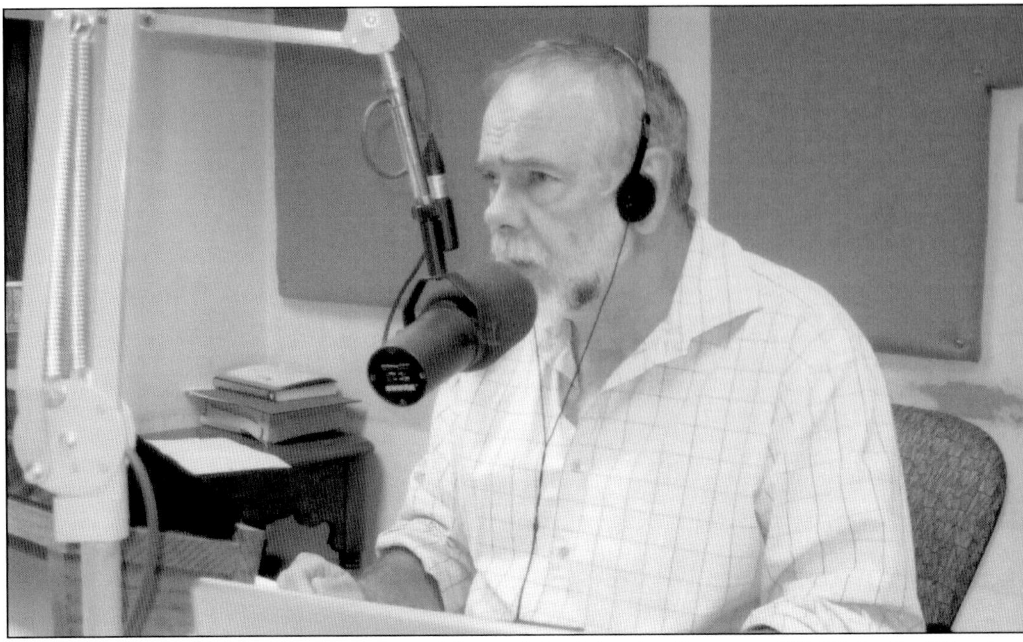

Dan Kennedy is the program director and host of the *Morning Report* on WOC Radio. The show features three and a half hours of news, weather, sports, and traffic reports. Kennedy also brings listener interviews with local and national news makers, authors, and people with great stories to tell. Dr. Laura, Rush Limbaugh, Jim Fisher, Sean Hannity, and Dennis Miller round out WOC's daily schedule.

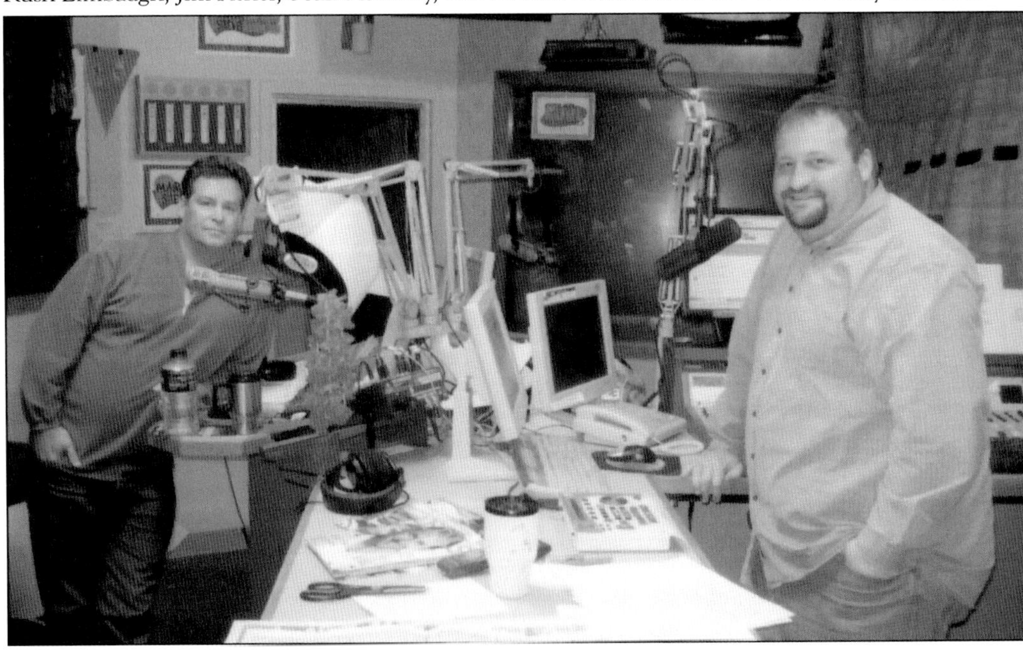

Steve Ketelaar (left) and Mark Manuel host the *KUUL Morning Guys* every morning from 5:30 to 10:00 a.m. The show features oldies/classic rock music, along with the news, weather, sports, and traffic reports. And the duo offers plenty of interaction with its listeners. Never afraid to offer a humorous comment on an interesting tidbit from the news, Mark and Steve encourage their audience to join in on the fun.

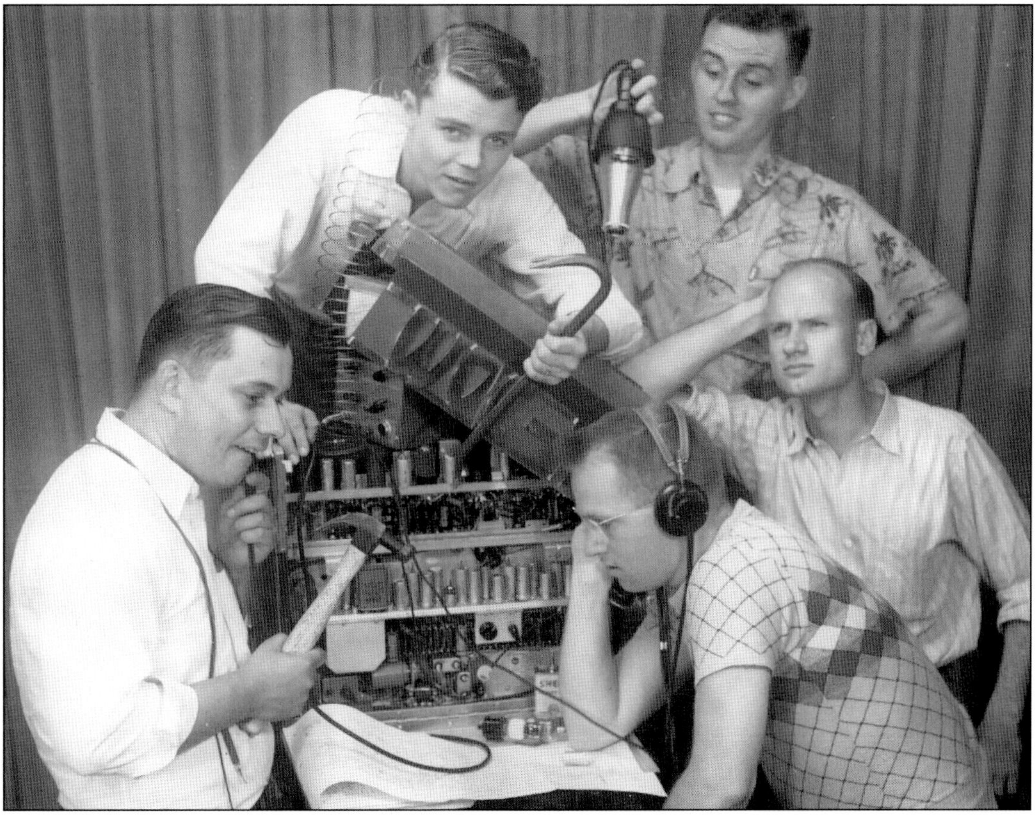

While the sales department and the talent might say that without them there would be no television to watch or radio to listen to, the true "stars" of any broadcast station are the engineers. These individuals not only operate much of the studio and transmission equipment, but they also perform the routine electronic maintenance to keep the station on the air. Their knowledge also allows them to quickly repair equipment that has failed and taken the station off the air. The photograph above was taken with a bit of whimsy. Pictured here are, from left to right, Bud Elliott, Russ Ide, Bob Trescott, Dave Hauser, and Bob Ramsey as they try to "repair" a television camera. Rest assured, these men know what they are doing. In the photograph to the right, Tom Innis is seen preparing to install a new signal modulation control. (Courtesy of KWQC-TV.)

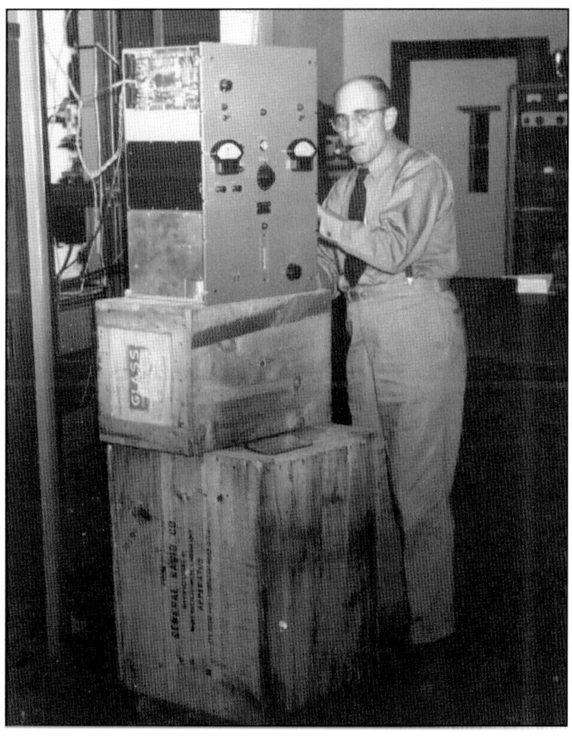